EVALUATING PROGRAM EFFECTIVENESS

Evaluation in Practice Series

Christina A. Christie & Marvin C. Alkin, *Series Editors*

1. Mixed Methods Design in Evaluation, by Donna M. Mertens
2. Facilitating Evaluation: Principles in Practice, by Michael Quinn Patton
3. Collaborative Approaches to Evaluation: Principles in Use, edited by
J. Bradley Cousins
4. Culturally Responsive Approaches to Evaluation, by Jill Anne Chouinard and
Fiona Cram
5. Experimental Evaluation Design for Program Improvement, by Laura R. Peck
6. Leading Change Through Evaluation: Improvement Science in Action, by
Kristen L. Rohanna
7. Evidence-Building and Evaluation in Government, by Kathryn Newcomer and
Nicholas Hart
8. Evaluating Program Effectiveness: Validity and Decision-Making in Outcome
Evaluation, by Marc T. Braverman

EVALUATING PROGRAM EFFECTIVENESS

VALIDITY AND DECISION-MAKING IN OUTCOME EVALUATION

Marc T. Braverman

Oregon State University

Los Angeles | London | New Delhi
Singapore | Washington DC | Melbourne

FOR INFORMATION:

SAGE Publications, Inc.

2455 Teller Road

Thousand Oaks, California 91320

E-mail: order@sagepub.com

SAGE Publications Ltd.

1 Oliver's Yard

55 City Road

London, EC1Y 1SP

United Kingdom

SAGE Publications India Pvt. Ltd.

B 1/I 1 Mohan Cooperative Industrial Area

Mathura Road, New Delhi 110 044

India

SAGE Publications Asia-Pacific Pte. Ltd.

18 Cross Street #10-10/11/12

China Square Central

Singapore 048423

Printed in the United States of America

ISBN 978-1-5063-5159-9

This book is printed on acid-free paper.

Acquisitions Editor: Helen Salmon

Product Associate: Audra Bacon

Production Editor: Vijayakumar

Copy Editor: Christobel Colleen Hopman

Typesetter: TNQ Technologies

Proofreader: Benny Willy Stephen

Indexer: TNQ Technologies

Cover Designer: Karine Hovsepian

Marketing Manager: Victoria Velasquez

22 23 24 25 26 10 9 8 7 6 5 4 3 2 1

• Brief Contents •

Acknowledgments   xv

Preface   xvii

About the Author   xxi

PART I • AN OVERVIEW OF VALIDITY CONCEPTS   1

Chapter 1 • Introduction: Why a Focus on Validity?   3

Chapter 2 • Validity in Testing and Psychometrics   17

Chapter 3 • Interpretations of Validity in the Theory and
              Practice of Evaluation   35

**PART II • VALIDITY APPLIED TO PHASES OF THE
              EVALUATION PROCESS   53**

Chapter 4 • Conceptualizing Your Intervention   55

Chapter 5 • Translating Your Constructs Into Variables   83

Chapter 6 • Measurement Strategies and Measurement
              Instruments   113

Chapter 7 • Evaluation Design   153

Chapter 8 • Data Analysis   187

Chapter 9 • Evaluation Conclusions and Recommendations   217

References   237

Index   251

• Detailed Contents •

Acknowledgments	xv
Preface	xvii
About the Author	xxi

PART I • AN OVERVIEW OF VALIDITY CONCEPTS   **1**

Chapter 1 • Introduction: Why a Focus On Validity?   **3**

What Is Accuracy in Evaluation?	3
Table 1.1 The Accuracy Standards of the *Program Evaluation Standards* (3rd Edition, 2011)	4
Evaluation Questions and the Evaluation Plan	5
Case Study 1.1 An Evaluation That Went Off-track	7
Case Study 1.2 Seeking a Measure of Career Awareness in Adolescents	8
Evaluation as Argument	9
The Role and Significance of Validity	10
Operationalizing in Evaluation	14
Chapter Summary	15
Questions for Reflection—Chapter 1	16

Chapter 2 • Validity in Testing and Psychometrics   **17**

Validity in the Psychometric Tradition	18
Tests and Their Constructs	19
Table 2.1 What Is a *Construct*? Some Variations	20
The Traditional, Tripartite View of Validity	22
The Current View: Validity as a Unitary Phenomenon	26
Approaches to the Process of Test Validation	26
The Argument Perspective on Validity in Measurement	31
Chapter Summary	32
Questions for Reflection—Chapter 2	33

Chapter 3 • Interpretations of Validity in the Theory and Practice of Evaluation   **35**

Validity Concepts Applied to Research Designs   35

    Case Study 3.1 The Generalizability of a Smoking Prevention RCT   39

Ernest House: The Validity of Evaluations   44

Cultural Influences in Evaluation and Validity   47

    Table 3.1 Kirkhart's Five Justifications Underlying Multicultural Validity   49

Chapter Summary   50

Questions for Reflection—Chapter 3   52

PART II • VALIDITY APPLIED TO PHASES OF THE EVALUATION PROCESS   **53**

Chapter 4 • Conceptualizing Your Intervention   **55**

What Exactly Is Your Intervention? The Intervention as Construct   55

The Interaction of the Intervention With Its Context   59

Understanding the Intervention as Planned: Program Theory and Logic Models   60

    Figure 4.1 A Sample Program Theory for a University Campus Media Campaign to Promote Students' Sexual Health   62

    Figure 4.2 Logic Model of a Water Quality Education Program for Farmers, Along With Sample Evaluation Questions   63

Understanding the Intervention as Implemented   65

    Case Study 4.1 A Multidimensional Evaluation of Implementation Fidelity   66

    Table 4.1 Potential Implementation Evaluation Questions for the Project 4-Health Evaluation, Based on the Type of Information Collected and Its Relationship to Program Outcomes   71

Multisite Interventions   72

    Case Study 4.2 An Evaluation of the Functioning of Foster Group Homes   73

Building the Knowledge Base: Comparing Interventions Across Evaluations   78

Chapter Summary   80

Questions for Reflection—Chapter 4   81

Chapter 5 • Translating Your Constructs Into Variables   **83**

Identifying and Specifying the Variables to Be Investigated   83

    Case Study 5.1 Pitfalls in the Interpretation of Constructs: Translating Claims About Parenting Styles   84

A General Model of Variable Selection and Measurement
Specification   86
   Figure 5.1 The Sequence of Moving From Construct to Measure   88
   Table 5.1 Measurement Planning: Identifying Potential Options in the
   Progression From *Construct* to *Evaluation Measures*   93
   Figure 5.2 Illustration of the Possible Progression From Construct to
   Instrument (Some Paths Left Incomplete)   94

Types of Variables to Account for in Your Program Theory   94

The Use of Proxy Variables to Represent the Primary Construct   96

The (Sometimes) Perilous Journey From Construct to Variable   97

The Understanding and Use of Constructs in the Political Domain:
An Example From California in the 1980s   105

Recommendations on Selecting Your Variables   109

Chapter Summary   110

Questions for Reflection—Chapter 5   112

Chapter 6 • Measurement Strategies and Measurement Instruments   113

Measurement and Validity   114
   Table 6.1 How Measurement May Affect Each of the Validity Categories   114

Identifying Your Measurement Strategies   119
   Case Study 6.1 A Comparison of Strategies for Measuring School-Based
   Cigarette and Alcohol Use   122

Identifying Your Specific Measures   123
   Case Study 6.2 Repeating versus Revising Questions in a Replication
   Study   125

Anticipating Potential Sources of Bias and Error   132
   Case Study 6.3 Dealing With the Possibility of Ceiling Effects on a Single
   Survey Item   137
   Case Study 6.4 Respondents' Tendencies to Answer Questions They
   Don't Understand   140
   Case Study 6.5 The Influence of Labeling Effects on Survey Responses:
   Opinion Polls About US National Health Policy   143
   Table 6.2 A Sampling of Types of Question Order Effects and How They
   Operate   150

Chapter Summary   151

Questions for Reflection—Chapter 6   152

Chapter 7 • Evaluation Design — 153

The Function of Evaluation Design — 153

Exhibit 7.1 Standard Descriptive Notation for Impact Evaluation Designs — 155

Case Study 7.1 Variations on the Standard Notation for Purposes of Presentation and Illustration — 156

Significant Elements of Impact Evaluation Design — 157

Evaluation Designs and Validity Theory — 163

Table 7.1 Threats to Internal Validity in Designs for Impact Evaluation — 164

What Makes a Design Strong? — 172

Figure 7.1 Design Options for Examining a Potential Selection-Maturation Interaction Effect — 175

Taking Account of Limitations and Weaknesses in the Evaluation Study Design — 179

Case Study 7.2 Assessment of a Regulation Requiring Menu Labeling of Calorie Information in Chain Restaurants in New York City — 179

Chapter Summary — 183

Questions for Reflection—Chapter 7 — 185

Chapter 8 • Data Analysis — 187

Data Analysis and Evaluation Validity — 188

Table 8.1 Type I and Type II Errors — 190

The Core Analysis — 192

Null Hypothesis Significance Testing and p-Values — 194

Case Study 8.1 Statistical Significance Testing: A True Story — 194

Exhibit 8.1 Recommendations for Reducing the Role of Statistical Significance Tests — 199

More Advanced Data Analysis Issues — 202

Post Hoc and Exploratory Analyses — 204

Case Study 8.2 Creating and Using an Ad Hoc Variable — 204

Analysis Decisions and Adjustments — 208

The Creation of New Evaluation Questions — 212

Chapter Summary — 213

Questions for Reflection—Chapter 8 — 215

Chapter 9 • Evaluation Conclusions and Recommendations — 217

Synthesizing the Evaluation's Results to Arrive at Conclusions — 218

Providing Recommendations — 220

Framing the Problem — 221

The Validity of Conclusions From Campbell's Validity Perspective   224
     Table 9.1 Data Interpretation Errors That Can Weaken the Validity of
     Evaluation Conclusions   224

The Validity of Conclusions From House's Validity Perspective   231

Chapter Summary   235

Questions for Reflection—Chapter 9   236

References   **237**

Index   **251**

• Acknowledgments •

I am grateful to Marvin Alkin, who originally recruited me for this book project, and to both Marv and Tina Christie in their roles as series editors. They have provided very helpful guidance along the way. Hearty thanks also to Jana Kay Slater, John Geldhof, and Yue Ni, who read all or parts of the manuscript and provided a great deal of important and insightful feedback.

I am very appreciative for the support of Helen Salmon, my SAGE editor, who has been a joy to work with. Helen has the perfect touch for encouraging projects to their completion. She is absolutely the best at what she does, and authors who work with her are very fortunate.

Finally, I would like to thank Michael Patton for counsel and advice in the early phases of writing the book. Michael is always accessible and is extremely generous with his time. He has been a mentor to more than one generation of young (and not so young) evaluators, and he is clearly very committed to that role.

Thank you all!

SAGE and the author are grateful for feedback from the following reviewers in the development of this text:

David Boyns, California State University, Northridge

Valerie Futch Ehrlich, University of Virginia

Abbie K. Frost, Simmons University

Barbara Holmes, Winona State University

Jitendra Kapoor, Alabama A&M University

Michael J. Lyman, Shippensburg University of Pennsylvania

Mitsunori Misawa, The University of Memphis

Leah C. Neubauer, DePaul University

Kathleen Norris, Plymouth State University

Jodi F Paroff, New York University

Rahbel Rahman, Binghamton University

Rohit Ramaswamy, University of North Carolina at Chapel Hill

Becky L. Thomas, The University of Akron

• Preface •

I heard a joke some years ago that goes like this. Three baseball umpires are sharing some beers after working a game. Around the third round of beers, their competitive juices are flowing and they start boasting about how they do their jobs.

> Umpire 1: There's balls and there's strikes, **and I call 'em like I see 'em.**

> Umpire 2: There's balls and there's strikes, **and I call 'em what they really are.**

> Umpire 3: There's balls and there's strikes, **and they ain't nothing until I call 'em.**

I hate to kill this joke by weighting it down with academic interpretations, and certainly my friend Terry, who told it to me and is also a social scientist, did not intend for the joke to be the carrier of symbolic meaning. Nevertheless, it has always seemed to me that these three umpires, each one taking a step further into a puddle of hubris, do a pretty good job of staking out positions within the philosophy of science about the nature of our interpretations of reality.

The first umpire suggests that a pitched ball will indeed be either a ball or a strike, and he does the best he can to figure out which it is and to get the label right. He's a hardworking stiff who, given the task of serving as the measurement instrument, may make a mistake here and there but he does his best. He believes that our measures are fallible but they represent our best attempts to understand an objective world that exists beyond our senses.

The second umpire claims to represent reality perfectly, without error. Reality exists beyond our senses, and all we have to do is get the measurements correct—which he believes is indeed within our powers—in order to understand that external reality with complete accuracy and confidence.

The third umpire seems to imply that labels such as balls and strikes are superfluous constructions. A ball travels through the air and lands in the catcher's mitt. There is nothing particularly dichotomous about that flight. To label it as a ball or a strike is a social construction, which doesn't exist outside of our human experience. We make it all up, and if it helps us to make sense of reality...well, good for us.

This book is about validity in program evaluation. Validity is concerned with issues of truth and accuracy—getting things right with the claims that we make from our inquiries—and therefore it has a lot to say about the accuracy, fairness, and value of our evaluation endeavors. How do we know if we are getting an evaluation right? To what degree are we introducing our own errors and biases into our pronouncements about what has been learned? Those are rather big questions, but if we are talking about them, then we are talking about validity. As are also the three umpires.

The book fills a niche in the evaluation literature that I believe has received little attention, in that it takes a detailed look at how to apply validity concepts every step along the way when planning and conducting an evaluation. Validity is very much discussed in the social sciences, but it is most often broached more generally, in relationship to tests and measurements, or to formal attributes of research and evaluation design, or, more recently, to cultural dimensions in evaluation practice. This book takes the approach that validity—including its varying conceptions in all of those theoretical subdomains—can be an organizing theme for any evaluation, making sure that the evaluation stays true to the critical purposes for which it was initiated. In this book, getting an evaluation right—that is, evaluating with validity—means being able to answer the evaluation questions in a way that is useful, accurate, and reflective of the information needs embedded in those questions. In my experience, this emphasis on practical guidance is an uncommon approach to the subject within the evaluation literature.

Audiences for This Book

I have aimed this book for practicing evaluators and users of evaluation. My perspective is practical, with the goal of helping evaluators to conduct high-quality outcome evaluations that are able to answer the evaluation questions that are posed. The subject areas explored are widely relevant to questions and decisions that evaluators face. With the multitude of decisions that must go into the planning of any evaluation, it is my hope that the concepts described can be helpful as an evaluator or evaluation team goes through the maze of decision-making in their planning and implementation of an evaluation.

The book is also appropriate for graduate students as a text in a second course on evaluation. The book does assume some knowledge of basic concepts in evaluation and the design of applied research, so it probably would not serve the purposes of a basic introductory text. But given a fundamental grounding in the concepts of evaluation, it can help students explore the material in ways suited to real-world applications.

A Focus on Outcome Evaluations

The book's focus is on outcome evaluations, rather than evaluation practice more generally. I cover ideas and practices that are relevant for examining an intervention's effectiveness and impact. Outcome evaluations tend to be marked by some consistent themes, although this takes place within a broad scope that allows for innumerable variations. Therefore the topic is very well suited for coverage in a book such as this.

Outcome evaluation has also been one of my primary areas of concentration throughout several decades of evaluation practice. I work in the land-grant university Extension System, and Extension is continually developing and delivering community-based programming across the United States in topic areas such as health promotion, youth development, community development, regional food systems, and many other topics, in addition to its longstanding educational and programmatic contributions in natural resources and agriculture. The personnel engaged with these Extension programs want to know how well their interventions work, how those interventions can be improved, and whether funding should be sought to expand the interventions to broader audiences. Therefore the study of intervention effectiveness is a major theme that has run through my professional work over the years.

Many of the examples in this book are drawn from my own evaluation work. This is not because I believe that my evaluation efforts represent higher standards of quality than everyone else's (although I have indeed striven to make the quality high). But there are several advantages to drawing on one's own past experiences. First, I understand the details of the studies and the irregular paths through which our planning decisions regarding design, measurement, analysis, etc., were arrived at. I can recount the points of argument and uncertainty, in addition to describing the final decisions. That inside story is not easy to obtain from other studies and reports. Further, I can criticize my own decisions more easily than I can somebody else's decisions. I can be brutal for the purposes of analysis and illustration.

Organization of the Book

The first part of the book, consisting of the initial three chapters, provides a general grounding in validity theory, including some distinct differences—but also through-lines—in the ways that validity is conceptualized and the uses to which it is put. Several distinct approaches and applications of validity are described, but they share a common emphasis on the truth and accuracy of inferences, judgments, and interpretations. Chapter 1 provides an introduction and overview of major themes and concepts that will guide later discussions. Chapter 2 describes the evolution of validity theory in the field of psychometrics, which is where it began and first evolved. The disciplines of psychology and education are prominently featured. Chapter 3 describes how social scientists and evaluators expanded the concept of validity in distinct ways, to broaden its applicability to include the design and assessment of research studies and entire evaluations. Several major theorists are highlighted. This chapter conveys the contributions that made validity a core component of evaluation theory and practice.

The second part of the book, Chapters 4–9, takes a pragmatic turn, analyzing separate phases of the outcome evaluation process and the design and analysis decisions that are characteristically required within those phases. Chapter 4 covers how the evaluation will conceptualize the intervention, including the need to specify what the intervention is and is not, and the implications that these considerations may have for what the evaluation study is being designed to learn. Chapter 5 presents a model for moving from general, intuitively worded constructs—which may be the primary coin of the realm when communicating with stakeholders about the evaluation—to the actual instrumentation that will be used for data collection. Chapter 6 covers the design and development of measures, including the need to anticipate potential biases in instrument development. Particular attention is given to those measurement strategies that involve asking people questions.

Chapter 7 discusses the components of evaluation design, including decisions about the sample(s), the timing of measurements, the critical planned comparisons, and other elements. The chapter focuses on how to do so in ways that can best allow for conclusions related to our questions about causality, that is, whether the intervention actually caused the changes in outcome status that may have been observed. Chapter 8 covers data analysis, addressing the many decisions that may be necessary during this phase. The chapter also discusses the relationship between analyzing our data set according to our original plan and analyzing it anywhere the data may take us. Finally, Chapter 9 focuses on our attempts to figure out what it all means, that is, how results are interpreted, how conclusions are reached, and how recommendations are developed and communicated.

• About the Author •

Marc T. Braverman is a Professor of Human Development and Family Sciences at Oregon State University, and an Extension Specialist in OSU's Family and Community Health program. Dr. Braverman has published in the areas of evaluation theory, applied research methods, measurement and survey methodology, tobacco control policy, health promotion, adolescent health, and other topics. He was the Associate Dean for Extension and Outreach in OSU's College of Health and Human Sciences from 2005 to 2011. Prior to coming to OSU, Dr. Braverman was an Extension Specialist at the University of California, Davis (1983–2005), and an evaluator at the Northwest Regional Educational Laboratory (now Education Northwest) in Portland, Oregon (1981–83). At UC Davis he established and directed the Tobacco Control Evaluation Center in 2004, with funding from the California Department of Health Services. In 1998–99 he was a visiting researcher at the Norwegian Institute of Public Health in Oslo, Norway. Dr. Braverman has received grants, as Principal Investigator or Co-investigator, from the National Cancer Institute, the US Department of Agriculture, the Robert Wood Johnson Foundation, the David and Lucille Packard Foundation, the California Department of Health Services, and other funders. He coedited the book *Foundations and Evaluation: Contexts and Practices for Effective Philanthropy*, published by Jossey-Bass. He has led numerous program and policy evaluations and has taught graduate classes on program evaluation, adolescent development, and research methods. He has a PhD in educational psychology from the University of Wisconsin–Madison.

An Overview of Validity Concepts

PART I

Introduction
Why a Focus on Validity?

Evaluation is often described as a practical discipline within the social sciences. It exists to answer questions. Other branches of the social sciences sometimes focus on discovering arcane, or abiding, truths about the world. Evaluation, by contrast, goes about trying to answer timely questions about social issues, social problems, programs and policies, and any number of things that people want to know.

Because the evaluation discipline is built around devising methods to answer pragmatic questions, its practitioners must place high priority on making evaluations both useful and accurate. Indeed, *utility* and *accuracy* are two of the four Program Evaluation Standards that have been developed by the Joint Committee on Standards for Educational Evaluation (Yarbrough et al., 2011). Of these two qualities, utility is the more encompassing one. For example, to be useful, evaluations need to understandable, perceived as relevant, and delivered on time, whether conducted inside or outside of a program or organization.

But clearly, to be useful, evaluations must also be accurate.

What Is Accuracy in Evaluation?

In an intuitive sense we might surmise that an *accurate* evaluation is one in which the technical aspects have been conducted with competence, resulting in a truthful and trustworthy representation of the program, policy, or other phenomenon under study. More specifically, we might conclude that the measures have been thoughtfully chosen, the data collection has proceeded competently, the analyses—quantitative, qualitative, or mixed—are thoroughly and expertly conducted, and the conclusions flow from those measurements and analyses. We might also suggest it means that the measurements and analyses are free from intentional bias (that is, attempts to arrive at a foregone conclusion), and that both measurement bias and random error are minimized to the extent possible.

In a nutshell, we may consider the information in an evaluation *accurate* to the degree that we believe it reflects the world in a truthful way. Each stakeholder, if they are paying attention, will have their own views on how successfully this requirement has been fulfilled. The opinions of stakeholders may well vary, but in making their judgments they will be working from a shared body of evidence.

The question of accuracy in evaluation has been directly addressed and examined in the 3rd edition of the *Program Evaluation Standards*, which identifies eight specific standards that relate to this category. In general, these standards "are intended to ensure that an evaluation will reveal and convey technically adequate information about the features that determine worth or merit of the program being evaluated" (Yarbrough et al., 2011). Table 1.1 lists the Joint Committee's accuracy standards and their descriptions.

TABLE 1.1 • The Accuracy Standards of the *Program Evaluation Standards* (3rd Edition, 2011)	
Standard	**Description**
A1. Justified Conclusions and Decisions	Evaluation conclusions and decisions should be explicitly justified in the cultures and contexts where they have consequences.
A2. Valid Information	Evaluation information should serve the intended purposes and support valid interpretations.
A3. Reliable Information	Evaluation procedures should yield sufficiently dependable and consistent information for the intended uses.
A4. Explicit Program and Context Descriptions	Evaluations should document programs and their contexts with appropriate detail and scope for the evaluation purposes.
A5. Information Management	Evaluations should employ systematic information collection, review, verification, and storage methods.

TABLE 1.1 ● *(Continued)*	
Standard	**Description**
A6. Sound Designs and Analyses	Evaluations should employ technically adequate designs and analyses that are appropriate for the evaluation purposes.
A7. Explicit Evaluation Reasoning	Evaluation reasoning leading from information and analyses to findings, interpretations, conclusions, and judgments should be clearly and completely documented.
A8. Communication and Reporting	Evaluation communications should have adequate scope and guard against misconceptions, biases, distortions, and errors.

Source: Yarbrough, D. B., Shulha, L. M., Hopson, R. K., & Caruthers, F. A. (2011). *The program evaluation standards: A guide for evaluators and evaluation users.* Sage. (p. 157)

Inspection of the accuracy standards conveys an appreciation of all the decisions required to achieve a suitable level of accuracy and verisimilitude. One thesis of this book is that the search for accuracy in evaluation—to whatever degree that may be achieved—depends, in part, on the sum total of the quality of the decisions in the planning, conduct, and interpretation of the evaluation study. Other determinants of accuracy include the skillfulness with which those decisions are implemented and the fair and just interpretation of the information that is thereby produced.

Evaluation Questions and the Evaluation Plan

In most cases, an early goal as an evaluation gets established is to determine a formal set of *evaluation questions* to be addressed. Most of my attention in this book will be focused on how the evaluation plan reflects and addresses the established evaluation questions. To reflect the complexity of interventions, most evaluations are multifaceted, involving areas of complexity and attention to a variety of the program's components and often examining those components from a number of angles. As a natural consequence, the set of evaluation questions will usually reflect this complexity, resulting in multiple questions that touch on numerous distinct dimensions of the program.

The ways in which evaluation questions get established, and the relation of those questions to the conduct of the evaluation, is a subject that deserves close attention. The process can be political to a significant degree because it depends on the sometimes diverging viewpoints of diverse stakeholders and other factors having to do with why the evaluation is being launched in the first place.

But once the evaluation questions are established, they provide a structure that guides the activities that follow. To be sure, an experienced evaluator will be alert to new knowledge and unexpected findings that arise from the evaluation process, even if they do not trace back to the themes of the questions. This process of serendipity and surprise can be invaluable—on occasion even the most lasting and significant contribution of the evaluation. But in the normal course of events, most of the evaluation plan and activities are geared toward addressing and answering the predetermined evaluation questions. A major concern of this book is that this process is conducted with accuracy, utility, and fairness.

The "evaluation plan" may be an actual document, which is usually most desirable. But there may be cases, especially when the program is small and the evaluation is undertaken for purposes of purely local utility, in which a formal, documented plan is lacking. Although it is far from an ideal scenario, it may happen that a program practitioner, called upon to evaluate their program as well as plan, conduct, fund, and otherwise ensure the program's existence, collects outcome data without any prior thought as to how those data will be analyzed. Nevertheless, if the evaluation is completed, at some point those analyses will have been conducted, presented, considered, and—with any luck—acted upon. In such cases the "plan" may be deduced from the activities and operations that have been carried out.

In this book, for purposes of simplicity, I will consider the existence of a distinct planning process, in which decisions are identified and represented. So whether the plan is a tangible document or a de facto set of decisions that must be reconstructed from what actually occurred—or some combination of the two—the evaluation plan is the focus of our attention and analysis for most of this book. In addition, the final two chapters discuss phases of the evaluation that occur in the course of implementing the plan: analyzing data, drawing conclusions, and making recommendations.

The evaluation planning decisions might involve the following areas, many of which will be examined in detail in later chapters:

- The determination of the primary evaluation questions to be answered

- The choice of primary outcomes

- The choice of measurement strategies to address those outcomes

- The choice of study participants

- The analytical design, whether based on quantitative or qualitative data, or a mixed-methods strategy

- The choice or development of instruments and other measures

- Timelines for tracking the outcomes

- The number of data points

Evaluations Sometimes Lose Their Way

Tolstoy's *Anna Karenina* famously begins: "Happy families are all alike; every unhappy family is unhappy in its own way" (Tolstoy, 1878/1961). In looking over the landscape of evaluations large and small, I am often reminded of this epigram and sometimes tempted to believe that every unsuccessful evaluation is unsuccessful for its own unique reasons. I am not sure that that is a defensible proposition, but it may serve to illustrate that there are a multitude of ways and reasons, frequently idiosyncratic, that evaluations fail to provide the understandings that are called for in their initial aims or in the original evaluation questions. An example of this phenomenon is provided in Case Study 1.1.

CASE STUDY 1.1   AN EVALUATION THAT WENT OFF-TRACK

In the 1990s I worked as an Extension 4-H Youth Development Specialist in University of California Cooperative Extension. In my capacity as a Program Evaluation Specialist, I advised a county 4-H program in southern California that had grant funds to hire an external evaluator to evaluate their 4-H afterschool program. I assisted my county faculty colleagues in drafting a Request for Proposals and provided some feedback in their team's selection of the successful proposer. Eventually they chose a fairly large research firm and awarded them the contract, which at $25,000 was one of the firm's smallest contracts. (It might be worth noting that $25,000 bought more in the 1990s than it does today.) The county 4-H team was interested in an outcome evaluation, and being responsive, the evaluation contractor proposed a prepost design. However, in the implementation of their design, they needed to deal with multiple challenges that are common to small afterschool programs, one of which is the lack of consistency in the attendance of participating children. If the time period between premeasurement and postmeasurement is long enough, this lack of consistency can result in highly attenuated, potentially biased, samples of children who have contributed scores at both time points.

The contractors began the evaluation. A few months into the process, they contacted the county 4-H team and me, to report that consistency in attendance was indeed a major impediment to their conduct of the evaluation as

(Continued)

(Continued)

planned. That news was not unexpected. The question was what could be done about it to arrive at some answers that could produce some degree of useful information however imperfect. As their preferred solution, the contractor suggested that the evaluation be changed to a series of focus group interviews, in which they could ask the afterschool staff, as well as the participating children and their parents, what they liked about the program. They provided no other options, based on the small budget. After some extended discussion the county team agreed, and that changed plan was followed.

When I heard this new proposal from the contractors I filed it in my memory bank as a glaring example of how an evaluation can lose its way. The evaluators steered toward a design that was possible and plausible, and that was economical within the constraints of the project budget. One might view all of these considerations as reasonable, under the circumstances. The one fly in the ointment is that their newly proposed design diverged radically from the original questions—which had reflected the needs of the program team—and, in essence, substituted a completely different set of evaluation questions, based on expediency. The evaluation was completed, and it was competently done in its way. The county team reviewed it briefly and didn't use it. For the purposes of their grant and their local information needs to gather evidence that might support program sustainability, their highest priority need was to assess program effectiveness. Thus, this evaluation must be considered a failure in achieving its aim of utility. Its implementation abandoned the original evaluation purposes.

In terms of losing sight of the original evaluation questions and losing the ability to answer those questions, Case Study 1.1 represents an example on a grand scale. But more subtle examples can also be cited. Case Study 1.2 describes a measurement-related decision that could have gone off-track with regard to what was being measured.

CASE STUDY 1.2   SEEKING A MEASURE OF CAREER AWARENESS IN ADOLESCENTS

Some years ago, in preparation for developing a youth development program on the topic of career development, I co-led a needs assessment study with Extension colleagues and graduate students, involving career development of high school seniors in northern California. We described our primary construct, *career awareness*, as follows:

> We use the term *career awareness* to refer to adolescents' reflectiveness about their future work lives. This may or may not include a specific career decision, in which a student can identify with certainty the career field that he or she wants to pursue. However, our definition does include

(Continued)

> students' active consideration of the elements upon which a decision can be based, such as understanding one's own talents and interests or understanding the opportunities and requirements of various career fields. (Braverman et al., 2002, p. 55)
>
> To examine this construct, we used an established instrument called the Career Decision Profile (Jones & Lohmann, 1998), a 16-item scale with six subscales including decidedness, level of comfort regarding vocational decision status, understanding of one's own interests and abilities, and other characteristics. We analyzed students' scores on these subscales in relation to their grades, part-time work experiences, and demographic variables. From these analyses, we drew some conclusions about school opportunities for career preparation programs.
>
> Our study, when completed, provided information that was considered valuable by the schools and our Extension colleagues at the University of California. But our team's path to understanding our variables was not straightforward and in fact the evaluation planning period proved to be a learning experience for us. We discovered a plethora of instruments relating to adolescents' vocational development, many of which varied, sometimes subtly, with respect to the variables on which we were focusing. Some of these identified constructs included career decision-making, career maturity, vocational identity, and career beliefs, among others. Thus, if we had accepted the first, or most convenient, instrument that turned up in our search, without intensive discussion and clarification of the specific variables that we wished to examine, we would have been misled.

Evaluation as Argument

Ernest House was an early proponent of the position that evaluation can be viewed as a process of argument, in which the evaluator presents evidence and builds a case toward a proposition or conclusion, e.g., regarding the value or effectiveness of a program. This position views evaluation as a particular form of inquiry and contrasts it with a view of evaluation as, for example, a fundamentally scientific endeavor. *Science* searches for enduring truths about the world—if not permanent truths, then truths that are sufficiently stable for the conditions of replicability to be determined and applied. An argument-based perspective, by contrast, relies on persuasion and the overall weight of evidence. House wrote:

> Evaluation aims at persuading a particular audience of the worth of something or that something is the case by an appeal to the audience's reason and understanding. For this purpose, uncertain knowledge is

useful although the ideas themselves are always arguable. The appropriate methods are those of argumentation, which is the realm of the "credible, the plausible and the probable" rather than the necessary....In summary, evaluation persuades rather than convinces, argues rather than demonstrates, is credible rather than certain, is variably accepted rather than compelling. (House, 1980, p. 73)

A more recent exposition of this viewpoint is provided by Thomas Schwandt (2015):

In its completed form, an evaluation is an argument for the value (or lack of value) of some particular program or policy. An argument is an attempt to persuade some particular audience of the conclusion about program value by giving reasons for accepting that conclusion as evident. The use of evidence in an argument demonstrates that evidence is not synonymous with data or information. Rather, evidence is data or information introduced at a specific point in an argument in order to persuade a particular audience of the veracity of the conclusion about program value. (p. 83)

Schwandt (2015) goes on to point out that an evaluation argument is notable in several respects. First, it does not purport to provide a proof of its evaluative proposition, but rather a credible, convincing case that can persuade a specific audience. Second, an evaluation argument is rooted in a particular context: it is concrete and immediate rather than abstract and universal. Third, Schwandt notes that such an argument is dialectical, meaning that it is part of an exchange of ideas. Fourth, the emphasis on persuasion as a goal requires that evaluation is concerned not just with accuracy and evidence but also, in part, with processes of communication, presentation, and rhetoric. Fifth, Schwandt notes that the argument itself can be the object of evaluation, in addition to the program or other evaluand.

The ideas and recommendations that I present in this book are consistent with the view of evaluation as a process of argument. My focus is on how evaluators can shape their evaluation plans with an eye toward building the most compelling, convincing case for the eventual interpretations of data and overall conclusions—well before data have been collected and certainly before those conclusions have been formulated.

The Role and Significance of Validity

The central concept in this book is validity, which relates squarely and directly to issues of quality, accuracy, and fairness in the evaluation process. Validity is a multifaceted construct that takes numerous forms, with a long history in the research tradition. As we will discuss more fully in Chapters 2 and 3, there are a number of perspectives as to what validity is, what it can do, and how it can contribute to the quality of research and evaluation efforts. But in the majority of its incarnations, validity refers to the adequacy of interpretations, judgments, conclusions, inferences, and knowledge claims. Validity is interwoven with the act of drawing interpretations from measurements, study designs, analyses, and entire studies.

In the social sciences, validity had its origins in measurement theory and practice, as will be discussed in Chapter 2. But if validity is a property of an inference rather than a measure, then it can be applied to other kinds of inferences beyond simply the meaning of test scores. As we will see in Chapter 3, Donald Campbell and his colleagues, particularly Thomas Cook and William Shadish, expanded the applications of validity to the research process itself, through the development of a four-part validity typology that they applied to research designs. Those subtypes were *internal validity, external validity, construct validity, and statistical conclusion validity*. Construct validity was already well established, having been introduced by Cronbach and Meehl (1955). But these theorists examined its use for purposes of assessing the quality of experimental and quasi-experimental designs in addition to the measurement context.

A different approach to validity, and one directly applied to the practice of evaluation, was offered by House, who approached the examination of validity in a way that is more connotative than scientific. He argued that the validity of an evaluation rests on a set of considerations on which the evaluation can be assessed overall, beyond attention solely to research rigor. Thus, he proposed that the quality of an evaluation can be judged with respect to three characteristics: truth, coherence, and justice (more in Chapter 3). One of House's unique contributions was to propose that in the determination of validity for an evaluation, accuracy is just one leg of a three-legged stool, accompanied by effective framing and communication (coherence) and the advancement of social justice. To the extent that these three cornerstones are well represented in an evaluation, the evaluation will be valid or, in House's words, worthy of recognition.

A final theoretical conception of validity, also described in Chapter 3, is multicultural validity. This form of validity is closely tied to the construct of cultural competence in evaluation, which was described as a critical skill set for evaluation professionals by the American Evaluation Association in a 2011 public statement (AEA, 2011). Originally developed and proposed by Karen Kirkhart, multicultural validity refers to the accuracy and fairness of evaluative inferences and conclusions considered in light of the specific, intersecting cultural contexts that characterize any evaluation setting (Kirkhart, 2010). It reflects a recognition that knowledge claims cannot be made in the absence of cultural understandings, and the validity of any evaluation is affected by how successfully those cultural dimensions have been incorporated into all phases of the evaluation. Multicultural validity also encompasses the promotion of social justice in evaluation, in common with House's validity model, and places high priority on the consequences of evaluations, including interpretations, conclusions, and actions that are taken in response to evaluation results.

Constructs and Construct Validity

Another central concept in this book is the understanding and analysis of *constructs*. A construct, as commonly understood in psychology, is an individual characteristic that exists only in a theoretical sense but can be useful in explaining patterns of activity, behavior, or abilities. General intelligence, reading ability, and mathematical aptitude are all constructs. So are all psychological traits, including the so-called big five traits of personality psychology (agreeableness, conscientiousness, emotional stability, extraversion, and openness; Poropat, 2009). Athletic ability is a construct, although running time in the 440-yard dash is an objective measure of running speed—at least as demonstrated on a particular day. In a psychometric framework, construct validity refers to the degree to which scores can be interpreted as providing information about the underlying theoretical construct. The validity theorist Bruno Zumbo (2009) observed: "In short, construct validity involves generalizing from our behavioral or social observations to the *conceptualization* of our behavioral or social observations in the form of the construct" (p. 68).

Outside of the realms of psychometrics and psychological theory, however, Shadish et al. (2002) argued that "...the creation and defense of basic constructs is a fundamental task of all science" (p. 65), and they defined *construct*, broadly and simply, as "a concept, model or schematic idea" (p. 506). They established the concept of construct validity as one component of the overall quality of research studies, and noted that the task of identifying, specifying, and describing relevant constructs applies not only to outcomes and variables but also to a study's units, settings, and treatments.

The specification of the constructs in an evaluation or research study is sensitive to larger contexts in ways that can be overlooked or that can rapidly change. An example is gender. Shadish et al., in describing the relationship between constructs and their conceptualization, wrote:

> It may help, however, to give examples of construct validity of persons, settings, and treatments. A few of the simplest person constructs that we use require no sophisticated measurement procedures, as when we classify persons as males or females, usually done with no controversy on the basis of either self-report or direct observation. But many other constructs that we use to characterize people are less consensually agreed upon or more controversial. (Shadish et al., 2002, p. 70)

Shadish et al. go on to describe the example of racial and ethnic identity as a type of construct, in contrast to gender, for which there is much less consensus and which presents challenges for determining the appropriate categories, the labels for those categories, and the best measurement procedures. It is striking that in the two decades after the publication of that volume, we can immediately recognize how much the concept of *gender* has changed, becoming a highly complex topic in society, politics, and social relations, as well as in research practice. Social conceptions of gender are transforming with remarkable rapidity, amid intense debate with consensus nowhere to be found. And in current research practice, a self-report survey item that inquired about gender by presenting the two-standard, mutually exclusive response categories would probably be viewed as unacceptable by most institutional review boards, as well as by many evaluators and researchers. Operationally in survey practice, the old construct of gender is now often divided into multiple variables (e.g., gender assigned at birth, followed by current gender identity). And recommendations for best research practice sometimes involve the presentation of multiple items with multiple response categories (GenIUSS Group, 2013). As this example illustrates, the quality and usefulness of a study, whether conducted for evaluation purposes or in a research context, can depend on considerations of its construct validity quite as readily as the more widely accepted considerations of its internal and external validity.

Construct Validity's Utility in Assessing Program Theory and Evaluation Plans

If we borrow the idea of trying to represent real, observable events through a theoretical or abstract conceptualization, we land very close to the purposes that evaluators ascribe to a *program theory* as the representation of a functioning program. A program theory is a schematic, highly simplified representation of how and why the program works (Chen, 2015; Lipsey, 1993). And for a given intervention, a program theory can be judged according to how well it succeeds in this task. Thus, it is reasonable for us to apply the concept of validity—particularly construct validity—to program theories as we seek to determine how accurately they help us to understand what is going on with the program on the ground.

The evaluation questions that an evaluation study is designed to answer or shed light on are characterized by constructs, including the program or policy being evaluated as well as its desired outcomes, and the relations between them. The decisions made in an evaluation plan represent the operational translations of these constructs in ways that allow investigation and examination through, in House's terminology, the logic of evaluative argument. A rigorous evaluation study, from this perspective, is one that preserves those intended core concepts and relationships in ways that create a strong evidence base for the process of evaluative inference. In this book we focus on how to build an evaluation plan so that its elements can adequately address the representations and assumptions inherent in our evaluation questions.

Operationalizing in Evaluation

It would be appropriate to consider much of the subject matter of this book as an analysis of the process of *operationalization* (Singleton & Straits, 2018). This can be thought of as the ways in which concepts and ideas get translated into real-world research or evaluation activities. Operationalization involves multiple, significant decisions by the evaluator, requiring expert judgment and sometimes entailing a degree of research creativity.

For target outcomes and other discrete variables examined in the evaluation, this process can be readily understood. For example, the evaluator of a nutrition education program that focuses on promoting "healthy eating" can measure that construct through survey self-report, detailed food logs, meal observations (e.g., plate waste), pantry inventories, and other strategies. Even within the confines of a specific measurement procedure (most notably survey self-report), the specifics of wording can produce significant alterations. For example, evaluations of smoking cessation programs can specify their definition of "current smoking" with wide variation on timeframe (e.g., past seven days vs. past 30 days), product (e.g., inclusion vs. non-inclusion of vaping products or hookah), and other particulars. These alternatives for representing what may seem like a clearly understood construct will result in very different choices regarding the operationalization of the variable. These topics are explored further in Chapters 5 and 6.

Beyond the specification of outcome variables, other aspects of an evaluation study also require skillful operationalization. For example, an evaluator who wishes to study whether the effectiveness of a community intervention strategy varies across different kinds of neighborhoods will need to identify the features and components that determine what a *neighborhood* actually is, and then decide which of those various features will be measured, and how that will take place (more on this in Chapter 5). Entire program treatments must be operationalized as well, in ways that may be more or less adequate for the purpose of addressing study questions, e.g., they may be oversimplified or instituted at sub-optimal levels (more in Chapter 4).

Because operationalization refers to the process of turning theoretical concepts into specific measures and other forms of practice, it is, by definition, perhaps the most fundamentally pragmatic of empirical activities relating to evaluation and research. Every evaluation plan must address the process in order to achieve on-the-ground implementation of the study. Therefore it is curious that the subject has received remarkably little attention in the evaluation literature, even though it can be done well or poorly, with significant implications for the eventual quality—the validity—of the evaluation study.

In the next chapter, we examine the development of validity theory in its original domain of psychometrics.

Chapter Summary

- Evaluation is a practical discipline within the social sciences that aims to answer timely questions about social issues, programs, and policies. Accuracy is an important value in evaluation. The Program Evaluation Standards, which are widely accepted within the discipline, include eight standards that relate specifically to dimensions of accuracy in evaluation.

- Validity is a multifaceted construct that addresses issues of accuracy, quality, and fairness in evaluation, research, measurement, and other endeavors. It usually refers to the accuracy and adequacy of judgments, interpretations, and conclusions.

- Once an evaluation study's primary evaluation questions have been determined, the evaluator develops a plan with the aim of answering those questions in the most accurate and valid way possible, within the limits of available resources. This book takes the position that validity in evaluation depends in large part on the quality of the decisions that are made in the planning, conduct, and interpretation of an evaluation study.

- Evaluation can be viewed as a process of argument, in which evidence and critical reasoning are used to build a case for evaluative conclusions. In outcome evaluations, those conclusions generally address the effectiveness of programs and policies. The perspective of evaluation as argument suggests that evaluation seeks to develop a body of evidence that can be persuasive to stakeholders and other audiences in making judgments about an intervention. This book focuses on how to design and carry out an evaluation plan that persuasively answers the evaluation's guiding questions.

- Operationalizaton is the process through which concepts and ideas get translated into real-world research or evaluation activities. Every evaluation study requires multiple decisions regarding how abstract constructs will be operationalized into variables, measures, designs, timelines, analysis strategies, and other activities necessary for the evaluation to be completed.

Questions for Reflection—Chapter 1

1. In your experience, did you ever encounter an evaluation that largely failed because it lost track of its original aims?

   • What were the ways in which it went off-track?

   • What were the reasons that this occurred?

2. The Accuracy standards shown in Table 1.1 are part of the *Program Evaluation Standards* (Yarbrough et al., 2011). In reading through these standards, do they expand the concept of *accuracy* beyond the ways that you would intuitively interpret that term as applying to evaluation? If so, in what ways do they expand it?

3. How might the conception of "evaluation as argument" change the ways in which evaluation is planned, conducted, and interpreted, in comparison to perceiving evaluation as a form of scientific investigation?

Validity in Testing and Psychometrics

The concept of validity originated and evolved within the fields of educational and psychological testing. In this chapter we will examine this evolution, with respect to how the concept has been applied to the interpretation and use of various kinds of tests.[1] In the first half of the 20th century validity was discussed and debated predominantly within a psychometric framework, relating to how the development and use of tests could be improved. In time it began to be applied in other contexts of social science inquiry, especially the assessment of research quality (covered in Chapter 3), but it continued to evolve within psychometrics as well.

In the psychometric uses of the concept of validity, one can see the priorities that have been applied to the term in all of its contexts. The specification and determination of validity are concerned with an appeal to truth and accuracy, and that orientation certainly describes its origins in psychometrics. As Angoff (1988, p. 19) wrote: "Validity has always been regarded as the most fundamental and important [concept] in psychometrics."

Many excellent texts on psychometrics discuss validity in detail (e.g., Bandalos, 2018; Cronbach, 1990; Urbina, 2004). Our purpose in this chapter is more selective: we discuss the psychometric view in a way that prepares for our discussion later in the book. Given that the point of validity is to assess the truth and accuracy of the use of a test, how has the concept needed to evolve in order to accommodate the steadily growing sophistication of test theory? Further, how can conceptions of validity take the leap

---

[1] In this chapter I use the term "test" as a shorthand to refer to a variety of measurement strategies, to which the assessment of validity can be applied. Thus a measure could consist of behavioral observations, observer judgments, etc., as well as a conventional test.

into other elements of social science methodology? We analyze how the "truth function" of validity has evolved to incorporate modern perspectives on testing and psychometrics.

Validity in the Psychometric Tradition

Beginning in the 1920s, validity was frequently defined as "the extent to which a test measures what it purports to measure" (Urbina, 2004, p. 154). That definition, although widely adopted and repeated in many textbooks, has long been abandoned by psychometricians as too simplistic. The scope of what *validity* should encompass—and, by extension, its definition—have been and continue to be debated, especially in light of current conceptions that view validity as complex and multidimensional. Related questions involve how validity should be assessed and what that assessment should include. The conceptualization has been provided some coherence by a consensus of social science organizations. A consortium of three leading societies—The American Educational Research Association, The American Psychological Association, and The National Council on Measurement in Education—first issued a joint statement of standards for educational and psychological testing in 1954 (AERA et al., 1954). Those standards have been revised and updated approximately every decade since.

The 2014 *Standards* define validity as follows: "Validity refers to the degree to which evidence and theory support the interpretations of test scores for proposed uses of tests" (AERA et al., 2014, p. 11). Several aspects of this definition deserve attention. First, it squarely consigns validity as a property of test score *interpretations* rather than as a static property of the test itself. Thus, it would be incorrect to make a single, initial determination of a test's validity and then accept it as a permanent feature of the test. Second, the definition also introduces the consideration of how the test will be used. This can include, for example, selection into a restricted program (e.g., entry into a program for students with special skills or talents, or conversely, into a remedial program for additional academic assistance), individual diagnosis of a student's current strengths and weaknesses (as in a classroom test of academic content), assessment of an individual's personality profile (e.g., for online matching of potential romantic partners), and innumerable others. By this definition, test validity will depend in part on the appropriateness of the decisions that will follow, which in turn are based on the interpretation of scores.

Evolution of the Conceptualization of Validity

Given the multitude of interpretations, uses, and functions of tests, it will not be surprising that the concept of validity—which targets the truth and accuracy of test score interpretations—would take on a wide variety of forms. Early conceptions of test validity, beginning in the 1920s, were based on the examination of correlational evidence, i.e., whether the test correlated with some designated criterion (Sireci, 2009). The correlation coefficient had been introduced by Karl Pearson at the turn of the century, and test validity was considered to be a practical application of that new statistical procedure. Sireci cites a 1946 quote from the psychologist J. P. Guilford that "a test is valid for anything with which it correlates."

The correlational approach was soon supplemented by a second technique, factor analysis, for other types of questions about tests. Factor analysis had also recently been introduced, by Charles Spearman, and it provided a completely different approach to determining the qualities of a test. Whereas correlational techniques focused on whether a test provided similar information to that from some other measure or criterion, factor analysis examined the internal structure of the test items.

For a variety of reasons, these early conceptions of validity and the corresponding methods of test validation were eventually judged to be inadequate and limited, and they came under increasing criticism by psychometricians. For example, with regard to the correlational approach, there were no standard expectations for how substantial a correlation needed to be before it could be considered as sufficient evidence to use a test in a particular way. This growing frustration led to the development of the Standards.

Introduction of the Standards

In the early 1950s, the American Psychological Association developed a proposal for common standards for the development and interpretation of psychological tests and measures. This led to the formation of the joint committee, which published its Standards in 1954. This document proposed four different types of test validity: content, concurrent, predictive, and construct. In later revisions through 1985, these were shortened to three categories—criterion-related, content, and construct validity—which form the basis of what is called the tripartite view of validity.

Following that initial appearance, revisions of the Standards were published in 1966, 1974, 1985, 1999, and 2014. Beginning with the 1985 edition, the Standards take a sharply different approach to validity. Rather than describing distinct types, it proposes that validity is a unitary phenomenon, and it describes five different kinds of validity evidence, as we will detail later.

Tests and Their Constructs

For a term that is used so frequently and with such import for the theory and practice of validity, the term *construct* is often used with little attempt to specify exactly what it means. Table 2.1 provides a summary of some of the definitions and explanations that have been offered for the term.

TABLE 2.1 ● What Is a *Construct*? Some Variations	
Source	**Definition**
Cronbach and Meehl (1955)	"A construct is some postulated attribute of people, assumed to be reflected in test performance. In test validation the attribute about which we make statements in interpreting a test is a construct." (p. 283)
Shadish, Cook, and Campbell (2002)	"A concept, model, or schematic idea." (p. 506)
Anastasi (1986)	"Let us consider the nature of the constructs employed in test development. Essentially they are theoretical concepts of varying degrees of abstraction and generalizability which facilitate the understanding of empirical data." (p. 5)
Embretson (1983)	"Here, *construct* refers to a theoretical variable that may or may not be a source of individual differences." (p. 180)
AERA et al. (2014)	"The term *construct* is used in the *Standards* to refer to the concept or characteristic that a test is designed to measure." (p. 11)
Messick (1981)	"Constructs thus provide organized interpretations of observed behaviors as well as a means of predicting previously unobserved behavioral consistencies from the theoretical implications of the nomological network." (p. 580)
Borsboom et al. (2009)	"[W]e do not know what constructs are, that is, we have rarely come across a clear description of what something should be like in order to deserve the label 'construct.' Constructs, as far as we are concerned, are truly shrouded in mystery,...in the sense that we don't really know what we are talking about in the first place." (p. 150)

In many cases, especially in years past, *construct* has been used to refer to latent traits and entities that don't have immediate and objective representations in the real world. Examples would be abstract concepts such as intelligence, sociability, aggression, attractiveness, or need for achievement. This was the approach originally taken by Cronbach and Meehl (1955): "A construct is some postulated attribute of people, assumed to be reflected in test performance" (p. 283). Their focus on constructs as latent traits was understandable since their paper, and their original formulation, was specifically focused on the domain of psychological testing. Thus the examples they cited involved trait-like characteristics: "The constructs in which tests are to be interpreted are certainly not likely to be physiological. Most often they will be traits such as 'latent hostility' or 'variable in mood,' or descriptions in terms of an educational objective, as 'ability to plan experiments.'" (p. 284) Cronbach and Meehl theorized that the focal construct of a psychological test should be supported by a body of theory and evidence, which they called a nomological network. In their formulation, the process of test validation consisted of identifying the nomological network and confirming its support of the construct.

This approach to terminology was more prominent in prior years when construct validity was seen as just one of several validity types, to be applied in some test settings but not others. In those cases it was invoked when the focus of testing was on an abstract and unobservable characteristic. With validity now being viewed as a unitary concept rather than a collection of types, and construct validity no longer seen as that specialized kind of validity that is invoked when there is a lot of debate about what exactly is being measured, the term *construct*—at least with regard to validity theory—is usually given a more universal role, reflecting the particular focus of any test that is under consideration. The 2014 Standards provide the following description: "The proposed interpretation [*of test scores*] includes specifying the construct the test is intended to measure. The term *construct* is used in the *Standards* to refer to the concept or characteristic that a test is designed to measure....Examples of constructs currently used in assessment include mathematics achievement, general cognitive ability, racial identity attitudes, depression, and self-esteem." (p. 11) Within this list, the inclusion of mathematics achievement—however hard it is to define—is noteworthy in its complete departure from the realm of latent psychological traits. Every test has its construct, whether that construct is steeped in psychological theory or behaviorally defined. There is no attempt to restrict the term to unobservable variables.

The psychometric theorist Anne Anastasi provided this elaboration:

[*Constructs*] are ultimately derived from empirically observed behavioral consistencies, and they are identified and defined through a network of observed interrelationships. In the description of individual behavior, such a construct corresponds closely to what is generally termed a trait. A simple example, with narrowly limited generalizability, is speed of walking. If we take repeated measurements of an individual's walking speed, we still obtain a whole distribution of speeds...Nevertheless, it is likely that an analysis of such varied measures would reveal a substantial common factor that reliably differentiates one person from another in overall walking speed. This common factor would be a construct; it does not necessarily correspond to any single empirical measure. (Anastasi, 1986, pp. 4–5)

Some constructs are highly general while others are more specific. The critical test is functionality. Cronbach (1990) noted:

> A formal construct is invoked when inference reaches out to diverse situations. "Musical talent" is a more convenient dimension than "talent for stringed instruments." That, in turn, is handier but less definitive than "dexterity in rapid finger movements" and "pitch discrimination." The broad construct is neither true nor false; it is adequate for some purposes and inadequate for others. (p. 52)

Some constructs invite definitional inconsistency not because of a theoretical debate about underlying components or a nomological network, but simply varied options for definition. However, it is important to conceive of the construct as existing apart from the test itself, such that the test is an attempt to capture it. In years past it was occasionally suggested that the construct and its test were identical, a concept known as *operationism*—famously illustrated in an early quote about intelligence by the American psychologist Edwin Boring: "...intelligence as a measurable capacity must at the start be defined as the capacity to do well in an intelligence test. Intelligence is what the tests test" (Boring, 1923). But operationism in measurement is now widely rejected.

The Traditional, Tripartite View of Validity

Until approximately the 1980s, the dominant view of validity was that it was a multifaceted concept comprising a collection of subtypes. The Standards adopted this view as well, beginning with their initial formulation in 1954 and continuing until the third revision in 1985, although the taxonomy varied to some degree over the revisions. For the most part, the major categories of validity were labeled as *criterion-related*, *content*, and *construct*.

Criterion-Related Validity

Criterion-related validity involves correlational approaches, and has been often conceived to encompass two subtypes, concurrent and predictive. As the names imply, *concurrent* validity refers to the degree to which the target test aligns with criterion variables measured more or less simultaneously, while *predictive* validity refers to the test's prediction of future events, such as success at a job, or its alignment with test scores obtained at a later point in time. In later versions of the Standards these were combined under the single heading of *criterion-related* validity. What the two types share in common is a reliance on empirical evidence from specific identified sources to arrive at a judgment about the test's validity status. This was historically the dominant view of what *validity* means, through approximately the 1950s.

For example, a newly developed measure of some construct of interest may be introduced into a crowded field in which other measures already exist. The supposed advantage of the new measure might involve a gain in practicality rather than improved truth or accuracy. Thus it may be shorter or less psychologically sensitive than existing measures. For example, the Rosenberg Self-Esteem Scale (Hyland et al., 2014) consists of only 10 items, considerably shorter than other available self-esteem measures, and is the most widely used scale for measuring that construct. As a different kind of advantage, it may be that the new test is designed for group-based administration whereas prior measures require individual administration by a trained tester. Or the new test might be less expensive to implement due to paper-and-pencil self-administration or savings on proprietary copyrights. For these or other reasons, the new test of a construct might be welcome even if other measures already exist. If the test is shown to correlate with one or more measures to some anticipated degree, that finding provides evidence for the test's validity, that is, the appropriateness of interpreting its scores as a measure of the construct in question. However, the level of that association with the criterion measures will be carefully considered and may be a point of contention among critics.

Concurrent and predictive validity typically have somewhat distinct purposes, despite their underlying similarities in perspective and approach. Predictive validity has an intuitively appealing functional clarity—specifically, the prediction of future status—that makes it well-suited for purposes of selection, such as hiring from among job applicants or colleges' selection of incoming students. By contrast, the classic purpose of concurrent validity is to make comparisons *between* tests. As noted, if an existing, well-established test is expensive or time-consuming to administer, a newly developed test can be used in its place, provided that a sufficient degree of equivalence or compatibility can be demonstrated. Thus the theoretical underpinnings of concurrent and predictive validity—that is, the assumptions about what "validity" means and the type of evidence it depends on—are similar and congruent, but the two types have distinct niches with regard to their purposes and uses.

Content Validity

Content validity makes no claims about correlational relationships, but rather addresses whether the test adequately captures, represents, or samples the universe of content that the test has been developed to measure. Content validity is most relevant for tests that are designed to assess the attainment of skill or mastery in some domain, and thus it is particularly applicable to educational achievement tests, which may be focused on knowledge acquisition (e.g., vocabulary), cognitive skills (e.g., long division), or motor skills (e.g., keyboard skills). Outside of the educational domain, content validity is also relevant for uses of tests that involve selection.

The assessment of content validity does not involve measuring congruence with an outside criterion, but rather focuses on identifying the hypothesized content domain and determining how well it is represented by the specific content of the test. The test represents a sampling from that domain, and therefore the content universe must be carefully defined and mapped. Once this is done, one can determine whether that universe is represented appropriately, with an appropriate balance of elements.

Another aspect of content validation is the determination that the cognitive processes required to answer the test questions, whatever they may be, are relevant to the abilities about which judgments are being made. For example, if a test item is intended to assess mathematical reasoning in answering a complex problem, producing the correct answer should require the replication of those reasoning processes. That process is subverted for a respondent who happens to remember the answer without needing to go through the reasoning.

These two sets of criteria for content validity—adequate sampling of the test items from a content domain and the requirement of engaging in specified response processes to arrive at the correct answer—are often assessed through expert appraisal, such as in the form of an invited panel of professionals with strong expertise in the relevant content domain. In sum, content validity focuses on the substance, selection, and composition of the test questions rather than agreement with an external comparator.

Construct Validity

This final form of validity in the conventional tripartite model was a new concept when it was proposed in the first edition of the Standards in 1954. Lee Cronbach and Paul Meehl, who were both members of the joint committee that produced the Standards (with Cronbach as chair), followed up the next year with a paper that has become one of the seminal articles in the history of validity theory (Cronbach & Meehl, 1955).

Construct validity refers to how well the test represents and measures an individual's status on the construct that comprises the focus of the test. Cronbach and Meehl did not identify a limited set of processes that could be used to establish construct validity for the uses of a test. Instead, they postulated that the validation process for construct validity requires the researcher to demonstrate that the test scores are consistent with the nomological network that already exists for the construct. For example, if a test is developed to measure a psychological trait such as sensation seeking (Zuckerman, 2007), construct validity will be confirmed if the test scores correspond to other measures in a manner consistent with the theoretical formulation. Another reason for the relative elusiveness of construct validity has been the sheer scope of the concept. Angoff (1988) wrote: "...we can see that construct validity as conceived by Cronbach and Meehl cannot be expressed in a single coefficient. Construct validation is a process, not a procedure; and it requires many lines of evidence, not all of them quantitative." (p. 26). Messick stated: "In its simplest terms, construct validity is the evidential basis for score interpretation. As an integration of evidence for score meaning, it applies to any score interpretation—not just those involving so-called 'theoretical constructs.'" (Messick, 1995, p. 743).

Limitations of the Tripartite View

Over time, the idea that there are different varieties of validity came to be seen as problematic. Despite the ubiquity of the tripartite view through the 1980s, the field of psychometrics was moving to abandon it. Lee Cronbach wrote, in 1988: "The 30-year-old idea of three types of validity, separate but maybe equal, is an idea whose time has gone" (Cronbach, 1988, p. 4).

A large part of that problem was in the pragmatic applications of the concept. Test developers tended to choose one or another of the subtypes for their validation studies, and then consider the case closed. Critics also noted that test developers, in their validation studies, tended to collect data that were most available and accessible—that is, easiest to collect—rather than data that conformed with a conception of what the test is designed to do, which would lead to a determination of which type of validity would be most appropriate to pursue. Another issue was that the validity types often overlapped, which made labels of construct, content, and criterion validity somewhat arbitrary.

The unit within the tripartite view that has the most in common with scientific inquiry, in general, is construct validity. Due to this perspective, many theorists had been moving toward a view that construct validity encompasses the other forms. The prominence of construct validity continued to rise in the second half of the 20th century, and because of the perceived similarity of construct validation to the overall research process, many psychometricians came to see it as central and essential to all forms of validity. For example, Zumbo (2009) wrote:

> Although it has been controversial, one of the current themes in validity theory is that construct validity is the totality of validity theory and that its demonstration is comprehensive, integrative, and evidence-based. What becomes evident is that the meaning of "construct validity" itself has changed over the years and is being used in a variety of ways in the current literature. Arguably in its most common current use, construct validity refers to the degree to which inferences can be made legitimately from the observed scores to the

theoretical constructs about which these observations are supposed to contain information. (p. 68)

Cronbach himself maintained this perspective as well, writing in the final edition of his textbook on psychological testing: "The end goal of validation being explanation and understanding, construct validation is of greatest long-run importance" (Cronbach, 1990, p. 152).

The view that "all validity is based on construct validity" presaged the unitary theory of validity, and made it a short conceptual jump to the view that validity itself cannot be divided into subtypes.

The Current View: Validity as a Unitary Phenomenon

Samuel Messick (1989, 1995) provided the most comprehensive rejection of the traditional view, advancing the idea that validity is a unitary concept. He wrote: "One or another of these forms of evidence, or combinations thereof, have in the past been accorded special status as a so-called 'type of validity.' But because all of these forms of evidence fundamentally bear on the valid interpretation and use of scores, it is not a type of validity but the relation between the evidence and the inferences drawn that should determine the validation focus. The varieties of evidence are not alternatives but rather supplements to one another. This is the main reason that validity is now recognized as a unitary concept." (Messick, 1989, p. 16).

Consistent with this view, the current conception of validity presented in the 2014 Standards does not enumerate separate kinds of validity. What used to be the different forms—content, predictive, concurrent, and construct—have been reconfigured to represent different *forms of validity evidence* (AERA et al., 2014).

Approaches to the Process of Test Validation

Traditionally, there have been several well-established approaches for assessing the validity of a test or measure. The approach that is most appropriate in a particular instance depends on the purpose of the test and the theoretical underpinnings of its target construct(s). Thus, for example, predictive and concurrent validity (both tied theoretically to external criteria) would typically be validated through correlational approaches: investigations would determine whether the test could predict the relevant event, or, alternatively, whether it would correlate with other tests that purport to measure the same construct. Tests that were intended to reflect a psychological construct would be subjected to factor analytic studies to determine the loadings of the items. Tests that purported to sample a universe of academic content would be subjected to content validity studies.

With the ascendance among psychometricians of the unified view of validity, many of these same approaches are still used, but they are considered to be simply different kinds of evidence rather than different phenomena. The 2014 Standards identifies five specific types of validity evidence, which, to some degree, are traceable back as restatements of the tripartite forms of validity.

1. **Evidence based on test content.** Consistent with earlier conceptions of content validity, this form of validity evidence is particularly suited to tests that are hypothesized to sample from a universe or domain of content. This includes educational achievement tests, which often sample from a body of knowledge or desired academic skills, as well as personnel selection tests, which sample from a domain of high-priority job performance skills. Rather than demonstrating the test's agreement with an external criterion or confirming its theoretical structure, content analysis seeks to demonstrate that the items comprising the test are a suitable representation of the larger domain of content from which it is drawn. This may be true for an area of subject matter knowledge or a type of skill set, such as various kinds of mathematical operations, the knowledge needed to be a lawyer in a particular state, and so on.

   The processes of content analysis often take the form of review by an expert panel, which can pass judgment on considerations such as the representativeness of the test content with regard to the content domain and the priority and relative weight of components of the test. A second approach is to develop a table of specifications (Bandalos, 2018), which details the scope and focus of the knowledge domain being measured, and, thus, what materials the test must sample. This table is then used to generate the specific content of the test, and the test content can be mapped onto the specifications.

   Two important concepts here are *construct-irrelevant variance* and *construct underrepresentation*, both of which are content-related threats to validity. Construct-irrelevant variance refers to differences between test scores that are due to something other than differences on the construct in question. As illustration, consider a carelessly constructed multiple choice test item. An alert student might recognize that one response option is longer and more detailed, or more carefully conditional, than the other options, and correctly infer that this option is correct. In that case, differences in students' scores might be due in part to their familiarity with the specific type of test, rather than whatever knowledge is presumably being tested.

Construct underrepresentation refers to a situation in which the construct is not fully represented. For example, a standardized test of math skills might include items related to arithmetic operations and fractions, but omit items related to decimals. In such cases score differences could indeed be due to differences in mastery of the construct, but if components of the construct are fully included in appropriate proportions, those differences will be more accurate, and possibly either larger or smaller.

2. **Evidence based on response processes.** This category of evidence refers to investigations of how the test takers answer the questions on the test, and is affirmed if it can be demonstrated that the processes necessary for arriving at correct answers on the test are those that are hypothesized for the target construct. For this category, reference to the underlying construct is key to providing evidence. For example, the determination of an answer to a question about long division should require going through the division process. The validation process involves task decomposition, that is, "an examination of test responses from the point of view of the processes, strategies, and knowledge stores involved in their performance" (Urbina, 2004, p. 159).

3. **Evidence based on internal structure.** This form of evidence relates to the relationships among the individual items in the test and the test's focal construct. The response patterns for the test items must demonstrate an internal organization or structure that conforms with the prediction of the construct. This evidence is based most commonly on some form of factor analysis, especially confirmatory factor analysis. The factor loadings, i.e., the correlations between the set of test items and the underlying dimension(s) of the test, can be examined to demonstrate evidence in support of the theory of the construct. Thus, if a construct is hypothesized to be unidimensional, a factor analysis should indicate that a single factor contributes to test scores. If the construct is presumed to be multi-dimensional, the factor structure would align with the theory underlying the construct, in terms of the number of factors (or subdimensions of the construct) as well as the items that load on each of those. Other kinds of analysis that demonstrate evidence based on internal structure include patterns of item difficulty and item response theory.

4. **Evidence based on relations to other variables.**
   Conforming with the older concept of criterion-related validity, this category of evidence for validation reflects the perspective that a test designed to measure a particular construct needs to demonstrate agreement with other indicators of that construct, which can include both other tests and different kinds of criteria. This form of evidence is correlational, examining whether the test takers' scores on the test conform with their status on other criteria relevant to the test's construct. A key distinction is whether we are talking about evidence that is predictive or concurrent, conforming with the traditional division within criterion-related validity that was presented earlier.

   Predictive evidence refers to the test's ability to predict test takers' status on some criterion that is measured at a later point in the future. This present-to-future relationship is the essence of a selection test. For example, the SAT test is designed to be administered to high school students with the purpose of predicting their future success in college, and has been used by colleges and universities as a part of the admissions process for many decades. Accordingly, for this test, the most direct form of validity evidence would be any of several indicators of later college success, such as grade point average, college graduation, or first year retention versus dropout. However, the SAT has been criticized as reflecting cultural and economic bias in its test scores and its susceptibility to test preparation courses that are more accessible to students from affluent families (e.g., Soares, 2020). The SAT has both detractors and supporters, but these concerns would constitute a threat to the test's validity based on the fifth form of evidence—the uses of test scores—discussed below.

   Concurrent evidence, by contrast, refers to the test's agreement with other measures that are assessed at approximately the same time as the test in question. For example, a test that is measuring a personality-related construct would be expected to correlate sufficiently well with other existing tests that purport to assess the same construct.

   Despite the emphasis on correlation in the description of criterion-related validity, some diversity exists in the potential methodological approaches that they employ, and the connection to "correlation" should not be interpreted as referring solely to a reliance on the correlation or regression coefficient. Besides straightforward correlational evidence based on criterion variables, the validation process can involve investigations of whether the test can distinguish between existing groups that would be expected to vary on the construct being measured. For example, a psychological test, e.g., of obsessive compulsive disorder, could be administered to a sample of known OCD individuals in comparison to a general population sample. The statistical analyses in these studies could involve t-tests or other tests of group differences. However, in this last case the conception of criterion-related validity begins to overlap with that of construct validity. Such ambiguity is one of the factors that led psychometricians to develop the view of validity as a unitary concept.

Donald Campbell, although best known for his contributions to the theory of validity in relation to experimental design (see Chapter 3), made a significant contribution to psychometric validity in a collaboration with Donald Fiske (Campbell & Fiske, 1959). Their procedure, called the multitrait-multimethod matrix, involves developing a pattern of correlational results based on other measures, some of which are hypothesized to measure the same construct as the target test and some of which are hypothesized to measure something else. In addition, the measures can differ from each other in their use of different methodologies, e.g., survey self-report, self-ratings, ratings by others, or essay examinations. A case for validity of the target test is demonstrated if the highest correlations exist for the measures of the same construct using similar methods, while measures of the same construct using different measures would be expected to display a somewhat lower level of correlation. Measures of different constructs using different measures should display the lowest correlations.

5. **Evidence for consequences of testing.** This form of evidence, introduced by Messick (1995), is the most recent of the five types. It refers to whether the uses of the test's scores—that is, the test's consequences—are appropriate. If it can be demonstrated that test-based decisions and other consequences of using the test have value compared to not using it (e.g., in producing more accurate hiring decisions), that will constitute evidence that these particular uses of the test are valid. It must also be determined that the uses and consequences of the test are fair, equitable, and free from bias to the extent possible.

This criterion is particularly relevant for tests that are used for purposes of selection, into either academic programs or employment settings. Thus this form of validity evidence is directly relevant to considerations of social justice in test use. As an example, consider again the SAT. Given the criticisms and extended debate about socioeconomic and cultural bias in the use of this test for college admissions decisions, an increasing number of colleges have dropped it as a requirement of the application process, either making it optional or eliminating it entirely.

The Argument Perspective on Validity in Measurement

Cronbach (1988) introduced the perspective that test validation should be viewed explicitly as a process of argument, rather than one that should adhere strictly to the procedures and protocols of scientific research. He noted, "Validation speaks to a diverse and potentially critical audience; therefore, *the argument must link concepts, evidence, social and personal consequences, and values.*" (p. 4, italics in original). He was making several points. First, the validation process must anticipate, and be responsive to, the perspectives of the audiences that receive the information. Further, it should incorporate elements of argument and persuasion that go beyond the presentation of empirical evidence. The argument perspective was offered in contrast to the perspective of scientific inquiry. Finally, the process must be able to accommodate and incorporate uncertainty with regard to the judgment. "'What work is required to validate a test interpretation?' That question, with its hint that we are after a 'thumbs up/ thumbs down' verdict, I now regard as shortsighted and unanswerable" (Cronbach, 1988, p. 4). His chapter went on to identify five specific perspectives that should be accommodated in the validation argument, which he labeled the *functional*, the *political*, the *operationist*, the *economic*, and the *explanatory* perspectives.

This view goes beyond what many other theorists were saying about validity, but it is compatible with the unitary view, and the central role of construct validity, because it speaks to the need for a wide array of types of evidence and the conception of validation as an ongoing process. In presenting his perspective Cronbach cited contemporary thinking in the field of evaluation as a model, particularly Ernest House. Cronbach wrote: "Validation of a test or test use *is* evaluation.., so I propose here to extend to all testing the lessons from program evaluation. What House (1977) has called 'the logic of evaluation argument' applies, and I invite you to think of 'validity argument' rather than 'validation research'." (p. 4). The argument view was taken up by Michael Kane (2013), who has become its most prominent proponent.

The perspective among some psychometricians that test validation is a process of argument opens a bridge to applying concepts of validity to other topic areas within the field of evaluation, including, e.g., recent scholarship on evaluative thinking (Buckley et al., 2015).

In this chapter we have reviewed the origins of validity theory in the psychometric tradition, and the evolution of the concept over the past century. A quote here from Messick (1989) is apropos: "Validity always refers to the degree to which empirical evidence and theoretical rationales support the adequacy and appropriateness of interpretations and actions based on test scores." (p. 13) In this book I try to represent that principle, with regard to other kinds of judgments. If we replace the term "test scores" with "elements of the evaluation plan," we have a concise summary of one of the themes of this book.

In the next chapter we will examine how the concept of validity was borrowed and extended beyond test scores to apply to an entirely different set of considerations: the adequacy of research, experimental designs, and evaluation studies.

Chapter Summary

- The concept of validity originated and evolved within the fields of educational and psychological testing. A consortium of professional societies—The American Educational Research Association, The American Psychological Association, and The National Council on Measurement in Education—first issued a joint statement of standards for educational and psychological testing in 1954 and have updated that statement several times since, most recently (as of this writing) in 2014.

- Validity refers to the truth and accuracy of test score interpretations. It is a property of those interpretations rather than a static property of the test itself. Validity also takes account of how test scores will be used.

- According to the 2014 Standards, a *construct* is "the concept or characteristic that a test is designed to measure."

- The traditional, tripartite view of validity recognizes three validity subtypes that are used to understand the accuracy of a test:

  - Criterion-related validity involves correlational approaches. It can refer to the test's correlation with criterion variables that are measured at the same time (concurrent validity) or in the future (predictive validity).

  - Content validity addresses whether the test adequately represents the universe of content that it has been designed to measure. Content validity is particularly appropriate for tests of skill or mastery.

- Construct validity refers to how well the test represents the individual's status on the construct that comprises the focus of the test.

- The modern view of validity rejects the idea of distinct validity subtypes and views validity as a unitary phenomenon. What used to be considered different forms of validity are now seen as different forms of evidence that supplement each other rather than serving as alternative approaches. Five specific types of validity evidence have been identified:

  - Evidence based on test content

  - Evidence based on response processes

  - Evidence based on internal structure

  - Evidence based on relations to other variables

  - Evidence for consequences of testing

- Lee Cronbach advanced the idea that test validation should be viewed as a process of argument rather than purely a process of empirical research. This view is consistent with Ernest House's view of evaluation as a process of argument, which is expanded upon in later chapters.

Questions for Reflection—Chapter 2

1. In your judgment, what are some constructs for which it would be relatively straightforward to develop measures? What are some constructs for which the development of measures would be particularly complex?

2. From your own professional experience, identify a measure that you have used or that you are familiar with. What is the construct that is addressed by this measure?

   - If you needed to gather evidence to demonstrate the construct validity of this measure, how would you go about the task?

3. As this chapter describes, testing theorists now generally view validity as a unitary phenomenon, which can be examined using different kinds of evidence. This replaces the older tripartite view, which tended to associate different kinds of evidence with different kinds of validity. What were the shortcomings of the tripartite view that led it to be eventually abandoned?

Interpretations of Validity in the Theory and Practice of Evaluation

Validity is a major topic of discussion among evaluators and in the evaluation literature, but its form and content differ considerably from the way it is discussed in psychometrics. The terms internal validity and external validity, so familiar to evaluators, do not apply to tests and measures. The person who made the leap was Donald Campbell, in a series of writings that are among the most important in the development of evaluation as a discipline. Evaluators have discussed validity primarily in relation to the design of evaluation studies: their accuracy, relevance, and capacity to shed light on causal relationships. In this chapter we explore these conceptions and note the threads that run through conceptions of validity in all of its guises.

Validity Concepts Applied to Research Designs

Donald Campbell and the Expansion of the Validity Domain: Internal and External Validity

In a 1957 paper in *Psychological Bulletin*, Campbell introduced a multidimensional conception of validity that was to transform the theory of social science research. He identified his domain as experiments and quasi-experiments. He expanded on that conception in a 1963 chapter with Julian Stanley that addressed designs for educational research and which was later reprinted as a monograph (Campbell & Stanley, 1966).

In these publications Campbell was concerned mostly with research designs that examined causality relationships, referred to by Mark (2000) as "cause-probing designs." Most of the research cases he cited were, in fact, outcome evaluations, in that the question was whether some intervention could produce some desired outcomes. The interventions were introduced in the designs as independent variables and the outcomes were included as dependent variables. One of Campbell's core ideas was the introduction of *plausible rival hypotheses* in the investigation of causality. For the researcher to be able to claim a causal relationship between the independent variable and the outcome variable, they would first need to demonstrate that there is indeed a correlational relationship between exposure to the independent variable and performance on the outcome, that is, scores of intervention group students are higher than scores of control group students. Beyond that, the researcher would need to identify those rival hypotheses that could *plausibly* explain the association (that is, in competition with the direct causal hypothesis, which claims that intervention exposure influences outcome status), and systematically rule out as many of them as possible. The degree to which that task could be successfully achieved determined the strength of the design in being able to support claims of causality. The correlational association was determined statistically, but the elimination of plausible rival hypotheses was accomplished primarily through processes of logic in relation to the characteristics of the design. The topic of rival hypotheses is covered in greater detail in Chapter 7.

In his writings through Campbell and Stanley (1966), Campbell posited that there are two general kinds of validity: internal and external. *Internal validity* refers to the conclusions that stem from the data analyses of the individual study. It was called "internal" because these conclusions do not look beyond the confines of the study. More specifically, internal validity refers to the strength of judgments about causality: Did the intervention cause a change in the outcome? Since this is the major purpose of cause-probing research, Campbell considered internal validity to be of paramount importance. Without the confidence to conclude whether or not the independent variable had in fact caused change in the dependent variable in the experimental setting, the study could not be successful in meeting its aims.

External validity—with "external" referring to issues and questions that lie outside the specific conditions of the research study—applies to the degree to which the study's conclusions can be appropriately applied to other scenarios, across changes in sample characteristics, program characteristics, outcomes, and/or settings. Thus, an external validity-related question might be: Given that this educational program successfully increased reading skills in this local sample at this point in time, can we conclude that the program would be similarly successful in a different educational setting, with children that varied in certain ways from the sample here, and perhaps with some differences in program delivery (e.g., absence of a pretest)?

Although Campbell explained internal and external validity in considerable detail, his early writings did not provide a definition of *validity* per se, that is, the superordinate concept of which internal and external were subtypes (Mark, 2000). These writings also did not explicitly acknowledge or draw upon the well-established theory of validity in psychometrics. However, in keeping with the modern theory of validity that became prominent decades later (see Chapter 2), Campbell nevertheless focused the meaning of validity on the appropriateness of *inferences* rather than tests—this at a time when validity was still spoken of as primarily a quality of the test itself. Indeed, Campbell knew the measurement literature well and he had made a major contribution to measurement validity in his paper with Donald Fiske, introducing the multitrait-multimethod matrix system for assessing criterion validity (see Chapter 2).

Nevertheless, Campbell's theory of validity had relatively little connection to the processes of educational and psychological measurement with which validity had been previously associated. It is true that attention to questions of measurement was contained within the theory, with regard to the content of several rival hypotheses (most notably *testing* and *instrumentation*), but it was only one component within a constellation of considerations. Furthermore, the relevant inferences to which validity applied involved the relationships between variables—independent and dependent—rather than the direct meaning of test scores. In that sense, the Campbell concept was an entirely different ball game from what had gone before.

The appearance of Campbell and Stanley (1966) was a watershed event in the development of social science research methods. The essay presented a theory about why experiments are structured in certain ways and what specific advantages can be gained from specific designs. It provided a basis for comparing different designs with respect to their rigor or quality, as well as a vocabulary for doing so. Researchers were introduced to the concept of threats to validity, and the various categories of validity threats were compiled into typologies. Campbell also introduced the concept of the quasi-experiment, which is a research design that approaches, but does not fully meet, the requirements for a "true" experiment, most commonly due to the use of nonrandomized comparison groups or some other form of comparator rather than randomly generated groups.

Because the experiments and quasi-experiments that Campbell presented typically examined program interventions that were intended to produce desirable changes in participants, the writings had immediate relevance for evaluation. Campbell is considered one of the pioneers of the field of evaluation, even though his early writings used the terminology of research rather than of evaluation per se.

Lee Cronbach (1982) endorsed Campbell's specification of two kinds of experimental validity, but in a famous critique, he argued that external validity is the more important of the two subtypes. Also unlike Campbell,

Cronbach explicitly couched his analyses within the frame of program evaluation. He wrote, "After reviewing the claims that have been made for its importance, I shall argue that internal validity is of only secondary concern to the evaluator" (p. 112). Thus a grand debate was launched. Campbell asserted that internal validity was the "sine qua non" of why a cause-probing study is done in the first place. The overall impact of the debate between these social science pioneers sparked a flood of intellectual activity and nourished the evolution of theory and practice within the field of evaluation. Indeed, the debate illustrates the value of another of Campbell's key ideas: the value and self-righting tendency of a "disputatious community of scholars" (Campbell, 1986).

Cook and Campbell (1979) and Shadish et al. (2002): The Validity *Full Monty*

Working with Thomas D. Cook at Northwestern University, Campbell presented a major revision of his work on experimental design (Cook & Campbell, 1979). Years later, William Shadish joined the partnership and they produced a second major revision of Campbellian theory (Shadish et al., 2002; referred to hereafter in this chapter as *SCC*). Campbell himself had died in 1996. These two volumes expanded Campbell's earlier conception of validity in experimental design to include two new components: *construct validity* and *statistical conclusion validity*. Thus, a four-part validity typology was established.

Construct validity. SCC defined *construct* as "a concept, model, or schematic idea" (p. 506). They provided the following context for construct validity:

> Scientists do empirical studies with specific instances of units, treatments, observations, and settings; but these instances are often of interest only because they can be defended as measures of general constructs. Construct validity involves making inferences from the sampling particulars of a study to the higher-order constructs they represent. (SCC, p. 65)

In the specification of units, treatments, observations, and settings, SCC cast their net to include all of the essential characteristics of a research study. The term *units* refers to the sample of individuals who are included in the study as participants, *treatments* to the programs themselves, *observations* to the measurement of the study outcomes, and *settings* to the specifics of the research study's locale—that is, the schools, classes, clinics, hospitals, community centers, offices, etc., in which the studied program is, or is not (in the case of control groups), being implemented.

To illustrate these concerns, consider a hypothetical evaluation study that aims to test the effectiveness of afterschool homework support on children's academic grades in seventh and eighth grades. If the results of this study are to have any bearing on whether such programs are a good idea in general, the particular sample of seventh-graders and eighth-graders who are participating in the study needs to be understood. The identification of the specific grades, though helpful and necessary, is insufficient. Perhaps these are rural, suburban, or urban youth. The sample will have a particular distribution with regard to gender, race, ethnicity, family income, family structure, and many other variables. If and when the evaluation leads to a conclusion such as that "afterschool homework support led to higher grades for seventh- and eighth-grade children," it must be understood that *seventh- and eighth-grade children* is being presented as a construct. Would a valid interpretation of the study be that the program can be helpful for seventh- and eighth-grade children in, say, your own school district? The use of this construct to generalize to many different populations of seventh- and eighth-grade children would probably be more justified—that is, more valid—if a similar positive effect could be demonstrated in multiple studies.

Similarly, the validity of the *treatment* construct in this study, with regard to its implications for interpretations of the results, also requires attention. This hypothetical program is full of specific individual characteristics, involving how often it was delivered and for how many total hours, how the time was used, the characteristics of the program delivery personnel, and numerous other attributes. Each of these characteristics may have a substantial impact on the overall effectiveness off the program, and thus it would probably be premature, and not justified, to consider any positive results to be interpretable for every program that gives itself the label of *afterschool homework assistance*. These considerations are linked to the construct validity of the treatment used in the study. This topic will be discussed further in Chapter 4. Case Study 3.1 provides an example from the smoking prevention research literature, illustrating the complexities that can arise with regard to the construct validity of inferences about educational programs.

CASE STUDY 3.1 THE GENERALIZABILITY OF A SMOKING PREVENTION RCT

I have worked in tobacco prevention and control for much of my career, starting in the 1980s with educational programming for youth in both school and out-of-school settings. In those years, educational programming was perhaps the most prominent strategy utilized for preventing youth smoking. Over time, however, it became apparent to prevention researchers that educational programming, implemented by itself rather than as part of a broad intervention strategy, has very limited effectiveness in preventing young people's tobacco use. Public health researchers increasingly turned

(Continued)

(Continued)

their attention to community-level and society-level strategies. Fortunately there were many of these strategies available, including limiting youth access to tobacco products, placing strong restrictions on tobacco advertising and promotion, implementing antitobacco media campaigns, manipulating the price of tobacco through taxation, promoting smoke-free public spaces, and pursuing legal actions against the tobacco industry to change their manipulative practices (U.S. Department of Health and Human Services, 2012). Smoking prevention programs were not abandoned entirely but they became one component of a far more comprehensive and sophisticated approach. In the ensuring years the rates of young people's tobacco use has declined very significantly, even though it is far from eliminated and remains a public health priority (National Institute on Drug Abuse, 2018).

As these trends were developing, in the 1990s there was considerable debate within the tobacco control community over the effectiveness and proper role of school-based educational programming. In this research environment, the report of a major study was published, conducted by the Fred Hutchinson Cancer Research Center in Seattle (Peterson et al., 2000). Funded by the National Cancer Institute, the Hutchinson Smoking Prevention Project was a 15-year group-randomized controlled trial involving 40 school districts in Washington State. A tobacco prevention curriculum was delivered to students in 20 of those districts that spanned ten years, from grades 3 to 10. The primary outcome variables were current daily smoking at grade 12 and two years thereafter. The trial was designed and implemented with the highest standards of methodological rigor in accord with state-of-the-art recommendations for methodological practice. The study had very satisfactory statistical power. The curriculum, focused on social influences theory, included 15 "essential elements" recommended by an expert advisory panel from the National Cancer Institute.

Despite the strong methodological foundation of this RCT, the results were highly disappointing. No significant differences whatsoever were found between the experimental and control conditions in either of the outcomes. For our current purposes, what particularly caught my eye was the set of conclusions that were drawn about what the study means. The authors wrote:

> The implications of our results for the field of smoking prevention among youth are considerable. These disappointing results raise serious concerns about the social-influences approach as presently conceived and applied to smoking prevention in the school/classroom setting, including those school-based interventions that comply with CDC's 'best practices' guidelines for comprehensive tobacco control programs (41). The HSPP intervention spans grades 3–12, covering virtually the entire period of smoking onset (40,82). It includes all of the components recommended by the NCI-sponsored Expert Advisory Panel (39) and by the CDC's guidelines for school tobacco use prevention programs (40). It was well implemented by trained classroom teachers and was evaluated rigorously. Nevertheless, the intervention had no

(Continued)

impact on smoking prevalence among youth. The HSPP results thus suggest that current school program 'best practices' are not strong enough to deter adolescent tobacco use..... Our judgment is that, given this major failure of the social influences approach despite the extensive nature of the intervention, the remedy should not be more of the same....It may be time for an altogether new approach that incorporates different theories, different intervention strategies, different venues, and/or different providers. (Peterson et al., 2000, p. 1988)

An editorial that accompanied the HSPP study called it the "gold standard" and noted: "Finally, what are the implications of these dramatic findings for prevention science and practice? The results provide compelling evidence of the need for a better understanding of the etiology of tobacco use and dependence...[A]s shown in the HSPP evaluation, existing discipline-specific theories about the causes of smoking among youth are not adequate" (Clayton et al., 2000).

In other words (my interpretation), school-based programming using the social influences approach should be declared dead and preparations should be made for its burial.

When I read this article at the time of its publication, several things seemed apparent to me. First, anyone could immediately appreciate what a tremendous disappointment it is to spend 15 years on a major study and obtain nonsignificant results. Second, this study was undoubtedly a mortal blow to proponents of the school-based social influences education approach. But I also thought, was it really also a *fatal* blow, as the comments seemed to be suggesting? Isn't it an overreach to conclude that the results from this study sound the death knell for the approach? Sophisticated and comprehensive as it was, this was a single program. Is it appropriate to consider it a stand-in for all programs using that approach? This objection is essentially a disagreement with the authors about the external validity of the broad conclusions stemming from this study. I felt that there was insufficient recognition that this experience represented a particular set of units, treatments, observations, and settings: Cronbach's paradigmatic U, T, O, and S. Some other observers agreed with this point of view as well. In a letter to the journal the following year, a group of prominent researchers noted that

The editorial accompanying the article (2) and recent media accounts may lead people to conclude that the social-influence approach is ineffective. That conclusion is unwarranted in light of the larger prevention literature....[I]t is worth considering possible alternative interpretations of these data. For example, it is possible that social-influence approaches do not work equally well with all youth (e.g., HSPP was conducted at small schools in primarily rural settings with primarily white youth). It is possible that youth did not like this particular program, since no process data are reported from youth. It is not clear how representative the HSPP intervention is of other

(Continued)

(Continued)

prevention approaches that include a focus on pro-smoking social influence. (Sussman et al., 2001, p. 1267)

Another letter stated: "Policy questions about tobacco prevention are too important to base on any single study, no matter how well designed" (Cameron et al., 2001, p. 1268).

Thus, this debate concerns the generalizability of a major study and the broad implications of its findings—in other words, the conclusions that can be drawn about external validity. The issue has high-stakes implications because it can influence the continuation of funding and the implementation of a widely delivered approach to youth smoking prevention. The issues about generalizability, or external validity, rest on the interpretations regarding the construct validity of the details of the research trial: the meanings of the units, treatments, observations, and settings. As Cronbach noted, conceptions about external validity are at the heart of judgments about the meaning of research findings.

The problem of variability of treatment across different sites becomes more complex when the study involves multiple program sites. In these cases the evaluator has a critical task in providing an accurate and detailed account of how the program can be conceived in the abstract, given that local sites may vary significantly in important characteristics. As Patton (2008) notes, in cases of extreme cross-site variability, local sites might share nothing more than the same program label. In such instances the construct validity of *treatment* can become an acute challenge for the interpretation of evaluation results.

The construct validity of *observations* is the component of the SCC model that is most intuitively parallel to the conception of construct validity from the psychometric literature, as discussed in Chapter 2. Variations in the conceived outcome variables for an afterschool homework assistance program might include end-of-year grades, levels of subject matter knowledge or skills, changes in skills involving homework independence, or records of homework completion. Further, options exist for how some of these variables can be measured. The ways that these outcomes are conceived and measured influence the nature of the judgments, interpretations, and conclusions that are made from the study.

Finally, the construct validity of the *settings* of the evaluation study relates to the nature of study conclusions as well. For this example, the afterschool setting into which the program is introduced might be small and intimate or large and impersonal; it may house several grades or just one or two; it may be situated in the school cafeteria, the gym, or a classroom. It cannot be assumed that these settings are interchangeable with regard to potential influences on program effectiveness.

Thus we see how almost every aspect of an evaluation study requires careful examination, and in each case considerations of construct validity will inform our interpretations of what has been learned from the study. Each aspect of the study that we will wish to describe involves processes of description and generalization, relevant to the specification of a construct. Construct validity also refers to the substance of our subsequent inferences.

It may seem apparent that construct validity in the SCC sense is closely related to external validity because both conceptions revolve around the adequacy and appropriateness of generalization processes: expanding out from the individual case to the larger set of which that case is a member. The difference is that external validity refers to the generalizability of the study's conclusions, particularly about cause and effect, whereas construct validity refers to the generalizability of study components: units, treatments, observations, and settings.

The Cook and Campbell and SCC volumes go into detail with regard to threats to validity. SCC note: "Threats to construct validity ... concern the match between study operations and the constructs used to describe those operations" (p. 72). SCC identify 14 specific potential threats, which in themselves are just a sampling of the threats that may exist. For illustration, a few of these threats are as follows:

- *"Construct Confounding*: Operations usually involve more than one construct, and failure to describe all the constructs may result in incomplete construct inferences."

- *"Mono-Operation Bias*: Any one operationalization of a construct both underrepresents the construct of interest and measures irrelevant constructs, complicating inference."

- *"Confounding Constructs with Levels of Constructs*: Inferences about the constructs that best represent study operations may fail to describe the limited levels of the construct that were actually studied." (p. 73)

Statistical conclusion validity. As its name implies, statistical conclusion validity refers to the accuracy of the study's conclusions based on the statistical analyses. SCC note that this validity subtype involves two kinds of inferences: first, whether there is covariation between the independent and dependent variables, and second, the strength of the relationship. With respect to the first question, they present a discussion of the classical distinctions of Type I and Type II errors, which draw on the tradition and methodologies of hypothesis testing (discussed in Chapter 8). The second question, regarding the strength of the relationship, is addressed by the estimation of the effect size. Some of the identified threats to statistical conclusion validity include low statistical power, unreliability of measures, restriction of range in the measures, and violated assumptions of the statistical tests.

In sum, validity in the Campbellian model is determined by examination of these four subtypes.

Ernest House: The Validity of Evaluations

In the evaluation literature, Ernest House has provided what is perhaps the most significant counterpoint to Campbell's model when it comes to our understanding of what validity is and how it applies to our evaluation efforts. *Evaluating with validity* (House, 1980) presented validity as a multi-faceted concept that extends beyond technical characteristics of design or measurement, to address the evaluation process as a whole.

In defining the term, House stated: "In a broad sense I take validity to mean something like 'worthiness of being recognized' ...The concept of validity that I have applied to evaluation is considerably expanded from the traditional notion of validity as prediction, although inclusive of it" (p. 249). House saw validity as a quality of an evaluation, with the evaluation study itself being the entity that must be judged with respect to worthiness of recognition and, ultimately, worthiness of being used for decisions or other actions. Thus his view stands in contrast to the definitions of validity as a quality of inferences, judgments, conclusions, and interpretations, e.g., with regard to test scores (the psychometric approach) or causal relationships between variables (the Campbellian approach).

House proposed that the validity of an evaluation is based on three dimensions: truth, coherence, and justice. The *truth* dimension is the one most closely aligned with the other conceptions of validity: the evaluation must present information that is accurate, at least within known and accepted limits. *Coherence* refers to the way the evaluation is framed and presented. It depends on communication and rhetorical choices. The communication of the evaluation-related activities must be compelling and enlightening. In discussing this dimension, House was particularly critical of evaluators who don't take the time, or don't have the skill, to communicate the methods and findings of the evaluation in a way that makes that information accessible to the critical stakeholder audiences for that information. Evaluators who speak from the confines of scientific method, e.g., emphasizing methodological details that their lay audiences might not have the background to understand, will fall short of this criterion.

Finally, the criterion of *justice* was concerned primarily with, in House's words, the political context: the consideration of whose interests are being served by the evaluation. The attention to justice within an evaluation depends on questions such as who the identified stakeholders are, how (and how well) their interests are represented by the evaluation, how their voices have been included in the phases of the evaluation process, and how the evaluation might have been constructed—consciously or unconsciously—to privilege the interests of some stakeholders over the interests of others. In House's analysis, implicit biases may be introduced into an evaluation by seemingly objective decisions about methodology, such as what forms of measurement are considered appropriate, what features of programs become the focus of observation, or what kinds of statistical interactions will be sought and examined. He also proposed that one's conception of justice can limit the approaches to evaluation that will be considered (House, 1980, p. 121). House continued to examine the intersection of justice and evaluation methodology in his later writings, including how randomized controlled trials (RCTs) are susceptible to forms of systematic distortion that can bias results in large drug studies (House, 2008).

House named his three dimensions *truth, beauty,* and *justice.* He later wrote:

> Put simply, my broadening of the concept of validity was based on the ideas that if an evaluation is untrue, or incoherent, or unjust, it is invalid. In other words, an evaluation must be true, coherent, and just. All three criteria are necessary....To add some flair, I talked about "truth, beauty, and justice" in evaluation. The underlying concepts were argument, coherence, and politics. Truth is the *attainment* of arguments soundly made, beauty is the *attainment* of coherence well wrought, and justice is the *attainment* of politics fairly done. (House, 2014, p. 10, emphases in original)

The catchy labels had staying power and took on extended life (e.g., Griffith & Montrosse-Moorhead, 2014). Perhaps this was a case of following one's own advice: We might surmise that the labels were generated by House with an eye toward establishing the coherence, i.e., beauty, of his own presentation of the three-part model.

Underlying House's presentation of the components of evaluation validity is his position that evaluation is properly viewed as a process of argumentation, a view he had long maintained, as described in Chapter 1. (As we have also seen in Chapter 2, a similar view is endorsed by some psychometricians with regard to test scores.) This is in contrast to couching evaluation in the scientific method. The differences between these approaches—evaluation as argument versus evaluation as science—can be profound with respect to the nature of the evaluator-stakeholder relationship. If evaluation is seen as an essentially scientific enterprise, the evaluator's task is to arrive at her/his conclusions through accepted principles of scientific practice. For example, a hypothesis testing procedure will produce evaluative conclusions that can be accepted as true within the accepted bounds of tolerance of uncertainty. The null hypothesis would be rejected or accepted based on predetermined criteria represented by alpha (α) being equal to .05, or .01, etc.—indeed, following standard practices in conformance with accepted principles of statistical conclusion validity (Shadish et al., 2002). Once this is done, if the stakeholders don't accept a finding as justified and—within the mutually determined limits—accurate and true, their lack of acceptance is *incorrect*. That is, they are wrong, based on the rules by which everyone has agreed to play. In this perspective, the essential critics for the evaluation are the researchers who have the specialized expertise to pass judgment on the study's methodology.

By contrast, if evaluation is a process of argument, then stakeholders' rejection of the evaluator's conclusions is, at least to some degree, a result of the failure of the evaluator to present the evaluation in a convincing manner. The stakeholders are not wrong in their negative assessment—they are just a tough audience. In this view, the evaluation is not a forum to demonstrate that a hypothesis, framed within the context of an evaluation question, is true or false. The uncertainty that unavoidably exists in any evaluation study is not there to be rejected based on the study's ability to minimize it beyond a certain threshold (e.g., $p < .01$, or less than 1 in 100 chance of being incorrect). Rather, it is there to provide a backdrop to the strength of the evaluation's argument. In this perspective, the essential critics for an evaluation are, potentially, all of the program's stakeholders.

But a caveat: viewing evaluation as a process of argumentation also assumes a willingness on the part of stakeholders to accept evidence if it is convincing. Stakeholders who reject evaluation findings simply because they don't want them to be true—for example, if they refuse to accept that their favored program failed to achieve its hoped-for outcomes—represent a different kind of problem. Viewing evaluation as argumentation is not an invitation to yield to existing biases. To be meaningful, the evaluation process requires that stakeholders are approaching the collection and interpretation of evidence in a fair and open-minded manner. They are willing to go where the evidence leads, but they are encouraged to apply their skepticism every step of the way.

> In summary, evaluation persuades rather than convinces, argues rather than demonstrates, is credible rather than certain, is variably accepted rather than compelling. This does not mean that it is mere oratory or entirely arbitrary. The fact that it is not limited to deductive and inductive reasoning does not mean that it is irrational. Rationality is not equivalent to logic. Evaluation employs other modes of reasoning. Once the burden of certainly is lifted, the possibilities for informed action are increased rather than decreased. (House, 1980, p. 73)

How can we reconcile the validity conceptions of House with those of Campbell and colleagues? It must be understood that House presented his conception in specific contrast with that of Campbell. He noted that "Campbell and Stanley's typology is a conception of experimental validity, not of evaluation" (House, 2011, p. 71). In presenting his model, House was intentionally attempting to go beyond Campbell's focus on experimentation, to offer a model that applied broadly to the theory and practice of *evaluation.*

Cultural Influences in Evaluation and Validity

Being sensitive to cultural contexts is an essential component of effective evaluation. Recent evaluation theorists have highlighted that evaluations must take account of culture in every phase of the process (Hood et al., 2015). Reflecting the emergence of the topic in evaluation theory and practice, the American Evaluation Association issued a public statement on cultural competence in evaluation in 2011, which describes the central role of cultural competencies and identifies skills and practices associated with those competencies.

The AEA statement defines and describes the concept of culture as follows:

> Culture can be defined as the shared experiences of people, including their languages, values, customs, beliefs, and mores. It also includes worldviews, ways of knowing, and ways of communicating. Culturally significant factors encompass, but are not limited to, race/ethnicity, religion, social class, language, disability, sexual orientation, age, and gender. Contextual dimensions such as geographic region and socioeconomic circumstances are also essential to shaping culture. (p. 2)

The statement also asserts that it is not possible for an evaluation to be culture-free. "Culture shapes the ways in which evaluation questions are conceptualized, which in turn influence what data are collected, how the data will be collected and analyzed, and how data are interpreted" (AEA, 2011, p. 2). Thus, every evaluation must take account of local cultural contexts and incorporate them into its planning and implementation.

Culturally responsive evaluation (CRE) is a term that reflects the application of these concepts to evaluation theory and practice. Hood et al. (2015) describe how CRE relates to each of nine stages of the evaluation process including preparing for the evaluation, engaging stakeholders, identifying the evaluation purpose, framing evaluation questions, designing the evaluation, developing instruments, collecting data, analyzing data, and disseminating and using results.

A CRE perspective also requires paying close attention to power dynamics within the evaluation setting. Power imbalances will typically exist between the funders of evaluation, personnel of the interventions being evaluated, the target audiences for those interventions, distinct stakeholder groups, and the evaluators themselves. These imbalances can influence decisions about an evaluation's goals, methodologies, interpretations, and applications (Hood et al., 2015). Sandra Mathison writes:

> Evaluation is a service bought and sold and while many evaluators frame their practice within larger principles of our professional organizations, evaluation and evaluators are nonetheless responsive to those who pay for their services. I believe it is difficult for most practicing evaluators to imagine that whoever has commissioned the evaluation does not have the most say in what the evaluation questions and preferred outcomes will be. Those with the money dominate the definition of what matters, what counts as success and how that is demonstrated. (Mathison, 2018, p. 116)

An example involving measurement choices is provided by Rodriguez and Acree (2021), who describe how culturally based power dynamics were manifested in the evaluation of a library program serving recently arrived immigrant youth. Program stakeholders disagreed about contentious issues such as the priority that should be accorded to acquiring English language proficiency and the meaning of one of the target outcomes, "belongingness." These disagreements worked their way into the development of a survey of the youth participants. The authors contend that the concepts that were communicated through the content and wording of the survey items were likely to influence the youths' emerging self-concepts of "newcomer identity" in deleterious ways.

Karen Kirkhart: Multicultural Validity

Insofar as cultural considerations are important components of sound evaluations, they also pertain to the validity of the evaluation process. Karen Kirkhart introduced the term *multicultural validity* in the mid-1990s, and describes it as referring to "the accuracy or trustworthiness of understandings and judgments, actions, and consequences, across multiple, intersecting dimensions of cultural diversity" (Kirkhart, 2010, p. 401). This perspective reflects a recognition that culture is imbued in discussions about social problems and society's attempts to address those problems. It is similarly imbued in evaluation efforts to study and understand those phenomena. As she has noted, "A key dimension of validity involves appreciating the culturally bound nature of understandings and judgments" (Kirkhart, 2005, p. 22).

Kirkhart views multicultural validity in terms of five justifications, or areas in which the construct has particular relevance for evaluation theory (LaFrance et al., 2015). These are presented in Table 3.1. She proposed the term "justifications of validity" over "dimensions of validity" (her earlier choice) because the latter term can be viewed as implying that there are distinct subcomponents to multicultural validity, which is inconsistent with the view that it is a unitary construct. In this regard her perspective is

TABLE 3.1 ● Kirkhart's Five Justifications Underlying Multicultural Validity	
Justification	**Focus**
Methodology	Epistemology and method: sampling frame, study design, measurement tools
Relationship	Interpersonal relationships, norms, cultural positions
Theory	Cultural traditions of participants, awareness of culturally bound biases, incorporation of culturally grounded social science theories
Experience	Life experiences of participants as well as evaluators, contributions to the evaluation process by participants and local citizens
Consequences	Promotion of social justice in the learning gained from the evaluation and the actions that taken as a result

Based on Hood et al. (2015) and LaFrance et al. (2015).

consistent with the evolution of the unitary view of validity in psychometrics. As described in Chapter 2, the components of the traditional tripartite view of test validity—criterion-related, content, and construct validity—were reconceived to refer to different types of validity evidence.

Kirkhart's "Consequences" justification indicates that a critical consideration underlying the multicultural validity of evaluations is the manner in which evaluation conclusions are applied. This also corresponds to current validity theory in psychometrics, which identifies one kind of validity evidence as "evidence for consequences of testing" (see Chapter 2). In both instances, the validity of inferences from a test or an evaluation relates to the qualities of fairness, equity, and social justice in the actions and decisions that follow from the evidence assembled and the resulting conclusions.

The concept of multicultural validity applies to both evaluation theory and evaluation practice. In assessing and understanding an evaluation theory, Kirkhart describes the importance of mapping its *cultural location*, that is, "the multiple intersecting identifications that position both an individual theorist and a piece of theory" (Kirkhart, 2010, p. 402). These identifications refer to, e.g., the backgrounds of the theorists themselves, the process of theory development and time period in which it took place, the theory's use of language, the way in which it positions the evaluator with respect to the intervention participants, and other features of the evaluation context. She provides an illustration from the Indigenous Evaluation Framework, a project begun in 2003 that operates from an American Indian and Alaskan Native worldview: "For example, where mainstream evaluation texts may speak of program theory and logic models, IEF expresses it as storytelling or creating a program story" (Kirkhart, 2010, p. 407).

The concept of multicultural validity adds a critical element to how we understand the contributions that validity theory can make to the planning, design, interpretation, and use of evaluations. Insofar as validity generally refers to the appropriateness, accuracy, and truth of evaluation results or measurement scores, a multicultural perspective reminds us that none of these qualities can be considered independently from the local cultural contexts within which evaluation takes place.

Chapter Summary

- Donald Campbell expanded the concept of validity beyond tests and measurement to apply to research designs, especially with regard to experimental studies that examine the effects of an intervention on participant outcomes. Consistent with views of validity in psychometrics, Campbell viewed validity as a property of interpretations, judgments, and conclusions that follow from a study.

- Campbell identified two types of validity that apply to research design:

  - *Internal validity* refers to the strength of judgments about causality: did participation in the intervention cause whatever changes were observed in the outcomes of interest?

  - *External validity* refers to the extent to which a study's conclusions about causality can be applied to other settings and scenarios.

- *Plausible rival hypotheses* are potential explanations for the obtained relationship between intervention participation and outcome change, which are alternatives to the direct conclusion that the intervention was responsible for the change. A strong research design will be able to rule out as many of these plausible rival hypotheses as possible.

- Campbell distinguished between true experiments and quasi-experiments. The latter are research designs that approach, but do not meet, the requirements for a true experiment, most commonly due to the use of nonrandomized comparison groups or some other form of comparator rather than randomly generated groups.

- Shadish, Cook, and Campbell (2002) expanded on the distinction between internal and external validity, to include two additional validity types applicable to research studies:

- *Construct validity* involves making inferences from the specific elements of a study—its units, treatments, observations, and settings—to the constructs that those elements represent.

- *Statistical conclusion validity* refers to the accuracy of a study's conclusions based on the statistical analyses performed. It includes two kinds of conclusions: first, whether there was any covariation between the independent and dependent variables; and second, the strength of that covariation.

- Ernest House introduced a view of validity that applies to the evaluation process as a whole, rather than to the characteristics of psychometric measurement or research design. House proposed that the validity of an evaluation is based on three dimensions:

  - The *truth* dimension requires that the information presented by the evaluation is accurate and that the arguments are soundly made.

  - The *coherence* dimension requires that the findings of an evaluation are communicated in a way that is compelling and enlightening for stakeholders.

  - The *justice* dimension requires that the evaluation is designed, conducted, and presented in a way that is fair and equitable to all stakeholders, and that the interests of some stakeholder groups are not being privileged over the interests of others.

- More recent theories of validity have emphasized that to be valid, evaluations must also be sensitive to the cultural contexts of the evaluation setting. It is not possible for an evaluation to be "culture-free." The American Evaluation Association issued a public statement on cultural competence in evaluation in 2011.

- *Multicultural validity*, a term introduced by Karen Kirkhart, refers to the accuracy of an evaluation's conclusions across dimensions of cultural diversity, which influence every component of the evaluation process. Kirkhart views multicultural diversity in terms of five justifications, which she identifies as methodology, relationship, theory, experience, and consequences.

Questions for Reflection—Chapter 3

1. As described in this chapter, the field of evaluation has conceptualized validity in ways that extend beyond the interpretation of validity as it relates to measurement.

   • What are the major differences in the various definitions of validity that have been applied in these two disciplinary traditions?

   • What are the similarities and links that draw the contrasting conceptions of validity together?

2. External validity refers to the attempt to apply the lessons learned from a completed evaluation study to a new setting in which the intervention is being delivered. What are the challenges that are typically involved in this generalization process? That is, what specific features of the intervention and its contexts must be considered?

3. What are the ways in which House's conception of validity radically departs from that of Campbell and his coauthors? What new dimensions does it add?

4. Reflecting on your own experiences or readings:

   • What were some instances in which cultural considerations were integrated into the evaluation process, with beneficial results?

   • What were some instances in which they should have been integrated but were not? What were the consequences for the evaluation?

Validity Applied to Phases of the Evaluation Process

PART II

Conceptualizing Your Intervention

An *intervention*, broadly speaking, consists of a set of organized strategies that are used to influence a current social condition and bring about desired changes. The term can be used to refer to a program, policy, funding initiative, or other set of activities.

It may not be intuitively apparent that, in the design of an evaluation, the intervention needs to be conceptualized as a construct. On the contrary, wouldn't the intervention be defined operationally as the sum of its component activities? If it is a program that has already been operating, it is an identifiable entity with tangible parts. Or, if a new program is being implemented for the first time, its characteristics are codified in its plan, curriculum, and other documentation. By all means, the intervention will need to be carefully documented and described. But as an actual set of activities, in what sense is it also an abstraction, as might be true for outcome variables such as skills, abilities, psychological characteristics, behavioral patterns, or community-level features?

This chapter addresses the need to consider the intervention as a construct, in the context of the validity of your potential findings and conclusions. I discuss the distinction between the intervention as it is planned and as it is delivered. I also discuss the considerations for interventions delivered across multiple sites, and for conceptualizing the characteristics of interventions across different evaluations. The chapter concludes with a summary and discussion of the implications of this issue for evaluation validity.

What Exactly Is Your Intervention? The Intervention as Construct

The rationale for viewing the intervention as a construct comes into play in several ways. First, it is germane for external validity. Consider: once our evaluation is completed and we wish to make claims about what we have learned, we must be clear and precise regarding the entity that we are making claims about. This can be illustrated from the example of the tobacco prevention education program examined in Case Study 3.1. As I had described, the authors concluded that based on their findings of a lack of program effectiveness, the entire category of school-based tobacco prevention education programs could thereby be considered unlikely to achieve their prevention aims. The authors' warrant for making their claim was that their program contained all the features that had been recommended for such programs by the National Cancer Institute's Expert Advisory Panel. My rejoinder was that in reality they had simply demonstrated the ineffectiveness of a single program, delivered in a limited number of instances by a specific instructional team.

This disagreement revolves around the issue of external validity. How broadly—that is, to how many other settings and populations—could those findings legitimately be generalized? Peterson et al. (2000) considered their school-based program to be a representation of all school-based programs. This difference of perspective boils down to the issue of the construct under discussion. For them the construct of "effective school-based tobacco prevention" was defined as programs containing those elements. However, one must consider the possibility that if another expert advisory panel were to be convened today, it might come up with a revised set of essential program features, based on new insights and discoveries from recent evaluations. In that event, it is possible that the construct of *school-based tobacco prevention* could become a new entity and receive new attention regarding its potential potency as a tobacco prevention strategy. In fact, several evaluations of tobacco prevention educational programs have been published since 2000, with conclusions that the programs have been effective in various ways (USDHHS, 2012). How can these results be aligned with the claim by Peterson et al. (2000) that this school-based strategy is functionally dead?

A second way in which intervention-as-construct is an essential concern involves multisite programs. The way that a program gets delivered will differ across sites in innumerable ways, no matter how precise the curriculum plan and the implementation guidelines. "Even when a treatment supposedly has been standardized, realizations are certain to vary" (Cronbach, 1982, p. 79). Adaptations of programs to meet the perceived needs of local settings may occur in haphazard and unpredictable fashion or, alternatively, may be anticipated and welcomed (Leviton, 2017). In such cases the entity about which conclusions are being drawn is indeed an abstraction, consisting of what are considered to be the essential common features across sites. This definition could well go beyond the contents of the implementation guidelines, e.g., to include physical features of the program locations. Thus the written program plan and implementation guidelines do not constitute a sufficient stand-in for this definitional process.

A third way in which the construct of "the intervention" must be nailed down is in the periodic and essential attempts to bring together independent evaluations to draw conclusions about entire categories of policies or programs. The example of school-based tobacco prevention education has already been discussed. If a research team wished to compile a literature review and draw conclusions about these programs *in general*, they would clearly and unavoidably be dealing with a construct, an abstract notion, that would need to be delineated, understood, and eventually accepted or rejected. Their notion of *school-based tobacco prevention program* would be open to debate and, ultimately, to judgments about validity: did they capture the construct in a way that could be accepted by individual educators, evaluators, funders, critics, and other stakeholders?

Distinguishing Between the Intervention as Planned and as Delivered

The intervention as planned and the intervention as delivered are distinct conceptual entitles. Both versions are potentially of high interest for the evaluation, depending on the evaluation's primary questions, the local project details, and the current state of relevant theory about the topic. Furthermore, they can be easily confused or conflated by evaluators, program personnel, and other stakeholders. A statement may be made about what has been learned regarding the effectiveness of the program, and the program plan may be held up as the entity about which we have learned, when in fact it is the actual delivery that should be the appropriate focus.

Interventions are difficult to implement as planned. This recognition is reflected in the well-known model of intervention trials in medicine and public health, which includes phases known as efficacy trials and effectiveness trials (Singal et al., 2014). Efficacy trials, occurring at an earlier phase in the development process, test whether the program can be successful when it is delivered under optimal conditions, e.g., conducted by the program developers or a team that has been intensively prepared. If these trials demonstrate that the program *can* be effective under the best of circumstances, the model proceeds to effectiveness trials, which test whether the program can also be effective under the normal conditions by which it might be disseminated. Thus, in efficacy trials, the conditions of program delivery are tightly controlled, typically trying to keep deviations at an absolute minimum. By contrast, effectiveness trials incorporate a larger number of sites, using program leaders with no prior familiarity with the program. These leaders have been prepared through curriculum guides or the standard methods developed by the program, rather than carefully and in person by the development team. In effectiveness trials there is an expectation that conditions will vary substantially across sites, and research interest turns to studying how those variations occur and what they portend for the operation and success of the program in field settings.

In place of the distinction between efficacy and effectiveness, some researchers and theorists prefer the parallel terminology of *explanatory* trials and *pragmatic* trials (Sedgwick, 2014). Explanatory trials are described as being able to provide causal evidence for the intervention's effectiveness, under controlled conditions addressing questions of internal validity, while pragmatic trials seek information about the intervention's delivery in the "real world," thus addressing external validity. The functional distinction is essentially the same as that for the classification of efficacy versus effectiveness.

The efficacy-effectiveness model applies to programs expected to receive wide dissemination. But the importance of understanding the range of potential differences between the intervention as planned compared to the intervention at various stages of implementation is equally important for local, single-site programs. After the evaluation has been completed and decisions about next steps are being made, the program stakeholders need to be clear about what they are referring to.

Construct Considerations Applied to Policies

Tobacco control advocates recommend that colleges and universities institute tobacco-free policies, which generally prohibit the use of tobacco in all campus locations (American College Health Association, 2012). Evaluation and research studies have generally found that these policies significantly reduce tobacco use on campus, reduce exposure to secondhand smoke, and promote cessation efforts by students, faculty and staff who use tobacco (Bennett et al., 2017; Fallin et al., 2015).

But what are the essential features needed to qualify as a tobacco-free campus policy? Do these policies all share similarities with respect to enforcement plans, communication efforts, and cessation support? For example, might the following features disqualify a campus policy from being considered "tobacco-free"?

- Allowing the use of e-cigarettes and other vaping products. E-cigarettes contain nicotine but no other parts of the tobacco plant. Most researchers, public health administrators, and policy advocates do classify e-cigarettes as a type of tobacco product, but that judgment is not universally accepted and endorsed. This is a significant definitional issue because in the mid-2010s, vaping became consistently more frequent among young people, including college students, than cigarettes and other traditional combustible tobacco products (USDHHS, 2016).

- Having a designated smoking area on campus where smokers can go to smoke but all other areas are tobacco-free.

- Allowing tobacco smoking on campus for ceremonial cultural uses, particularly involving Native American communities.

In the case of campus tobacco policies, there happens to be an arbiter of such questions that has gained broad acceptance. The organization

Americans for Nonsmokers' Rights (ANR; www.no-smoke.org) tracks the number and types of policies on university campuses in the United States, and maintains a list of smoke-free and tobacco-free campuses (American Nonsmokers' Rights Foundation, 2022). By their definition, a campus that includes designated smoking areas does not receive a designation as tobacco-free. However, a campus that allows vaping outdoors can indeed be considered tobacco-free as long as it prohibits the use of all other forms of tobacco in all locations. ANR tracks and reports this distinction among the campuses on its list. ANR's tobacco-free designation also allows for exceptions to be made in limited instances for tobacco use based on Native American cultural traditions.

In the case of most interventions, such a referee does not exist to make these judgments of inclusion and exclusion. Thus, when considering these questions, stakeholders are on their own to interpret definitions and criteria.

The Interaction of the Intervention With Its Context

Any delivery of an intervention takes place in a certain location and time, involving a host of unique characteristics. This combination of characteristics forms the context for that specific instance of implementation—what Cronbach (1982) called a "realization of the treatment." If a program has been found to be effective, an important line of inquiry will be to determine the degree to which that set of results was dependent on the elements surrounding that particular delivery.

As we saw in Chapter 3, the conception of internal validity focuses exclusively on the delivery under study: how valid are the conclusions about program effectiveness in this single instance, with all of its specific details intact (Shadish et al., 2002)? To the degree that an experiment or quasi-experiment can supply a strong inferential conclusion on this question, the internal validity question has been answered. The question of how well the program will work elsewhere is the domain of external validity. Cronbach made the argument that external validity is the essential concern of an evaluation study, because most audiences examining the completed study will be doing so to determine that program's future prospects in another time and place; the primary value of an already-completed realization is to shed light on that issue. "Insights applicable to units, treatments, variables, and settings not directly observed are, I shall argue, the principal yield of an evaluation—more important than answers about the domain directly sampled" (Cronbach, 1982, p. 83).

Virtually all evaluation theorists and practitioners recognize that the contextual elements and prosaic details of program delivery can play a hugely influential role in the success of the intervention. For example, at a pragmatic, nontheoretical level, a classroom that is too warm or too cold can easily suppress the attention and concentration needed for effective education.

One of Campbell and Stanley's (1966) illustrations of program–context interaction involves the potential influence of a pretest that is administered for purposes of the evaluation study but is not a feature of the program itself. As they describe, the experience of taking a pretest could potentially affect students' posttest scores by creating a practice effect, especially if the evaluator uses the identical test for both pre- and posttest. Thus it may be the pretest that accounts for the gain in scores, rather than the program. This falls into a category of validity threats, or plausible rival hypotheses, that they called *testing*.

Another possibility could be that the program is indeed effective, but *only* if it preceded by the pretest. For example, the combination of pretest plus program could be particularly effective if the pretest provides a sensitization to the upcoming content that promotes the direction of the student's attention in a beneficial way. Put another way, pretest plus program is educationally effective, but program alone is not. This is a validity threat called program–pretest interaction. If such a relationship exists, an inattentive evaluator might conclude that the program is effective, but this would be an incorrect and invalid conclusion. This example of a pretest being appended to a program, with potential confusion about how they interrelate, provides another illustration of why the construct of the *intervention* is consequential—as well as often ambiguous.

In this hypothetical example the pretest—a component of the evaluation that is artificially added to program delivery—winds up becoming an essential ingredient for intervention success. But the larger point is that there are innumerable other contextual elements that may also be operating to influence effectiveness. Leviton and Trujillo (2017) note that one of the challenges implicit in external validity is to determine which contextual elements are helpful, harmful, or irrelevant.

The ways that context and setting will influence the intervention delivery are not entirely predictable. In the next two sections I discuss the need to understand the intervention from two different perspectives: as planned and as implemented. It is useful to distinguish these because different forms of information are involved. The intervention as planned is an abstraction. Even if it is a program that has previously been delivered many times, you as the evaluator are interested in the delivery that is about to happen. The plan is a set of expectations, most of which may well be realized if implementation is reasonably effective. By contrast, the intervention as delivered during the evaluation study will be a one-time empirical event, full of surprises, to be observed, recorded, and interpreted.

Understanding the Intervention as Planned: Program Theory and Logic Models

In developing an understanding of the intervention as it has been planned, before it becomes sullied by the surprises and imperfections of actual implementation, several sources can be consulted. Primary among these are the intervention's program theory, logic model, and logistical plan for implementation.

Program Theory

An intervention is built on a theory about what activities, events, etc., need to occur in order to achieve the desired results. These are sometimes called *small theories* (Lipsey, 1993), in the sense that they have limited scope, referring simply to the intervention's activities, anticipated mediating processes, and anticipated outcomes. Program theories are sometimes built from grander, well-known theories in the research literature that seek to explain patterns and processes of development, various behaviors, family functioning, human learning, social interaction, media communications, adoption of innovations, and so on. An intervention's program theory, sometimes called a *theory of change* (Funnell & Rogers, 2011; Patton, 2008), is a causal model depicting the expectation that participation in the processes of the intervention will lead to the desired outcome(s), often through the operation of intermediate processes.

As a simple illustration, a statement of the program theory underlying drug prevention programs from decades ago may have been:

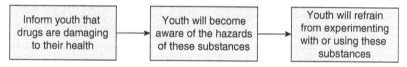

This theory has generally been found not to work, as evidenced by many years of ineffective programs that have (one hopes) been long abandoned. The good news, however, is that the longer that creative program development goes on in a field, the shared understanding of what must occur to promote success becomes steadily more sophisticated. The field of prevention science, including strategies to deter young people's use of tobacco and other drugs, is now complex and multidimensional, as reflected in the program theories of contemporary interventions. This is not meant to imply that opinion will necessarily trend toward unanimity over time; debates and differences of opinion will certainly continue. However, those debates will themselves become more sophisticated, based on a growing evidence base that compels them to evolve. This accumulation of knowledge will result to a large degree from a growing scrap heap of debunked hypotheses—sometimes in the form of program theories—that have been found to be inadequate or simply wrong.

A program theory describing a university campus media campaign to promote sexual health is displayed in Figure 4.1.

The program theory is an essential part of the intervention plan, and as an evaluator, it will be important for you to know it. It may sometimes

FIGURE 4.1 ● A Sample Program Theory for a University Campus Media Campaign to Promote Students' Sexual Health

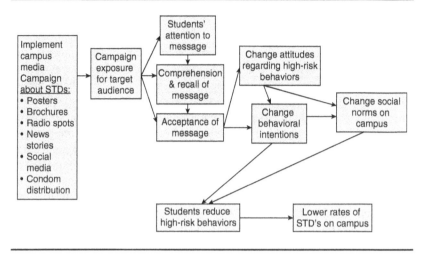

Source: Adapted from McKillip (1989).

happen that there is no existing, explicit statement of a program's underlying theory, although this situation is found less frequently than in years past. A more common occurrence than the complete absence of a program theory may be that the program theory, in your judgment as the evaluator, is inadequate to serve as a useful blueprint for the program or for the evaluation plan. When a program theory is absent or underdeveloped, there are almost always implicit, undeveloped theories that guide the actions of program personnel. Unfortunately, different individuals' implicit theories will not always be consistent or compatible. It can be a useful function of the evaluator to bring an explicit program theory to the fore and to achieve buy-in by key program stakeholders. Funnell and Rogers (2011) describe several approaches for doing so.

The Logic Model and the Logistics of Implementation

The program theory is a conceptual, thematic representation. The plan for the intervention will also require information about resources, specific activities, and expected outputs such as people served or materials produced. For example, the plan for establishing a counseling drop-in center or a telephone hotline will include hours of operation, staffing plans, resources for distribution, a core of providers, training procedures, certification procedures, and so on. An instructional program will entail a certain number of sessions, an expected amount of time, and an expectation for the program leaders, among many other details.

These key features of the intervention plan are often detailed to some degree in the intervention's *logic model*. The logic model is a close cousin of the program theory. Both of these can take many diagrammatical forms, but in most instances the logic model will provide more of the necessary logistical details. A program's logic model will usually be an excellent source of information on what the program planners consider to be the essential components of the program. Typically it will include descriptions of the program's required resources, planned activities, and expected outputs, as well as a chain of expected outcomes, often subcategorized as short-, medium-, and long-term. An example of a logic model for a water quality education program for farmers, designed by University of Wisconsin Cooperative Extension, is shown in Figure 4.2. The figure also shows sample evaluation questions that could potentially be generated from the logic model.

FIGURE 4.2 ● Logic Model of a Water Quality Education Program for Farmers, Along With Sample Evaluation Questions

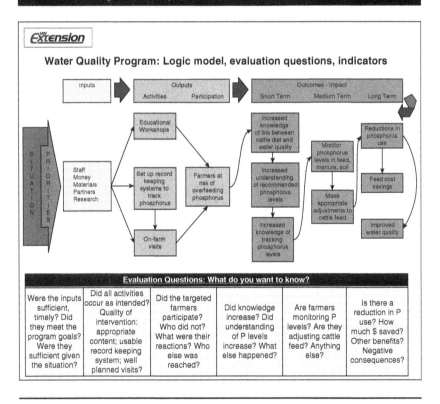

Source: Taylor-Powell (2002).

The example in Figure 4.2 follows the most common format for logic models, consisting essentially of a sequence of lists; Funnell and Rogers (2011) refer to this format as a *pipeline logic model*. "We refer to these as pipeline models because they represent the program as a linear process where inputs go in one end and outputs and outcomes come out the other end" (p. 32). Detailed treatments of logic models are provided in numerous excellent resources available both online and in print (e.g., Funnell & Rogers, 2011; Knowlton & Phillips, 2013). A caveat, however: the terminology of program theories is sometimes inconsistent.

Knowlton and Phillips describe the differences between the two types of planning models. They use the terms *theory of change model* and *program logic model*, respectively, to describe what I have been referring to as *program theory* and *logic model*:

> Theory of change models display an idea or program in its simplest form using limited information. These models offer a chance to test plausibility. They are the "elevator speech" or cocktail napkin outline of an idea or project. Program logic models vary in detail but offer additional information that assists design, planning, strategy development, monitoring, and evaluation. Program models support a display that can be tested for feasibility. They are the proposal version of an idea or project because they have fleshed out far more detail that often includes activities, resources, outputs, and other elements of interest to those creating and/or using the model. (Knowlton & Phillips, 2013, p. 5)

Both the program theory and the logic model can be valuable tools to support the generation of the guiding questions for an evaluation study. Many of the links in a program theory—represented by the arrows between elements—can be conceived as causal hypotheses, with the suggestion that the antecedent element is necessary to bring about the desired change in the subsequent element. (Some links, however, are just intended to represent a time-based or logical sequencing.) All of these links can be legitimate targets of inquiry for an evaluation. Carol Weiss expressed these relationships in her aptly titled article, *Which links in which theories shall we evaluate?* (Weiss, 2000).

Other Information About the Intervention as Planned

The intervention's program theory and logic model—in whatever forms in which they are expressed and available—are primary sources for developing the construct of the intervention, prior to its actual implementation. But there are often other sources as well, such as curriculum plans and other documents. In addition, the intervention plan will by necessity involve logistical, on-the-ground details that are not included in the formal statements. For example, a program will take place at a particular place and at a particular time, delivered by a particular individual or set of individuals. These details, often prosaic, could conceivably influence the intervention's operation and effectiveness, and it is not always possible to predict accurately which factors will be influential and which inconsequential. For example, the person or team delivering the program will almost always be an important and influential feature of delivery. The space in which a program is delivered *might* be important: e.g., the extent to which a physical space encourages or discourages active participation may be relevant to program success. Thus, one function of the evaluation plan is to attempt to identify and stipulate as many features as possible that can influence successful implementation. And a function of the program description, after delivery has taken place, is to try to understand the interactions and influences of as many program delivery features as possible. This process often demands powers of perception, insight, and awareness.

Understanding the Intervention as Implemented

In most instances, understanding the intervention as it was actually delivered will be a more central concern than the intervention as planned. This is the domain of implementation evaluation. Let's take a closer look at three frequent functions of implementation evaluation: program monitoring, fidelity assessment, and, more generally, investigation aimed at understanding the operation of the program in action.

Program Monitoring

This term refers to a class of evaluation strategies aimed at ongoing, routine tracking of the program's activities. Patton (2008, p. 324) describes: "Monitoring program implementation is typically an internal management function. An important way of monitoring implementation is to establish a management information system (MIS) that provides routine data on client intake, participation levels, program completion rates, caseloads, client characteristics, and program costs." In organizational applications of evaluation, "Monitoring and Evaluation" is a well-established subfield in which routine assessment strategies are applied (e.g., Chaplowe & Cousins, 2016).

Braverman et al. (1993) described evaluation strategies for a ropes course program that was administered by the 4-H Youth Development Program in San Francisco. In the ropes course, trained leaders guided groups of youth or adults through a series of outdoor physical challenges in a forest environment. Some of the challenges took place as high as 60 feet in the air, so safety was a prominent concern and, thus, a focus for program monitoring. Therefore, in addition to monitoring activities that included standard types of information such as enrollment numbers, participant demographics, and mechanisms for collecting participant feedback, the program's monitoring procedures also included information feedback systems about safety and leader effectiveness. One such mechanism, simple but effective, was an "accident/close call report," which program staff were trained to complete for any incident that in their judgment reflected a threat to participant safety. In addition, the professional program staff routinely completed several forms requiring the assessment of group leader effectiveness, including an emphasis on how the leader ensured the safety of participants. As this example illustrates, individual program settings may establish the need to institute unique monitoring strategies to collect specific forms of information that are necessary for their local purposes.

Intervention Fidelity

Fidelity refers to the match between intent and delivery, or the accuracy with which the delivery adhered to the plan. "Intervention fidelity" itself is a complex, potentially multicomponent construct that will vary across evaluation settings. Its definition for a particular evaluation study depends entirely on the factors that the evaluator and critical stakeholders identify as most relevant for their purposes. Conceptualizing what fidelity will mean for your evaluation involves determining the intervention's essential components. The process may also include specifying standards for assessing the accuracy or comprehensiveness with which those components are delivered (e.g., "at least 80% of the session's major points were introduced in the discussion"). These standards will allow for a summary judgment to be made about the overall adequacy of delivery. Fidelity may be conceptualized as a single variable (e.g., consistency with the curriculum's session delivery plans) or as an aggregation of several component variables. Case Study 4.1 presents an example of a particularly detailed, multicomponent conception of program fidelity.

CASE STUDY 4.1 A MULTIDIMENSIONAL EVALUATION OF IMPLEMENTATION FIDELITY

Esbensen et al. (2011) described their process evaluation of the Gang Resistance Education and Training (GREAT) Program. GREAT is delivered in middle schools by law enforcement officers and consists of 13 lessons designed to be delivered in 40–45 minutes. The two primary goals of the program are "to help youths avoid gang membership, violence, and criminal activity" and "to help youths develop a positive relationship with law enforcement." The evaluation covered the implementation of the program in the 2006–07 school year, in seven cities: Albuquerque, Chicago, Dallas-Fort Worth, Greeley, Nashville, Philadelphia, and Portland, OR. The unusually comprehensive implementation evaluation concentrated on three areas: (1) officers' preparedness and commitment to leading the program; (2) support

(Continued)

and involvement of classroom teachers and school administrators; and (3) the delivery of the program.

Data for the evaluation included both quantitative and qualitative measurement strategies, grouped into four distinct components:

- Observations of 8 training sessions for officers to learn to deliver the program (either 40 or 80 hours, depending on whether the officers had prior teaching experience);

- Surveys and interviews of all officers in the 7 cities trained to lead the program and their supervisors. Surveys were returned from 137 officers (67% response rate). Interviews were conducted with 27 officers and 5 supervisors in the evaluation study schools.

- Mailed surveys of teachers and administrators in the 31 evaluation schools; 230 surveys were received (29.1% response rate).

- Observations of program delivery in 31 schools. Altogether, 492 onsite observations were made of 33 officers in 31 schools in 7 cities; 26 lessons were double-observed to determine interrater reliability. The observation protocol included checklists, ratings, qualitative comments, and notation of unexpected occurrences. In rating the implementation quality, fidelity was judged to have been achieved if 5 conditions were met, including 70% of the lesson content being covered, a total lesson time of at least 20 minutes; lesson content covered in the recommended sequence; student participation; and observer rating of implementation quality of at least "good" (3 on a 5-point scale).

From the analyses of implementation data, the evaluators concluded that overall, the fidelity of program implementation was strong. Twenty-seven of the 33 officers delivered the program with fidelity that was rated adequate or higher. However, the analyses revealed numerous insights regarding implementation issues and potential for improvement, including the following:

- The training sessions consistently overestimated the time that would be available to teach the lessons. The trainings typically took about 1 hour to complete a lesson, while the average time permitted by the schools for lesson delivery was 40 minutes.

- As a result of the reduced teaching time, lesson adherence was adversely affected, in ways that could include combining lessons, reducing coverage, or eliminating activities.

- Apart from the time available, some of the officers had problems with time management. These problems stemmed primarily from two causes: disruptive students and unexpected occurrences (such as schedule changes, the officer being interrupted to respond to a school disturbance, etc.).

(Continued)

(Continued)

- Classroom management problems were sharply reduced when the classroom teachers were involved in the lesson, but this only occurred in some of the classes.

- There were variations in officer enthusiasm for teaching the GREAT program. The officer surveys revealed that involvement in the program does not generally improve chances for promotion, allows fewer opportunities for overtime, and is not perceived well by other officers.

The evaluation produced a number of valuable recommendations. Among these were to modify the officer training to reflect that actual time that is typically available for lesson delivery, to potentially build in strategies to uniformly shorten lessons when necessary, and to strive to promote greater teacher involvement in program delivery.

This unusually wide-ranging implementation evaluation illustrates the variety of dimensions that can be ascribed to the construct of "fidelity," and the ways that data collection strategies follow from that definition. It also illustrates the significant level of resources that is sometimes required to conduct an implementation evaluation.

Measuring fidelity. The variety of ways to measure fidelity reflects the complexity of the concept. The specific method will depend on the specification of the fidelity components, the resources available at your disposal, the planning time available to develop the measures, and the logistical considerations required to implement the measures during program delivery. Some general rules of the road can be suggested for developing this part of the evaluation plan:

- Give careful consideration to what the fidelity constructs will be.

- Collect input from the primary evaluation users and other critical stakeholders.

- Develop a process of developing measures that parallels the development of your outcome measures.

The importance of these processes is underscored by a variety of potential functions that the assessment of intervention fidelity may have. For example, a clear understanding of fidelity will be essential if you find that the intervention did not succeed to the degree that was desired or expected. In that eventuality you will need to tease apart the possible reasons underlying this failure to achieve results. Some possibilities are theory failure, implementation failure, and measurement failure, among others.

Standards of fidelity. Once you have determined what your fidelity variables and measurement strategies will be, you will need to determine how the data from these measurements should be interpreted. That is, how should these scores be mapped onto your expectations and definitions of what the program should be? Several approaches are possible:

- *A dichotomous standard.* For a particular fidelity variable, you may wish to set a single threshold value for whether fidelity has been achieved. This may be most relevant for multisite programs in which each site can be assessed in this way. This assessment could be used, for example, to set up a series of outcome analyses that take fidelity into account: e.g., a primary analysis in which *all* sites are included, followed by a secondary analysis in which the passing sites are included. (This gets into issues of *intent to treat* analyses, described in Chapter 8.)

  A complication for using a dichotomous fidelity standard occurs if multiple fidelity constructs are identified and measured. In those cases, the attempt to label a delivery instance in a binary capacity will be obscured by the possibility of scoring adequately on some of the variables and inadequately on others.

- *A graded standard.* Expanding this idea to more than two levels, fidelity can be conceptualized in three levels or more (e.g., *strong, adequate, unacceptable*). This approach will be more sensitive to site variations and will probably yield more useful information than a dichotomous approach.

- *A pseudo-continuous range of values, without application of adequacy judgments.* Levels of one or more fidelity variables can be identified across a range of values (designated here as "pseudo" because the variable would probably take on some limited number of values rather than being truly continuous), without a judgment necessarily being made as to the adequacy of those values. These variables can then be included as site-level components in multilevel analyses.

  The complexity of this question is enhanced by the fact that it doesn't necessarily require a straightforward answer in every case. Many high-quality implementation evaluation studies identify the components of fidelity and examine how they have influenced and interacted with program effectiveness vis-à-vis the intended outcomes. This provides an understanding of the operation of the program, and if this is the main kind of information required, there may not be a need to deliver a judgment about the "level" of fidelity that was achieved. To be sure, in many cases this will indeed be desirable, but that depends on the stakeholders and audiences for the evaluation, so it is a locally determined desideratum.

These considerations will be particularly important for the evaluation of multiple sites because different sites will be characterized by different levels of effectiveness on the intervention's target outcomes. You will need this information to try to understand why those differences between sites occurred.

Evaluation Activities Aimed at Understanding the Intervention's Operation

The field of evaluation has largely moved on from the days in which interest centered around a program's effects without consideration for how those effects came about – the so-called "black box" approach that treated a program as an impervious whole (Mead, 2016). Most evaluators are keenly interested in delving into the reasons for the presence or absence of effectiveness. Indeed, numerous evaluations focus primarily on the operation of program elements.

Implementation evaluation and *process evaluation* are terms often used inconsistently; some evaluators treat them interchangeably while others draw distinctions between them. A critical point is that these evaluations focus on aspects of program operation, generally going beyond the mere documentation of program activities that characterizes program monitoring. Implementation evaluations often seek to provide explanatory analyses that can either confirm or disconfirm the explicit program theory.

One way to view the extensive variety of implementation evaluation approaches is to look at their purposes on a continuum, with straightforward documentation and accountability on one end and explanation, insight and theory enhancement on the other. Questions focused on program documentation may aim to track benchmarks or the achievement of program goals (Rossi et al., 2019). In that case, data collection may be concerned with issues such as the following:

- Reaching the program's intended target population: Is the target population being reached? How many of the program's participants are part of the target population?

- Delivery of program components: Is the program plan being implemented as it was intended? Are all aspects of the plan being implemented thoroughly?

- Are there any challenges—anticipated or unanticipated—involving program implementation?

- (For a media campaign) How many people viewed or engaged with each component of the campaign (e.g., public service announcements, website content, social media, etc.)?

A second dimension on which implementation evaluation questions can be distinguished is whether or not they incorporate judgments about sufficiency or adequacy. Components of program delivery may be assessed in light of standards that have been developed by either the evaluator, the program's personnel, other administrators, prior literature, or other stakeholders (Rossi et al., 2019). For example, if an estimate is calculated regarding the percent of the target population that is being served, these standards could be used to determine whether that proportion is very successful, reasonably adequate, or unacceptable.

Third, implementation evaluation questions may vary in the degree to which they seek to identify and explain the linkages between program components and program outcomes. For example, a variable that distinguishes between program sites may be included in the data analysis in order to examine whether it covaries with scores on the primary outcome variables. The explanatory power of these linkages can be valuable for program revision and refinement.

Table 4.1 provides some further examples of implementation evaluation questions that are categorized by, first, the degree to which they involve

TABLE 4.1 ● Potential Implementation Evaluation Questions for the Project 4-Health Evaluation, Based on the Type of Information Collected and Its Relationship to Program Outcomes			
		Type of Implementation Information Collected	
		Straightforward Documentation	Interpretation
Linked to program outcomes?	No	• What was the space in which the program was delivered? • In the discussion periods, what were the levels of parent participation in the discussion?	• What were the levels of youth attention and engagement during the presentation?
	Yes	• Was the size of the space correlated with the attention of participants? • At the site level, was parent participation related to higher or lower outcomes?	• Did sites with higher levels of youth participation have better results on the educational outcomes? • What aspects of curriculum delivery were associated with higher outcomes?

interpretation versus documentation, and, second, their reference to program outcomes. The table refers to a tobacco prevention program called *Project 4-Health*, which was delivered to 4-H youth in 36 sites across California (D'Onofrio et al., 2002). The program delivery settings varied widely, including schools, libraries, and gyms. Parents were invited to sit in on the program, and the levels of parent attendance and participation differed across sites. The numbers of youth and parents at each site was also highly variable. Thus there were numerous factors relating to the conditions of program delivery that could conceivably influence the measured effectiveness of the program across sites, and the evaluation team was attentive to the need to measure dimensions of program implementation. Table 4.1 illustrates some of the implementation questions that were addressed in the evaluation.

Insightful treatments of implementation evaluation are provided by Patton (2008) and Rossi et al. (2019), among other evaluation texts.

Multisite Interventions

The question, *What is the intervention?*, is rendered more complex for interventions delivered at multiple sites. As we have seen, the delivery at each site will be unique in numerous important respects. In such cases the construct of "the intervention" will demand particular consideration and will depend on what we specifically want to know. To cite a few potential options, "the intervention" might be considered to be:

- The activities at a single site, in which case the sites will have thematic similarities but must be considered separately.

- The sum of activities at all sites.

- The sum of activities at all sites, but including only those sites that have achieved a satisfactory (to be defined) level of fidelity.

- The set of core elements of the intervention plan.

Evaluating Independently Functioning Sites

Case Study 4.2 describes an evaluation of foster group homes for youth offenders that was conducted by Michael Patton (2008). This evaluation project is a good example of the process of identifying critical features of intervention sites that may be related to successful outcomes. In this case the foster homes were pre-existing, so this is not an instance of sites coming into existence and conforming to an overall original program blueprint. However, the analytic process illustrates a common theme in the evaluation of multiple-site interventions: through a variety of techniques that may include observation, theory-based insight, stakeholder discussions, statistical analysis and other processes, characteristics of the intervention are identified and studied. These characteristics may be preidentified in the evaluation plan or discovered post hoc.

CASE STUDY 4.2 AN EVALUATION OF THE FUNCTIONING OF FOSTER GROUP HOMES

Michael Patton (2008) describes an evaluation of foster group homes, which he conducted on behalf of the Community Corrections Department in a Minnesota county. One of the program's primary objectives was to reduce criminal recidivism in the youth. "The theory undergirding the program was that juvenile offenders would be more likely to be rehabilitated if they were placed in warm, supportive, and nonauthoritarian environments where they were valued by others, could therefore learn to value themselves, and were provided caring guidance about how to make responsible decisions" (p. 329). The evaluation investigated the quality of care in the group homes and its relationship to positive outcomes for the youth.

Patton's evaluation team examined 50 group homes. At each one they collected data on the youths' recidivism and other indicators relating to successful adjustment, and they administered a questionnaire to the youth, foster parents, natural parents, and corrections personnel. The items on the youth questionnaire addressed their perceptions of relationships with the foster parents, their inclusion in family decision-making, and other indicators of the foster home environment. The data analyses included a factor analysis of the youth questionnaire responses, which identified one dominant factor on which 19 items loaded above .45. This factor accounted for 54% of the variance in youth recidivism.

The evaluators then convened a half-day meeting with community corrections staff, welfare department staff, court services staff, and members of the county board. "That meeting included some 40 of the most powerful elected and appointed officials in the county as well as another 160 field professionals" (Patton, 2008, p. 488). In an interesting twist on the usual roles taken on by evaluators and stakeholders, a primary purpose of this high-level meeting involved an activity that typically is done exclusively by the evaluation team: to have these professionals discuss the findings and identify the primary factor. Through a process of coordinated discussion, the group arrived at a conclusion, specifying *supportive-participatory* as the descriptor of the group home environment at one pole and *nonsupportive-authoritarian* as the descriptor at the other pole. The data analysis revealed that this dimension was strongly associated with recidivism, with recidivism occurring in 56% of the *nonsupportive-authoritarian* homes and only 24% of the *supportive-participatory* homes.

The group meeting participants were also asked to develop recommendations that would be included in the final evaluation report. Following the evaluation, local policymakers used this information and the recommendations

(Continued)

(Continued)

to improve the quality of foster home environments and the training of foster parents.

In this example, the evaluators knew, from the program theory for the group homes, what they were looking for: dimensions of warmth and support in the group homes. They developed their measures to assess this quality. Because of its inherent complexity, they did not treat it as a single variable but rather subjected participants' opinions to factor analysis, allowing for the possible emergence of more than one important dimension. Through this process they were able to categorize the group homes on the variable of interest. The inclusion of primary stakeholders is a central tenet of Patton's *utilization-focused evaluation* approach, but this evaluation took the unusual step of actively including stakeholders in the process of data interpretation.

In initial analyses of this type, we aim to identify site features linked to success. But as the intervention becomes refined in future cycles, these features can be built into the plan as essential core components. The intervention construct evolves to incorporate the lessons gained from practice.

Another point about this example is worth mentioning: exceptional time and effort were put into creating and leading a meeting of busy people, for the purpose of engaging in a task—interpretive data analysis—that is usually the province of the evaluators. Further, in addition to participating in this facet of the data analysis, this group followed up by developing the evaluation's recommendations. The extra effort paid off. One can imagine that the commitment of local decision-makers to put this new knowledge to use was significantly enhanced by their inclusion.

Local Adaptations

Conventional wisdom holds that for programs delivered at multiple sites, the program administrators should strive to achieve maximum fidelity at all of those sites. In this way, we can be confident that to the best of our knowledge, program participants are undergoing the best experience that can be provided to them. From the point of view of the evaluation, striving for maximum fidelity at all sites will create the most valid test of our program theory, and we will have the strongest warrant to draw conclusions about the program's operation, effectiveness, and impact.

This view certainly makes sense. But it is counterbalanced by a recognition that if the participants and settings at the different sites are dissimilar, there may be value in allowing the program to be adapted to local circumstances. Adaptations can take many forms, major and minor. To cite a few examples:

- The participants at a particular site may be from a cultural group that differs from the other sites, creating problems of cultural relevance for some of the activities as written in the script.

- The participants at one particular site, relative to other sites, may be unusually knowledgeable about the subject matter, suggesting that the introductory presentation of information should be shortened from the prepared script, to avoid their getting bored and distracted.

- The group at a particular site may be unusually large, which may make one or more of the planned activities, e.g., asking everyone to contribute to discussion, logistically unworkable.

Those examples involve situations that may possibly be foreseen and planned for. In other cases, program delivery will be unexpectedly forced to adapt to local circumstances. An educational program may be developed for school-based delivery under the assumption of a fixed time period for each session, but it may turn out that for some schools the available time period is shorter or longer, either for all sessions or on a particular day, as was found in Case Study 4.1. As another example, the expected educational technology may be missing or malfunctioning at a particular site, forcing the presenter to improvise from the original plan.

For these reasons, program designers and evaluators sometimes plan for, and even welcome, the possibility of local adaptations to the program plan. In any case, adaptations will often be possible or necessary. The extent to which this occurs depends in part on the control of the program delivery process. Strict centralized control can be expected in an efficacy trial, while more control is afforded to local sites in an effectiveness trial.

The presence of local adaptations to an intervention—whether anticipated or not, welcome or unwelcome—presents complications for both the construct validity of that intervention and the external validity of evaluation inferences. Regarding construct validity, the status of "the intervention" becomes harder to understand, identify, and establish. Regarding external validity, stakeholders must determine how the intervention, in whatever form it is understood, will translate into new settings with new audiences.

Laura Leviton (2017; Leviton & Trujillo, 2017) has recommended that program designers work closely with local practitioners—those who know the local audiences and who may be delivering the program—to develop functional adaptations that can increase the effectiveness of programs in those local contexts. As a senior evaluator with the Robert Wood Johnson Foundation (RWJF), Leviton has worked to institute a research program that studies the process of adaptation, with the support of RWJF-funded programs.

External validity acknowledges the fact of variation, which increases uncertainty for both decision makers and practitioners about where an intervention will be effective, for whom, and in what context. Because the number of combinations of populations, settings, practitioners, and treatment variations is endless, external validity is always an inductive process. Program theory is essential to identify the regularities across contexts where an EBI [*evidence-based intervention*] is used. Then, the populations, settings, and other context features that have a greater importance and frequency can take priority for assessment. (Leviton & Trujillo, 2017, pp. 442–443)

The Evaluand as Label

Policymakers and funders of large projects, especially at the national level, will often consider the focus of an evaluation to be all of the sites under the funding umbrella. However, many large funding initiatives result in sites having little in common. Patton (2008) has cautioned against conducting large evaluations without understanding site-level differences, which he likens to the evaluation of nothing more than a label. "What a program calls its intervention is no substitute for gathering actual data on program implementation. Labels are not treatments. I suspect that over-reliance on program labels is a major source of null findings in evaluation research. Aggregating results under a label can lead to mixing effective with ineffective programs that have nothing in common except their name" (Patton, 2008, p. 327).

My own view is that the truth of this perspective lies in the danger of misinterpreting one thing (the label) for another (a cohesive intervention construct). But there may be times when the evaluation of multiple sites linked by an organizational affiliation is precisely what is desired, with full understanding that the sites are strikingly different from each other. The great hazard with evaluating a label that connotes little substantive information regarding actual services (e.g., "in-home care," "afterschool instruction," "school-based nutrition education") is that stakeholders will mistake the label for the intervention and believe that they are being told something about the on-the-ground activities. By contrast, if it is recognized that nothing specific is to be inferred about local site delivery, the common thread is the inclusion of the larger initiative. In these cases, the "label" may itself be the target of inquiry, and the construct being examined is the funding initiative.

An example of this issue, with respect to complex funding initiatives, is the Children, Youth and Families at Risk (CYFAR) initiative of the National Institute of Food and Agriculture (NIFA). Since the 1990s, CYFAR has provided grants to every state's land-grant university Extension Service. The grants are used to develop and deliver innovative projects that serve—as the name says—at-risk children, youth, and families. "The projects are planned at the state level, and thus there is no expectation of continuity or coordination of specific program activities from one state to another. Further, within a state, there is often diversity in how the program is shaped and delivered across counties, and even between community sites within counties" (Braverman, 2019, p. 100).

Within the CYFAR initiative, there is no misunderstanding about whether these state sites are delivering the same program. They are not. And yet, because Congress has funded the CYFAR initiative every year (at varying levels), CYFAR's administrators and national evaluators are accountable to show the results and impacts of these programs. The theme tying the programs together, besides the target populations and the Extension grantee organizations, is the funding umbrella. As with all government programs, there is a need to examine whether the money is being well spent. As part of the response to this mandate, the CYFAR program has developed a set of common measures to be used across sites. As I wrote on a previous occasion:

> This broad tapestry of projects, many of which share common aims, presents a daunting challenge for the task of measuring their impact on target outcomes. In response, a national CYFAR evaluation team developed a series of scales to be used as common measures across sites.... The use of common measures across program sites can be enormously valuable, by providing continuity and standardization in the evaluation process.... Results at different sites can be aggregated to allow for evaluative conclusions at the level of the broad program initiative, while different program delivery options can be compared for relative effectiveness. Thus, the credibility and actionability of evaluation evidence will often be considerably enhanced, especially for program funders and other stakeholders at levels of administrative and policy decision-making. For example, the use of common measures to assess critical program outcomes across states allows NIFA to report about the broad impacts of the CYFAR initiative to its parent agency, the U.S. Department of Agriculture. Common measures can enhance the credibility of evaluation data at the community site level as well, if it is communicated that the data stem from highly regarded, widely used instruments. (Braverman, 2019, pp. 100–101)

The use of these measures to tie the project sites together for evaluation purposes is, in one way of looking at it, evaluating the CYFAR label. But the difference from the previous examples is that there are no misunderstandings about the level of consistency in the site interventions lying behind that label. Indeed, each of the individual grantee states must conduct its own evaluation of its program activities, in addition to participating in the national effort. This is due to the recognition that putting all of these apples and oranges together into a single data analysis is an inadequate way of understanding what is occurring at the program level, even though there is a separate logic that dictates the "lumping together" process. In this case the construct under evaluation is "CYFAR," but it is identified and understood clearly as a funding stream, not an individual intervention.

Building the Knowledge Base: Comparing Interventions Across Evaluations

The concept of intervention-as-construct comes fully into view when we try to build knowledge by comparing results from different interventions, which are thematically related in pursuit of the same general goals but independently developed and implemented. As we have discussed in this chapter, it is no small task to specify even a single intervention as a construct. When we create a conceptual umbrella that combines independently developed interventions, we clearly are talking about an abstraction. What caveats and interpretations are necessary when we talk about, e.g., the limitations or failures of school-based tobacco education (see Case Study 3.1), or the successes of tobacco taxation policy in reducing tobacco use (Chaloupka et al, 2019)? A literature review may report inconsistent patterns of success for interventions that share the same goals; to what degree might those inconsistencies be traceable to identifiable variations across the interventions?

Attempts to summarize across interventions, and to build a construct that encompasses a collection of independent interventions, necessarily rely on descriptions of the core elements and critical features, which have been developed and identified through a combination of program theory and practice. As Laura Leviton describes:

> Better descriptive frameworks to assess generalizability would be helpful, but they are not enough. A general failing of descriptive frameworks is their focus on surface similarity: attending to features that are most readily available on the surface. These may not be the features that make an EBI [*evidence-based intervention*] effective; indeed, some notable failures to replicate based on simple descriptions support this contention (28). Program theory specifies the core components of an EBI (also known as essential program elements as distinct from peripheral or incidental program elements) (44). Core components are necessary to achieve intermediate program objectives....

The underlying challenge involves construct validity: the ability to make inferences from specific activities back to the theoretical concepts on which they were based (11, 23, 26, 76). Although construct validity is often discussed as a measurement issue, in fact it applies just as much to treatments: assessing whether theory has been made operational. As in measurement, the challenge is to infer from specifics back to underlying concepts. Knowledge about construct validity is essential to expanding knowledge about external validity. (Leviton, 2017, pp. 374–375)

What are the practical implications of the challenges involved with developing an adequate construct for a class of interventions? If you are developing or evaluating an intervention, and attempting to build on existing knowledge from past research and evaluation activity to inform your work, it may be helpful to keep the following recommendations in mind.

- **Don't accept a research summary conclusion unless you are clear on how it defines the relevant class of interventions.** A research summary will generalize; that is the task at hand. If the reviewers are doing their job well, they will be crystal clear—to the degree possible—about the specifics of their generalizations. But that is not always the case. In digesting their information, you won't have usable information unless you come away with a good sense of how they are conceptualizing the intervention construct. In large part, that means identifying what they see as the core elements of the intervention and identifying how those elements contribute to the various incarnations that they are reviewing.

- **Be aware of how your intervention conforms to and differs from the interventions being summarized.** The summary conclusions will only be relevant to the degree that your intervention is consistent with those prior interventions. If there are areas in which your intervention is unusual, you may be able to build an argument that your intervention might improve on the level of past success. Alternatively, you might decide that you need to alter your intervention to take advantage of information that has already been learned.

- **When you are designing an evaluation of an intervention, look for the edges of theory, with regard to the core elements.** That is, be aware of what is known and not known, which kinds of elements are established with relatively strong confidence, and which ones are either the subject of some debate or even entirely new. Those spaces are the places where your evaluation may be most likely to contribute to advances in program theory and research knowledge about that type of intervention.

Chapter Summary

- An intervention is a set of organized strategies used to influence a current social condition and bring about desired changes. The term can refer to a program, policy, funding initiative, or other set of activities.

- Conceiving of the intervention as a construct involves identifying the core elements that are essential for effectiveness. This is important for several purposes, including developing program theory and logic models, understanding differences between the intervention as planned versus as delivered, planning for implementation evaluation, understanding the operation of an intervention delivered at multiple sites, and generalizing from a particular evaluation study to other settings.

- Program theories and logic models are schematic descriptions of how an intervention is expected to work and the resources that it requires. There are numerous variations in how these are designed, but typically a program theory is a conceptual representation of the mechanisms through which an intervention is expected to result in its desired outcomes. A logic model is usually more detailed, describing the program's required resources and planned activities in addition to the expected outputs.

- If a program theory or logic model for a planned intervention does not exist, it can be a useful function for the evaluator to work with key stakeholders to develop one.

- Understanding the intervention as it has been implemented is an important evaluation focus. Some useful approaches for doing so—which differ from each other in terms of their specific purposes—include program monitoring, tracking fidelity of delivery, and studying the role and operation of critical intervention components.

- Fidelity of program delivery can be conceived in different ways. The plan for evaluating fidelity can incorporate the use of standards for judging the sufficiency or adequacy of that delivery, based on a variety of different dimensions.

- It can be challenging to address the question *What is the intervention?* for interventions delivered at multiple sites, because the sites will differ in numerous ways, large and small. Some of these variations will influence intervention effectiveness and others will not. Administrators of multisite programs may strive to achieve maximum fidelity at all sites or they may allow for the possibility of local adaptations and deviations from the original plan. Both of these approaches can have potential benefits as well as challenges.

- Understanding an intervention's delivery as a specific case of a more general intervention construct becomes particularly important when attempting to build the knowledge base about entire categories of programs or policies (e.g., "parent education programs," "university smoke-free campus policies") from multiple evaluation studies. Which general program or policy approaches can be effective in achieving a desired goal? To build theory, evaluators and social researchers must attempt to identify the core elements and features that are essential for intervention effectiveness. In these instances, construct validity can be thought of as the attempt to categorize and understand the critical similarities linking a collection of distinct interventions.

Questions for Reflection—Chapter 4

1. As illustrated in Case Study 4.1, the measurement of intervention fidelity can comprise multiple dimensions. Consider one or more programs that you are familiar with.

   - What are some distinct dimensions of program fidelity that would be important to track for assessing the quality of delivery?

   - How would you measure each of those dimensions?

2. Program theories can be developed with greater or lesser levels of detail.

   - Devise a simple program theory or theory of change for a program or policy with which you are familiar. Identify the most important outcomes and mediating processes.

   - Now expand it, introducing additional outcomes and breaking down the mediational chains into finer units.

   - How would the more detailed and less detailed displays of the program theory differ with regard to their usefulness for evaluation planning and for communication?

3. In the coordination of multisite programs, what is the value of maintaining strict control over program operations at the various sites?

   - By contrast, what is the value of allowing local sites to exercise a free hand in adapting the program? What do you see as the correct balance?

   - Suggest some examples of how local program contexts may alter this balance for different kinds of programs.

5

Translating Your Constructs Into Variables

This chapter is about identifying and defining the variables in your model with a degree of specificity and clarity that is sufficient to accurately represent their underlying constructs. Proficient specification of your constructs can promote consensus and understanding among the critical stakeholders in your evaluation study, as well as situate your evaluation within the broader research and evaluation literature.

Identifying and Specifying the Variables to Be Investigated

The variables in an impact evaluation study are those characteristics, properties, and features that differ among participants and whose interrelationships enable us to answer our evaluation questions. In the very simplest of impact evaluations there might be only two variables involved. The first would describe the relationship of the participants to the program. This could be expressed in binary format (e.g., being a member of the treatment group vs. a member of the control group) or it could take on multiple values (e.g., an indicator of program dosage such as the number of sessions attended). The second variable in the evaluation would be the primary outcome that the program is designed to influence.

Of course, most evaluation studies are more complex and involve multiple variables. There will often be outcome variables, including some theorized to change over the short, medium, or long term following program participation. There will be one or more variables representing exposure to the treatment. There may also be proposed mediating variables that appear in the hypothesized outcome chain, potential moderator variables that could influence who will be impacted by the program, and variables upon which participants' selection into the program or study was based. There may be demographic variables included for the purpose of documenting who participated. There may also be variables representing potential undesired (known as *iatrogenic*) effects, which the program designers hope are unaffected by the program and are included to confirm whether this is the case. And finally, there may be variables that *might* be related to the treatment experience in some way, and which have been included in the study in an exploratory capacity to increase understanding about the program.

The identification of variables to include in the study, and the determination of how they will be represented and measured, is a major component of evaluation planning. If this is done carelessly, we might wind up with measures that bear little resemblance to the constructs in which we are most interested. Thus construct validity is a significant part of this process. Case Study 5.1 provides an illustration of the misapprehension of a construct from the research literature on parenting.

CASE STUDY 5.1 PITFALLS IN THE INTER-PRETATION OF CONSTRUCTS: TRANSLATING CLAIMS ABOUT PARENTING STYLES

A column in the *New York Times* in February 2019 had an intriguing headline: "The Bad News About Helicopter Parenting: It Works" (Druckerman, 2019). The subhead read: "New research shows that hyper-involved parenting is the route to kids' success in today's unequal world."

"Helicopter parenting"—a parenting style marked by the metaphor of a hovering helicopter, always ready to come to the rescue when kids encounter a problem—is not a construct that appears in the social science literature to an appreciable degree. But it does show up in the public consciousness with some frequency, almost always in a disparaging light. The usual critique is that kids need to be given space to make their own mistakes and learn from them. Citing the conventional wisdom, the columnist noted: "Psychologists, sociologists and journalists...insist that hyper-parenting backfires—creating a generation of stressed-out kids who can't function alone." So the suggestion that it may actually be beneficial accounted for the headline's counterintuitive hook.

For our purposes, the article gets interesting when it brings in a contrarian analysis from a recent book by two economists (Doepke & Zilibotti, 2019). The book examines historical shifts in parenting styles since the 1970s, arguing that those shifts are influenced by growing economic inequalities in Western societies. Low inequality in the 1970s led parents to be more permissive, "giving children lots of freedom with little oversight." [All quotes are from the Times article, rather than the book.] When inequality grew in the 1980s, "permissive parenting was replaced by helicopter parenting.

(Continued)

Middle- and upper-class parents...began elbowing their toddlers into fast-track preschools and spending evenings monitoring their homework and chauffeuring them to activities." The column reports that the book's authors found that "an 'intensive parenting style' correlated with higher scores" on an international test of 15-year-olds' academic achievement in 2012.

The column continues: "It's not enough to hover over your kids, however. If you do it as an 'authoritarian' parent—defined as someone who issues directives, expects children to obey and sometimes hits those who don't—you won't get the full benefits. The most effective parents, according to the authors, are 'authoritative.' They use reasoning to persuade kids to do things that are good for them. Instead of strict obedience, they emphasize adaptability, problem-solving and independence."

Here is where I believe the interpretation of these constructs becomes murky.[1] The typology of "authoritative," "authoritarian," and "permissive" parenting comes from the influential model of parenting styles originally proposed in the 1960s by developmental psychologist Diana Baumrind (1991). These categories derive from a crossing of the general parental characteristics of warmth (or responsiveness) and control (or demandingness). *Authoritative* parenting, which is indeed the recommended style according to developmental psychologists, is a combination of high warmth with high control, as well as the gradual granting of autonomy as children become older (Baumrind, 1991; Crockett & Hayes, 2011; Martin et al., 2011). *Authoritarian* parenting is characterized by high control but low warmth, while *permissive* parenting is high warmth but low control. Both of these styles have been found to be generally less effective than the authoritative style.[2] (A fourth style of parenting, termed "neglectful," is low on everything.)

The parenting model presented in the column, which follows the presentation in the economists' book, is that authoritative and authoritarian parenting are both subtypes of a high-intensity parenting approach, to which they affix the well-known label "helicopter parenting." Permissive parenting is classified as low-intensity and is therefore non-helicopter. In this way, however, parenting style constructs that have been studied by developmental researchers for decades have been conflated with a construct taken from the popular press. To my knowledge, there is no research that has empirically demonstrated a positive association between authoritative parenting and "helicopter" parenting. In fact, the concepts are incompatible, among other reasons because authoritative parenting promotes children's self-reliance and age-appropriate autonomy, which does not fit with the intensive attempts

(Continued)

---

[1]This is just my opinion, of course, based on my understanding of the research on Baumrind's parenting styles model.

[2]One exception to the critical verdict on authoritarian parenting is that it can be seen as protective for children living in high-crime neighborhoods (Baumrind, 2013). In those cases, what is seen as "overprotective" in other environments can help to ensure the child's safety.

to solve children's problems connoted by helicopter parenting. Numerous detailed descriptions of the parenting styles by developmental psychologists do not mention the concept of "helicopter parenting" (e.g., Baumrind, 1991, 2013; Crockett & Hayes, 2011; Martin et al., 2011). In arriving at this joining of "authoritative" and "authoritarian" with "helicopter," the economists substituted the concept of parental "intensity" for parental "control." In fact, decades of developmental research do not support the idea that authoritarian parenting—presented here as a subcategory of helicopter parenting— "works," as declared by the article's headline.[3] And it is not an accurate interpretation of the parenting styles research to claim, in effect, that you should hover over your kids in an "authoritative parenting" way to get the full benefits—of helicopter behavior.

This example illustrates how constructs can get lost in translation as they migrate from their originally assigned meanings into the public sphere. Terminology is misinterpreted and given idiosyncratic interpretations. As a result, summary claims can be made that are inaccurate and invalid from the perspective of construct validity.

The identification of variables and the approaches used to measure them are interconnected in a multistep process. In this chapter we will examine the processes of specifying constructs and variables. In the next chapter we will look at how these variables, once identified, are operationalized into measures and measurement strategies.

A General Model of Variable Selection and Measurement Specification

As discussed in Chapter 4, the intervention's program theory lays out the relevant constructs and the processes through which the program is hypothesized to affect outcomes. An impact evaluation is designed to examine at least some of those processes. Depending on the time and

---

[3]The claim that helicopter parenting works calls up an entirely different set of questions regarding what is meant by "works." That is, what are the hallmarks of children's developmental success? The varied ways of conceptualizing success can also be a fruitful examination of construct definition. In Doepke and Zilibotti's book, as reported in the New York Times column, "works" takes the forms of academic achievement and adult earning power—which is understandable given their disciplinary orientation as economists. In any case, the present discussion focuses only on the ways that the parenting style constructs are being interpreted, condensed, and presented.

resources available, the evaluation's guiding questions may be broad in scope or tightly focused on covering just one corner of the program theory. For example, the evaluation team might choose to focus on those links in the program theory that are considered most critical for program success, or most dubious, or least examined by prior evaluations (Weiss, 2000). Based on that decision process and the resulting evaluation questions, the evaluators will decide on which constructs in the program theory will be addressed in the evaluation study. Those constructs will, eventually, be represented by the evaluation's measures and observations.

The relationship between the ways that we conceptualize constructs for purposes of understanding, discussing, and theorizing, and the ways that those constructs become operationalized for measurement in research and evaluation is a topic that has received limited attention in the evaluation literature. But the sociologist Hubert Blalock wrote insightfully on the subject years ago:

> Conceptualization involves a series of processes by which theoretical constructs, ideas, and concepts are clarified, distinguished, and given definitions that make it possible to reach a reasonable degree of consensus and understanding of the theoretical ideas we are trying to express...Thus, conceptualization refers to the theoretical process by which we move from ideas or constructs to suggesting appropriate research operations, whereas measurement refers to the linkage process between these physical operations, on the one hand, and a mathematical language on the other. (Blalock, 1982, pp. 11–12)

The process of conceptualizing variables and arriving at measures can be thought of as occurring in four major steps or stages (Braverman, 2013, 2019). Each of these stages is marked by a series of options, choice points, and necessary decisions. The steps are illustrated in Figure 5.1, along with some sample questions that may drive the decision process. Ideally, these decisions would be made by the evaluators working together with primary stakeholders (Braverman, 2013). The four steps are to (a) identify the target construct, conceptualized in a form that is clear, unambiguous, and conducive for discussion, (b) identify the variable, or variables, that will be used in the evaluation to represent that construct, (c) determine the general measurement strategies that will be used to measure the variables, and (d) select or develop the actual measures, protocols, forms, and other instrumentation that will produce the data to be analyzed.

Step 1: Specifying the Constructs for the Evaluation

The target constructs in an evaluation are usually worded in everyday language, often representing concepts that people are colloquially familiar with. The constructs may be stated at the level of the individual, group, organization, institution, or community. For example, at the individual

FIGURE 5.1 ● The Sequence of Moving From Construct to Measure

Identifying the construct of interest	Identifying variable(s) to represent the construct	Selecting the measurement strategy(ies)	Developing or selecting the measure(s)
Guiding questions: At what level of generality is this construct? Is there research precedent for studying this construct?	Guiding questions: Are multiple variables needed to represent this construct? Is the relationship between this variable and the construct direct or indirect? Is it an indicator? If so, what is the level of correspondence between construct and indicator? What assumptions are needed to accept this variable as a stand-in for the construct?	Guiding questions: Are there one or more approaches that are typically used? How resource-intensive is this strategy? Can multiple strategies be used? Is this variable important enough to justify triangulation? What types of bias are associated with this strategy?	Guiding questions: Are there measures already well-established in the research literature or evaluation practice? If so, are they adequate for the present purpose? How well does this measure represent the variable? How resource-intensive and time-intensive is this measure? What types of bias are associated with this measure? If this is self-report, is it reasonable to expect honest and accurate responding?

level, funders and other stakeholders may be interested in patients' skills to manage their diabetes, students' motivation to attend college, parents' disciplinary practices, farmers' knowledge of pesticide regulations, or job seekers' employment success. At the institutional or community level, stakeholders may be interested in a university's student retention and graduation rates, a community hospital's emergency room utilization patterns, county incidence rates of Lyme disease, the month-by-month utilization of a regional hotline, or community levels of opioid abuse and physician prescribing practices.

The evaluator's task at this stage is to ensure that stakeholders feel clear in their own understanding of the construct and that there is at least a rough consensus among the primary stakeholders about what the construct means. If an intervention aims to "build parenting skills," discussion may reveal that different stakeholders are not really clear, or are not in agreement, about what that means. Some further discussion may reach consensus that the construct should be made more specific, e.g., to refer to dimensions of the parent-child relationship such as disciplinary practices, communication, monitoring, and so on.

If a construct becomes refined through this process, the evaluator must also make sure that it remains consistent with the aims, content, and operation of the program itself. For example, at the evaluation planning stage for an ongoing parent education program, a discussion with stake-holders may conclude, "OK, by *parenting skills*, we are really talking about *communication and discipline*." But if the program activities concentrate on other aspects of parenting, this will lead to a mismatch between the foci of the program and those of the evaluation. Thus the evaluator must perform a balancing act in building a consensus about how the primary constructs are to be conceived.

There may be an existing statement of the program theory that already identifies the primary outcomes, mediators, program elements, and other constructs to guide the evaluation plan. The constructs as worded in the program theory will constitute key input for the planning process, but the evaluation team may still find that those terms need to be refined in order to provide clear guidance and a common understanding among stake-holders of how the evaluation should proceed.

Step 2: Identifying Variables

At the level of generality with which constructs are often stated within an evaluation context, it can be hard to conceive of how they can be measured. (This is not universally true; some constructs will be precisely described and operationally self-evident. But those cases tend to be exceptions.) Therefore, for purposes of the evaluation, a construct will be represented by one or more variables on which measurement operations and data analysis can take place. A *variable* is defined as an attribute of a unit—such as a person, family, school, neighborhood, etc.—that takes on different values within a sample or population of those units.

In the translation from construct to variable, the variable might be seen as a direct expression of the construct, simply a version that is specific and suitable for measurement. For example, the construct of "college graduation" is self-explanatory and will require no additional translation, unless the stakeholders wish to specify a timeframe, type of institution, or other condition; either the individual has graduated or they haven't. The construct of "daily exercise" might be changed to "average number of minutes of moderate to vigorous exercise per day." Here, "daily" is just being particularized as "average number of minutes per day." This would be more informative than a binary version of the construct such as whether the individual engages in moderate to vigorous exercise every day (or alternatively, "most days"), for which the scoring options would be simply Yes or No. In these examples there is little new information being added to the mix.

In other cases the translation process will involve the addition of particular details. For example, a decision may be made to operationalize "college success" as "graduation from college within five years, with a GPA of at least 3.0." This case is a compound set of requirements, but nevertheless the variable could be binary: Yes [1] if all conditions are met, No [0] if otherwise. Or "regular smoking" might be operationalized as "having smoked a cigarette or used a vaping product on at least 20 out of the past 30 days." In these cases the added detail may be necessary to enable measurement. Stakeholders might generally agree that the new details maintain their overall intended meaning of the construct. However, the additional information represents choices from among a set of alternatives, and there may be disagreements about what those choices should be. In the college case, some stakeholders may think it best to use a graduation window of four years, or six years, instead of five. In the smoking case, there may be some preference for stipulating, as the definition of "regular" smoking, that smoking should take place every day instead of only a proportion of days.

A construct may be inherently complex or compound, so that the evaluation team may choose to represent it using multiple variables. An education intervention that aims to influence the construct "quality teaching" could break it down into variables that address components such as effective engagement of students, clarity of communication, the use of appropriate teaching strategies, strong command of subject matter, provision of constructive feedback, fair grading practices, and so on. As another example, the construct "illegal drug use" might best be operationalized by creating a variable for each of several drug categories: cocaine, methamphetamines, opioids, hallucinogens, cannabis (although its illegality is dependent on geography and is evolving rapidly), and so on. Each of those could be further split according to timeline, e.g., past-month use, past-year use, and/or "ever" use. Thus, the evaluation team might choose to capture a construct through a dozen or more separate variables.

The overall point is that the evaluation team should be aware of the multiplicity of choices in this process. There is usually not a single choice that stands out as unquestionably best. As House (1980) and others have proposed (see Chapter 3), the validity of these choices is largely based on argumentation: which choices make the most sense and stand the best chance of providing the information we need with least bias? Evaluators should be prepared to defend their choices and recommendations as reasonable. For example, the choice may reflect the precedents that have been commonly used in prior research and evaluation studies. Evaluators should also make sure that the choices make logical sense and are acceptable to the evaluation's primary stakeholders.

Step 3: Choosing the Measurement Strategies for the Variables

For a given variable, the potential options for measurement strategy will depend on the nature of the variable, the time and resources available for data collection, and the evaluation context. By "measurement strategy" I am including the information source, the format of the instrumentation, and the data collection activity. For example, obtaining information about children's study habits by interviewing their teachers and their parents would constitute separate strategies.

For variables that reflect individual behaviors, the options for measurement approach might include self-report by the participant, direct observation by the evaluation team, mechanical or electronic trackers (e.g., pedometers), objective indicators (e.g., plate waste in nutrition programs), reports by others (e.g., children's parents or teachers), or physiological measurement, among others. For variables that reflect participants' skills, knowledge, or aptitudes, the options might include direct tests, self-assessment by the individual, assessments by others, or existing indicators such as standardized test scores. For variables that reflect internal psychological states such as behavioral intentions, personal values, interest levels, or motivations, there will probably not be viable alternatives to self-report. For variables at the organizational or community level, the available options for measurement strategy might include key informant interviews and inspection of public records.

To measure variables that reflect presumably objective kinds of information such as body mass index, weight, or school grades, there might seem to be little choice with regard to available measurement strategies. But even in these cases, decisions must be made that will affect the reliability and accuracy of the results. In the case of weight, for example, the evaluation team will need to decide how carefully to control the time of day of the measurement, and whether the weight should be self-reported or recorded by a member of the team. In the case of grades, they may decide to ask the student or, alternatively, seek direct access to grading information (Braverman, 2013).

Step 4: Selecting and/or Developing Our Instruments

The choice of measurement strategy for a given variable will usually not dictate what the actual measure will be. Thus the final step is to determine the specifics of the instrumentation. This may consist of individual questions, multi-item scales, protocols, rubrics, structured observation forms, instructions for free-form observations and notes, electronic monitors and other devices, performance indicators, and/or other instruments that will directly form the basis for the evaluation data.

Many, possibly most, of the measures and instruments used in evaluations involve the production of data by people answering questions or otherwise responding to structured stimuli. In these cases, attention must be given to the development of questionnaires, scales, and forms. This extends to both the wording of questions and the structure of response options, as discussed with regard to validity issues in Chapter 2. In developing scales and individual items, the evaluators must take account of characteristics of their participants such as reading levels, cultural backgrounds, and prior knowledge of the topic.

Any given measure will have limitations, which might include its cultural appropriateness for use with various populations, its reliability (as measured by internal consistency, interrater consistency, consistency over repeated administrations, etc.), its dependence on human memory or other fallible sources, the specificity of information it provides, and so on. When warranted, the use of more than one measure can help to neutralize the limitations or weaknesses of any single measure (Braverman, 2013). As noted earlier with regard to measurement strategy, the evaluators need to be alert for likely forms of bias associated with any instrument, response format, or question wording.

Table 5.1 and Figure 5.2 provide illustrations of the four steps described here. Table 5.1 provides potential sequences for several sample constructs: *parenting skills*, *physical activity*, and *healthy eating*. Figure 5.2 goes into more depth on how this could look for deciding on measures that will be used to address the construct of *healthy eating*.

The remainder of this chapter focuses primarily on the second of these steps: the identification of variables to represent our constructs. Chapter 6 will cover the final two steps: choosing the measurement strategies and developing the actual measures. My focus is on how we can preserve the original intent of the constructs, identify and minimize bias as much as possible, and make sure that the data, the analyses, and the conclusions match the intent of the guiding evaluation questions. In other words, we will examine these processes from the perspective of maintaining and optimizing the validity of our constructs and our conclusions.

Levels of Specificity

When concepts are discussed in ordinary conversation, a level of ambiguity or vagueness can be tolerated which would not be feasible for social science investigations. Indeed, when a program is being conceived and initially developed, the goals of the program are described in non-specific terms. For example, we may wish to institute a homework assistance program in order to improve our students' *academic success*; we may deliver a program on civic engagement in order to *build future citizens*; and so on.

Note the vagueness. Of course, this is not always the case. We may institute a safe pesticide handling program for farm workers because we want to minimize the incidence of pesticide-related illnesses. Similarly, a nutrition education program aimed at "reducing levels of obesity" has a fairly unambiguous aim, even if there are definitional details still to be resolved.

But once we are putting the program into place and designing a study to measure its effectiveness, we need to be considerably more precise.

TABLE 5.1 ● Measurement Planning: Identifying Potential Options in the Progression From *Construct* to *Evaluation Measures*

General Construct	Specific Variables that Might be Used to Represent the Construct (Selected)	Related Variables that Could Potentially Also be Used as Relevant Outcomes (Selected)	Potential Measurement Strategies
"Parenting skills"	<ul><li>Identification of parenting style</li><li>Parenting self-efficacy</li><li>Parent–child communication</li><li>Parent–child interactions<ul><li>expression of warmth</li><li>empathy</li><li>responsiveness</li></ul></li><li>Discipline practices</li><li>Monitoring</li></ul>	<ul><li>Parental stress</li><li>Parenting satisfaction</li><li>Parent–child relationship quality</li><li>Positive child behaviors</li></ul>	<ul><li>Survey self-report questionnaire (scales or specific items):<ul><li>Self-ratings of knowledge gain</li><li>Behavioral self-report</li></ul></li><li>Observation of parent-child interaction:<ul><li>Live observations</li><li>Videotaped interactions</li></ul></li><li>Interview</li></ul>
"Physical activity"	<ul><li>Daily, weekly, or monthly total minutes of *Moderate to Vigorous Physical Activity* (MVPA)</li><li>Number of days per week with at least 1 hour MVPA</li><li>Average or total number of steps per day</li><li>Physiological tracking (heart rate)</li></ul>	<ul><li>Body mass index</li><li>Sedentary behavior (e.g., sitting time) per day</li><li>Overall physical fitness</li></ul>	<ul><li>Survey self-report questionnaire (scales or specific items):</li><li>Activity logs or diaries</li><li>Interview</li><li>Activity monitors:<ul><li>Pedometers, accelerometers</li></ul></li><li>Direct observation</li></ul>
"Healthy eating"	<ul><li>Overall eating patterns</li><li>Food consumed in the past week (or day or month)</li><li>Meal observation</li><li>Food available at home</li><li>Eating intentions</li></ul>	<ul><li>Family eating practices</li><li>Knowledge of...<ul><li>Nutrition</li><li>USDA's MyPlate</li></ul></li></ul>	<ul><li>Survey self-report questionnaire (scales or specific items):<ul><li>Food frequencies</li><li>Dietary recall (e.g., over 24 hours)</li></ul></li><li>Tracking of food purchases (e.g., from debit card)</li><li>Pantry inventory inspection</li></ul>

Source: Braverman (2019).

FIGURE 5.2 ● Illustration of the Possible Progression From Construct to Instrument (Some Paths Left Incomplete)

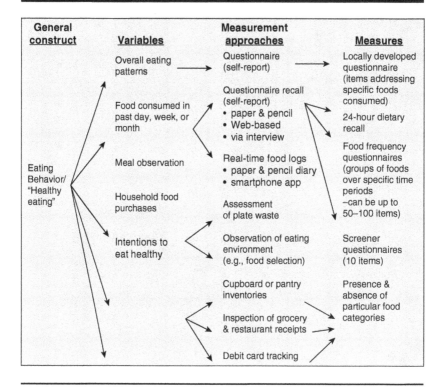

Source: Braverman (2013), p. 103.

Types of Variables to Account for in Your Program Theory

Desired outcomes are the constructs that get most of the press with regard to variables in the program theory, but other kinds of variables are important parts of the evaluation model as well. Some of these categories are as follows:

Outcomes. These are the characteristics for which we wish to produce change as a result of our intervention. In most cases they are qualities of individual participants such as their diet, exercise levels, college readiness, civic engagement, skills in particular subject matters, and so on. But community-level outcomes are common as well. Interventions might be designed in order to increase viability of farmers markets in a neighborhood, change tobacco policies at community housing sites, or reduce opioid prescribing levels within a healthcare system. Some variables might concern individual behaviors while being measured at the level of the community. For example, a vaccination program might measure its success by the number of schools with a target proportion of youth who have been vaccinated.

The evaluation's findings regarding change—or the lack of change—in the outcome variables will constitute the critical core of the evidence base that supports arguments for or against the success of the intervention. For that reason, very often the greatest level of attention during evaluation planning goes into the specification of outcome variables and measures—and quite justifiably so. This means that the measures of target outcomes will often be extensive, leading to longer questionnaires or other measurement activities. In addition, evaluation plans often include multiple ways of measuring the primary outcomes. This can entail measurement time and resources, and the other families of variables, described below, may suffer as a result. This is one common type of trade-off in the evaluation plan.

Hypothesized causal variables. In most outcome evaluations, the core causal variable is participation in the program. Several factors make the specification of this variable more complicated than it may seem at first sight, including the operationalization of the program or levels of it, the operationalization of the comparative conditions, and the meaning of "participation." We will treat this topic in detail in Chapter 7 on evaluation design.

The program theory may also identify other independent variables that influence the outcomes. These other variables might include characteristics of the participants and the program setting. If the program is delivered at multiple sites, it will be possible to identify numerous descriptive variables that may influence post-program outcome status. For example, in multiple sites, a program may be delivered by different teachers, for which distinguishing variables may be prominent (experienced teacher vs. new teacher, teen vs. adult, trained via method A vs. method B, and so on).

Selection variables. These may be variables that dictate which individuals get selected into a program. For example, school-based gifted and talented education programs typically require some kind of threshold score level to gain entry. Similarly, for low-achieving students, remediation programs that provide extra assistance to youth may base their selection on a particular type of score, though in this case it would be at the low end of the academic achievement distribution rather than the high end. As another example, some programs are designed for low-resource families; in these cases, the eligibility variable may be some measure of income or socioeconomic status.

Other correlates. These variables may be used to help understand the program model, e.g., which kinds of participants benefit the most and least from participation in the program. Demographic variables are often included as correlates, which might include race, gender, geographic location, income level, and family structure. Correlates may be entered into the data analyses as control variables, which would sensitize the statistical tests of relationship between the intervention and the outcomes. Correlates may also help to understand the mechanisms that are operating to make programs successful. They will be helpful in identifying mediational processes, which could lead to important program refinements. We will return to this topic in more detail in Chapter 7.

The Use of Proxy Variables to Represent the Primary Construct

Sometimes, for reason of logistics or feasibility, variables are selected that don't represent the target construct directly but rather serve as proxy stand-ins for the construct. In such cases, there must be confidence that these "proxy variables" are highly correlated with variables that would directly represent the construct. For example, the evaluation of a program aimed at producing behavioral change might not have the resources to follow participants for the long term, necessitating that data collection end at the time of the program's conclusion. Therefore, the evaluation might identify a short-term outcome and use it as a proxy for the behavior variable that is of real interest. For example, the behavioral construct of healthy eating might be replaced by dietary intentions, hypothesized as a psychological mediator, as the evaluation's primary outcome variable. In other words, the hypothesized mediators replace the original outcomes in the assessment of program success (Braverman, 2013).

Programs and policies aimed at preventing smoking by elementary or middle-school children often engage the youth before the ages of most extensive smoking uptake. A comprehensive evaluation would need to follow a sample for several years to determine their uptake rates. In the mid-1990s, John Pierce and colleagues at the University of California, San Diego (Pierce et al., 1996) developed a measure of a psychological variable, youths' susceptibility to smoking, which can be assessed earlier in the uptake process than actual tobacco use. In its recent form (Strong et al., 2015), the *susceptibility to smoke* index consists of four items that ask about the respondent's expectations about smoking in the future, potential acceptance of an offer from a best friend, and curiosity about smoking. The potential responses range from "definitely not" to "definitely yes." Respondents who answer each item "definitely not" are classified as *not susceptible* to smoke, and respondents who provide any other answer to any of the questions are classified as *susceptible*. A good deal of research has demonstrated the validity of this measure's prediction of later smoking uptake. Thus the susceptibility measure has been established as a legitimate target outcome that can be used in the evaluation of youth-focused smoking prevention programs and policies.

These shorter-term variables may be identified in a program's logic model as a short-term outcome that mediates the relationship between the intervention and the long-term outcome that appears further down the outcome chain. That is, desirable change in the short-term outcome must be achieved if there is hope of achieving desirable change in the long-term outcome. As one can see, this relationship depends on the accuracy of the program theory's outcome chain (see, e.g., Funnell & Rogers, 2011; Weiss, 2000).

The (Sometimes) Perilous Journey From Construct to Variable

This chapter emphasizes the importance of consistency, clarity, and transparency in the specification of variables. Unfortunately these guideposts are not always reached. Several examples can be found, in the social science literature or in evaluation practice, of significant errors in interpretation that have led to compromised studies. Let's consider a few examples, which are grouped according to the primary reason for the error.

Convenience

In *Utilization-Focused Evaluation*, Michael Patton (2008, p. 35) recounts a Sufi story in which a man searches for his lost key, not in the dark pasture where he dropped it but rather under a street lamp. His reasoning is simple: "Because there is more light here." It may be convenient for this fellow to do his searching in an area where he can see, but unfortunately he will never find his key. Patton uses this parable to make a point about evaluation use: that we might look for the utilization potential of a particular evaluation *after* the evaluation has been completed, but the more productive time would be before any data are collected. However, I have always thought that this story is a perfect example of a different kind of faulty substitution, involving the measurement process: choosing to measure what you're not really interested in rather than what you truly need to know, simply because it is easier to do so. I have seen this "convenience principle" play out on numerous occasions, sometimes involving the choice of which variable to focus on, and sometimes the choice of which measure to use for a given variable.

Self-assessments of learning. For educational programs, the desired outcomes will typically include one or more types of skills or knowledge, e.g., knowledge about *X*, or ability to do *Y*. Evaluators are then faced with the task of deciding how to assess these variables. A relatively rigorous approach would be to identify or develop a reliable test of the outcomes and apply it in a pre-post design, which allows for the determination of the amount of change that occurred over the course of the program. Further, if this measurement of program participants could be combined with a similar pre-post measurement in a control group, the design would allow for conclusions about how much of the change (if indeed there is change) can be attributed to program participation, since the control group provides a no-treatment expectation.

However, the use of such tests to measure outcomes can involve considerable resources of time and money. It may be challenging to find an established test that covers the program's specific content, and, once identified, the test might cost money to use. If an adequate existing test cannot be found, time and expertise will be needed to develop a test specifically for the project. From the perspective of participants, they must consent to completing the test at both time points—pre and post—which represents a cost in terms of their time.

Therefore, some evaluators, especially if they are strapped for time, funds, and personnel, may choose to dispense with a skills test. Instead, at the program's conclusion they may simply ask participants to assess the degree of their acquisition of skills or knowledge. This might be done, e.g., with one or more items that ask some variation of, "How much have you learned about X in this program?", using a point scale that might range from "very little" to "a great deal." This type of self-assessment is considered to be a form of *indirect* rather than direct measurement (Banta, 2004). Despite its convenience, I have previously pointed out several reasons why self-assessment is a far less rigorous method of skills assessment than direct testing (Braverman, 2013). For our present purposes, the pertinent point is that a specific decision has been made as to how to represent the target construct as a variable to be measured in the evaluation. The target variable has been changed. Rather than participants' actual knowledge (or skill) level, as might be demonstrated through use of a direct test, it is now their self-assessments of that knowledge gain. The consequences of this choice will need to be dealt with later, when the evaluator must conjecture about how closely the self-ratings of knowledge gains match the actual gains, or when the choice to use a less rigorous strategy may have to be defended to outside audiences for the evaluation. I have also seen unfortunate instances where the original measured variable gets lost in the data interpretation process, such that the qualifier "self-assessed" gets dropped along the way and the outcome is eventually interpreted, incorrectly, as a directly measured gain in skill or knowledge.

Organizational and Administrative Decisions

Giftedness. The process of selecting participants into a widely administered program, e.g., one that encompasses a school district, requires an operationalization of the selection construct. One may expect that well-established programs tend to use relatively more systematized and well-defined selection processes, due to the need for transparency, organizational accountability, and equality of opportunity. An example is the construct of "giftedness" and/or talent, which schools or school districts may use to determine children's eligibility for their "gifted and talented" programs. Giftedness is generally understood to refer to intellectual ability, in either an overall or specific capacity, and multiple models of the construct have been proposed (Worrell et al., 2019). Some models of giftedness focus on a single kind of general cognitive ability while other models are more complex. Renzulli (1986) proposed a three-part definition that included commitment and creativity as well as ability. Sternberg's "triarchic" model (Sternberg, 2011) also has three components, identified as analytical, creative, and practical intelligence. Gardner's theory of multiple intelligences (Davis et al., 2011) identifies eight independent intelligences, or types of ability, though he asserts that only two of these—linguistic and logical-mathematical—tend to be prioritized in school settings. Worrell et al. (2019) describe 16 models of giftedness in three groupings. The models tend to vary according to the degree to which giftedness is recognized as unidimensional versus multidimensional, as well as the value placed on students' achievement, performance, or productivity in addition to their "inherent" cognitive ability.

The federal government has established a definition, but state agencies and local school districts are free to use it or adopt their own definitions (McWilliams, 2018). As Worrell and Erwin (2011) note:

> [T]he definition of giftedness will help to shape the gifted program's goals and curriculum and will dictate which students are selected for and excluded from gifted instruction....At present, the federal government defines gifted students as those who give evidence of high achievement capability in areas such as intellectual, creative, artistic, or leadership capacity, or in specific academic fields, and who need services or activities not ordinarily provided by the school in order to fully develop those capabilities....[but] in practice, schools tend to focus almost exclusively on general intellectual capability when identifying gifted learners. (pp. 320–321)

In developing their selection procedures, school districts' decisions must include both a clear definition of the giftedness construct and the way it will be operationalized in the selection process. Critics of gifted and talented education programs have noted that the selection process can be arbitrary and unfair, and that there is often disproportionate representation in gifted programs with regard to race, family income, and other demographics (e.g., Peters, 2022; Roda, 2015). From the perspective of the children and families who would be served by the program—*if* the children get selected—the way that giftedness gets operationalized is often viewed as a high-stakes determination.

"Evidence-based." In recent decades, evidence-based decision-making has become an important priority across numerous fields (Rousseau & Gunia, 2016). First taking root in the practice of clinical medicine, the trend rapidly spread across professions and disciplines, to include policy and program interventions as well as professional practice. Proponents of evidence-based decision-making try to ensure that those decisions are based, to the extent reasonable and possible, on objective evidence rather than tradition, anecdote, habit, or various kinds of professional biases.

Thus there is a wide consensus that being "evidence-based" is a desirable quality to be attached to an intervention. But what exactly is it? The concept is ambiguous with regard to the nature of the evidence in question, its strength, and its relevance to the decision at hand (Pawson et al., 2011). Thus, how does that global construct get translated into a form that can be applied in practice?

Carol Weiss and her colleagues described these issues with regard to administrative efforts to require evidential support for the use of drug prevention programs. They concluded:

> [B]asing policy on evidence requires somebody, or some body, to ordain and proclaim the 'best evidence.' An authorized group has to select that evidence which is worth attending to and give it visibility and standing. If evidence-based policy is to be 'imposed,' organizational arrangements have to be made to reach an authoritative answer—or set (or range) of authoritative answers. Here again our case suggests some frailty. (Weiss et al., 2008, p. 43)

I saw some of these complications firsthand when I served on a California panel that examined educational drug prevention programs in the late 1990s. The panel was charged with determining which programs should be approved for use by local school districts with state drug prevention funds. A major criterion for approval was that the program had some demonstrated evidence of its effectiveness. What constituted satisfactory evidence? Our panel was free to make that determination, but our general guidance was that there should be at least one published and refereed journal article reporting a statistically significant level of effectiveness for the program, with regard to at least one outcome variable.

In practice, we found this guidance to be more ambiguous and less helpful than might appear at first glance. One reason was that it is not very difficult for researchers to obtain evidence of significance for a single variable within a study (e.g., Gorman & Huber, 2009). One could attempt to do so by testing for a great many outcomes and dividing the program audience into a great many slices. It becomes quite likely that at least one of the *outcome x audience* combinations will return a significant finding—due either to a Type I error or a highly localized actual program effect. In addition, we were determining the adequacy of evidence with regard to fixed grade groupings (corresponding to high school, junior high school, etc.), whereas a published finding of significance might have applied only to a single grade (e.g., effective for fourth graders but not for fifth graders). Thus this type of pattern would not provide a strong warrant that the program would be similarly effective for all grades within the groupings we were dealing with.

In sum (and simplifying somewhat for the purposes of illustration), the guidance that was provided to us operationalized the important guiding construct of "evidence-based" into the dichotomous variable "demonstrates significance in a journal article." Our panel discussions determined that this substitution was far from satisfactory in terms of its validity for representing the essential construct.

Changes in Conceptualization in the Translation From Research to Intervention Practice

Resilience. The construct of "resilience" is extensively encountered in the context of child and adolescent development, and its enhancement in young people is a prime goal of many program interventions offered for youth. However, the construct is particularly challenging to pin down because it is, by most definitions, compound in nature (Masten & Monn, 2015; Rutter, 2012). Ann Masten, a leading resilience researcher, summarized:

> Identifying resilience in a person's life requires two kinds of evaluation: judgments about exposure to adversity and judgments about how well a person is doing in the midst or aftermath of the adversity. In other words, resilience is inferred from two sets of evaluations, one concerning the nature of threat posed by their life experiences (has there been risk?) and a second one about the quality of adjustment or a person's development (is this person doing okay?)....If there is little or no threat in an individual's life, or if there is not (yet) evidence of recovery or good outcome, then there is no observed resilience (at least not yet). This sounds obvious and straightforward, but the devil is in the details of defining risk and good outcome, and who gets to decide on these criteria. It has become clear in the study of resilience that these decisions can be complex and controversial. (Masten, 2014, p. 13)

Similarly, Masten and Monn (2015) noted: "Resilience is not construed as a trait, though numerous individual and family attributes are associated with the emergence of positive adaptation in the presence of threats and elevated risk" (p. 6). Thus, from this research perspective, the assessment of resilience is a multi-step, inferential process based on the assessment of its component constructs: (1) risk or adversity, in conjunction with (2) competence, adaptation, or developmental success.

The resilience construct, understandably, has had a powerful appeal for youth practitioners because of its obvious value for young people facing difficult circumstances. And a range of attempts to incorporate it into intervention development has led to some reinterpretation and, possibly, simplification of the construct. In intervention practice, it has largely been reconceptualized as a trait-like characteristic (despite Masten and Monn's admonition, above) that numerous interventions aim to instill in children, e.g., through outdoor adventure and other experiential education experiences (Overholt & Ewert, 2015; Whittington & Aspelmeier, 2018). And efforts to evaluate these programs have created a need for scale-like assessment strategies that are suitable for rapid administration and pre-post designs. In these cases, the idea of identifiable adversity needing to be a prerequisite for the possibility of resilience has been dropped.

Indeed, a great many instruments have been developed to measure resilience (Windle et al., 2011). Some of these measures are quite short, consisting in the most extreme cases of less than 10 items. Many of them have been developed with methodological care and attention to the resilience literature. However, for the most part, these scales address assets and competencies that have been associated with resilient outcomes—such as self-efficacy, problem-solving, future orientation involving goals and aspirations, and so on—rather than the resilience construct itself. They typically do not measure past or present exposure to adversity. Thus the evaluations of these programs are based on a particular logic: (1) certain personal competencies have been found to promote resilient outcomes, (2) the programs have led to increases in those competencies, and therefore (3) it can be surmised that resilience itself has been enhanced.

I do not mean to assert that this approach is completely incorrect. Many competing definitions of resilience exist, and the tent of resilience scholarship has grown large, diverse, and unwieldy. But it does appear that in these cases the term *resilience* is being loosely used to refer to specific forms of competence in children, rather than the original definition of resilience found in most developmental research. The assessment of that logical link becomes essential to the decision as to whether this substitution and the resulting claims about resilience are warranted and valid.

The Evolution of Concepts over Time

Tobacco use. The cessation or prevention of *tobacco use* is an aim of a great many health programs. Until recently the term was unambiguous. Tobacco is a plant that is processed to make a wide variety of products that can be either smoked or consumed orally. The products include cigarettes, cigars, pipes, moist and dry snuff, loose leaf and plug chewing tobacco, and dissolvable lozenges. The psychoactive ingredient in tobacco products, nicotine, is extremely addictive and makes it exceptionally difficult to discontinue tobacco use despite severe and extensively documented health risks (U.S. Department of Health and Human Services [USDHHS], 2014). *Tobacco use* refers to the consumption of these products.

The tobacco industry was upended with the introduction to the market of electronic cigarettes, known more formally as electronic nicotine delivery systems (ENDS), in the late 2000s. These devices contain a battery-powered heating element that vaporizes a liquid containing nicotine and delivers the aerosol to the user through a mouthpiece. Early ENDS products resembled conventional cigarettes but quickly diversified to take on a wide assortment of shapes. Most of them now feature refillable cartridges for the e-liquid, which typically contains nicotine, chemical flavorings, and propylene glycol or other solvents. In addition to nicotine, the ENDS vapor or aerosol can contain volatile organic compounds, carcinogens, heavy metals, and other toxic substances (USDHHS, 2016, 2019).

The use of e-cigarettes, known as *vaping*, became remarkably popular in a few short years, especially among adolescents and young adults. Since 2014 its use has consistently outpaced conventional cigarettes in these audiences (USDHHS, 2016; Wang et al., 2018). ENDS have been marketed by their manufacturers as a health-enhancing product aimed to help adult smokers quit cigarettes, but their extraordinarily rapid uptake by youth has created a new public health crisis in the judgment of most of the medical and public health communities, due to the strong potential for nicotine addiction and other health risks (Glantz & Bareham, 2018).

The introduction and proliferation of e-cigarettes and ENDS raised the question: These are nicotine products, but are they also tobacco products? If you vape, are you using *tobacco*? The question has crucial policy implications: it determines whether restrictions on tobacco use extend to vape products, as well as how the packaging, marketing, labeling, and distribution of vape products are regulated.

In most instances the question has been answered in the affirmative, although not without debate. Most notably, in 2016 the US Food and Drug Administration (FDA) announced that it would classify e-cigarettes containing nicotine as tobacco products for regulatory purposes. But the designation has not been unanimous. Some states classify ENDS as tobacco products while others classify them as "alternative nicotine products" or a similar designation (National Conference of State Legislatures, 2017). And a leading scientific journal, *Nicotine & Tobacco Research*, decided that it would define e-cigarettes as distinct from tobacco products, largely because of the lack of international consensus. Explaining the journal's position, the editor wrote:

> [*The FDA's classification*] is the product of policy developments around the role of the FDA and their ability to provide regulative

guidance and authority relating to a range of products. ...However, describing e-cigarettes as tobacco products is a particularly US phenomenon. Some countries include e-cigarettes in tobacco product regulation, but others do not. ...Our preference is for the term "tobacco products" to be reserved for those products that are made from and contain tobacco (rather than contain constituents such as nicotine extracted from it). ...[*This position*] reflects our status as an international journal with contributions from many countries, each with their own legal and regulatory frameworks around tobacco and other nicotine-containing products. (Munafò, 2019)

This example illustrates how a construct's generally accepted meaning can become muddled due to technological changes, with resulting confusion between people using the same terms in different ways.[4] One very practical consequence is that policies that place prohibitions on smoking or tobacco use, e.g., in parks, housing developments, schools, hotels, and other public spaces, need to be explicit in how they define terms such as *smoking, tobacco use,* and *tobacco products.* Otherwise the policies may well be misunderstood, misinterpreted, and inadvertently (or deliberately) violated. Similar confusions may exist when the construct is invoked in evaluation and research contexts.

Gender. Gender is often a relevant variable for program and policy evaluations because it can be a predictor of how much participants may benefit from a program or how much interest participants have in a program. It is also used to determine equity in serving target populations from a social justice perspective. For example, if a school-based program does not adequately engage either girls or boys, that will be a sign that the program may need revision.

In the first two decades of the 21st century, previous interpretations of the construct of gender were exploded. These changes involve a growth in the complexity of interpretation. What had once seemed the clearest and most straightforward of demographic concepts was beset by debate. The scientific community is largely in agreement about the broadening scope of the construct. Current research investigations and debates focus on what the parameters of the construct should be.

One distinct development, on which there is basic consensus, is that what had previously been considered "gender," or, equivalently, "sex," has

---

[4]A parallel challenge has come from some advocates of ENDS products as to whether *vaping* can be considered distinct from *smoking,* since it does not involve burning or combustion; the implication is that vaping may be allowable in places where smoking has been prohibited. In addition, tobacco companies are developing products that are designated as "heat-not-burn," with the intent that tobacco is vaporized at levels that do not involve combustion. If these products gain popularity and market share, they will further complicate the debate about what exactly is being restricted by prohibitions on *smoking.*

largely been split into two constructs, which are often identified as *sex* and *gender identity*. A website of the American Academy of Pediatrics describes it as follows:

> Being a boy or a girl, for most children, is something that feels very natural. At birth, babies are assigned male or female based on physical characteristics. This refers to the 'sex' or 'assigned gender' of the child. Meanwhile, 'gender identity' refers to an internal sense people have of who they are that comes from an interaction of biological traits, developmental influences, and environmental conditions. This may be male, female, somewhere in between, a combination of both or neither. (Rafferty, 2018)

A 2018 editorial in the journal *Nature* stated: "The research and medical community now sees sex as more complex than male and female, and gender as a spectrum that includes transgender people and those who identify as neither male nor female....The idea that science can make definitive conclusions about a person's sex or gender is fundamentally flawed" (Nature This Week, 2018).

Given the radical evolution of the gender construct, its representation in the program evaluation planning process can be a source of confusion, disagreement, or misunderstanding if there are multiple, inconsistent interpretations among the team members or primary stakeholders.

The Understanding and Use of Constructs in the Political Domain: An Example From California in the 1980s

In 1986 in California, Assembly Bill 3659 was passed by the state legislature and signed by the governor, creating a body called the California Task Force to Promote Self-Esteem and Personal and Social Responsibility. The guiding concept behind the bill was that low self-esteem and a sense of low individual self-worth appear to be linked with many intractable social problems, and may in fact be an underlying cause of some of those problems. It followed that by studying and fully understanding this psychological characteristic, it may be possible to devise strategies and policies that ultimately have greater success in ameliorating these societal concerns than previous approaches had been able to achieve.

As described by the bill's author and primary sponsor, Assemblyman John Vasconcellos, the new legislation...

> ...directed the task force to carry out three charges. The first was to compile research concerning the role of self-esteem as a possible causal factor in six areas of major social concern: crime and

violence, alcohol and drug abuse, teenage pregnancy, child abuse, chronic welfare dependency, and educational failure. These are among the most compelling and the most lamentable social ills we face, and they are certainly problems on which we spend billions of tax dollars without seeming to make much headway. Collecting and analyzing research on the role of self-esteem in these areas could provide a foundation for designing more effective public policy strategies.

...The second charge given to the task force was to compile current knowledge about how healthy self-esteem is developed, how it is damaged or lost, and how it can be revitalized....The task force's third charge was to identify model self-esteem programs, including institutions to which people can turn when they need help for themselves or their families. (Vasconcellos, 1989, pp. xviii–xix)

At the time of its passage, the legislation was met with various levels of excitement, open-minded curiosity, and skepticism. Most famously, it was mercilessly lampooned over a period of months in Garry Trudeau's popular *Doonesbury* comic strip. But other commentators described it as a bold new direction for social policy, and whatever one's perspective on the wisdom of the legislation, that designation was hard to dispute. The funding attached to the legislation was not extravagant; the 25-member task force was empaneled for three years, with an annual budget of $245,000 (Vasconcellos, 1989). But the commitment of state tax funds to this unusual concept placed the bill's sponsor and supporters out on a limb. It was a high-stakes bet on the part of political leaders and other proponents—in terms of reputation, visibility, and political capital—that a psychological approach to solving high-visibility social problems, never before undertaken in quite this way, might be able to pay off where standard approaches had failed.

For our current purposes, the relevant question from this story is: What exactly *is* self-esteem? Or more to the point, given the steady evolution of social science theory, what was self-esteem circa 1986? The chair of the task force wrote: "The gathering of data and testimony at public hearings...built a consensus that a *primary* factor affecting how well or how poorly an individual functions in society is self-esteem" (Mecca, 1989, p. vii; italics in original), Such claims suggest that members of the policymaking community generally knew and agreed on the meaning of the term, at least to a workable extent, and were ready to move on to the task of solving problems.

Nailing Down the Construct

Shortly after formation, the task force commissioned research reviews by University of California researchers on the relationship between self-esteem and each of the six identified social problems. Those reviews (Mecca et al., 1989) revealed self-esteem to be a murky concept, largely dependent on the orientation of the individual research study. Here are sample descriptions from the papers:

> Self-esteem is currently an ambiguous and poorly defined construct in the literature. Numerous conceptualizations, operational definitions, and measurement methodologies exist and often vary depending on the theoretical orientation of the research, the context of measurement, and the research goals (Schneiderman et al., 1989, p. 221; from the review on self-esteem and welfare dependency).
>
> ...[W]e have a fairly firm grasp of what is meant by self-esteem, as revealed by our own introspection and observation of the behavior of others. But it is hard to put that understanding into precise words....In addition to self-esteem, our authors have identified the ideas of self, self-concept, self-respect, awareness, identity, image, congruence, and consciousness. None of these hits the nail on the head. ... Is there anything we can salvage from this definitional maze? ... Greater definitional difficulties arise when we consider the stability of the concept of self-esteem. Should it be regarded as some kind of global attribute, one that enjoys a constant strength and level of organization for the individual? Or should it be treated as largely situational? (Smelser, 1989, pp. 9–10; from the research overview).

A review of the research reports, all of which addressed the task of defining self-esteem, builds an overall picture of a construct encumbered by lack of uniformity. The most succinct definition was provided in the review on alcohol and drug use: "Self-esteem is the *experience* of one's personal self-worth" (Skager & Kerst, 1989, p. 249). But other discussions were diverse and inconsistent, depending to some degree on differences in disciplinary traditions, particularly those of psychology and sociology. All of the reviews describe self-esteem as a complex, multi-dimensional concept, and there are differences with respect to what those dimensions are. For example, in one report self-esteem was hypothesized to encompass both an evaluative dimension, involving perceptions of competence, and an affective dimension, involving self-acceptance (Crockenberg & Soby, 1989, p. 128). Other conceptions differentiated between dimensions such as inner and outer self-esteem, and sense of power and sense of worth (Bhatti et al., 1989, p. 36). Researchers also differed regarding the degree to which self-esteem should be viewed as a global attribute of the individual, as opposed to existing in separate dimensions of daily functioning such as academic, social, athletic, artistic, etc., as well as the degree to which self-esteem should be conceived as a stable attribute of the self, maintaining some measure of consistency over time.

Beyond the difficulties of definition, the reviews also described difficulties in measurement and mixed results regarding the contributions of self-esteem to each of the social problem areas. A common conclusion was that more research is needed, both to understand the construct and to determine its relationship to areas of social functioning. On the other hand, most of the reviews also recommended that progress should continue on the development and testing of interventions that address self-esteem as one target outcome, if not necessarily the primary target outcome.

The Task Force's Treatment of the Construct of Self-Esteem

In its final report, issued in January 1990, the task force reported its definition of self-esteem as follows: "Appreciating my own worth and importance and having the character to be accountable for myself and to act responsibly toward others" (California State Department of Education, 1990, p. 18).

In reading this definition, one is struck by its compound nature, consisting of multiple components that themselves require clarification: *appreciating, having character, being accountable*, and *acting responsibly*. The definition has little connection with the research studies that were commissioned to help understand the nature and function of self-esteem. Further, the parts of the definition involving accountability and responsible action bear no resemblance to the conceptions presented in the research reviews. Thus, the Task Force's report gives no indication that the group considered and learned from the complexity of the reviews issued by the researchers.

One might ask, why was such an awkward definition adopted, especially following the delivery of in-depth reviews of existing research? In developing its definition, why didn't the task force hew more closely to what had been learned from those reviews? That question is open to speculation, but I would suggest—purely an outsider's vantage point—that one potential reason was the need for the definition to serve purposes beyond simply the accurate representation of a difficult, complex construct. It is to some degree a political definition, formulated so as to be able to justify the expenditure of public dollars. Assemblyman Vasconcellos, in describing his reintroduction of the bill after two previous versions had failed to gain passage, recounted: "In an attempt to speak to the concerns of more conservatives, the bill's title and purpose were broadened to include the promotion of 'personal and social responsibility'" (Vasconcellos, 1989, p. xvi). *Personal and social responsibility* and being *accountable for myself* suggest financial self-reliance, a desirable trait from a political perspective. The lack of research-based precedent for their inclusion into the construct of self-esteem becomes a secondary concern.

The Legacy of the Task Force: A Failure to Clarify

The task force ended its work with the issuance of its 1990 report, which generated high interest and was widely distributed. It was reported in 1990 that the state of California had sold 60,000 copies, making it the state's biggest seller of all time (Billingsley, 2010). The report listed multiple recommendations for what could be done in relation to each of the target areas. However, inspection of these recommendations shows that they are difficult to isolate and to implement meaningfully, due to a high level of generality.

The legacy of the California Task Force to Promote Self-Esteem and Personal and Social Responsibility is thin. Several reasons could be offered—including politics and budget—for its failure to leave a mark on the state's legislative priorities and the programmatic priorities in education, criminology, welfare, and the other domains it explored. As far as one can tell, no recommendations were implemented. But I would submit that one reason it failed is that it didn't leave a usable core of knowledge to advance social programs and policy. Given the challenges of mobilizing concerted action, the task force failed to develop a core construct and establish its validity, ultimately leaving nothing for people and organizations to work with. Apart from not incorporating the research findings on the relationships of self-esteem with the social problems identified, the three years of effort by the task force did not make progress in clarifying self-esteem or helping the research and policymaking communities come to a consensus about how it could be defined going forward. This case example illustrates the difficulties that can be encountered in moving from the level of global everyday construct, informed by our personal introspections, to the level of a researchable and actionable variable.

Recommendations on Selecting Your Variables

Know the Field and the Literature

We begin our thinking with constructs. To the experienced evaluator, the path from an initial construct to the variable that will represent it in the evaluation study can be fairly well trodden. (Sometimes this translation involves more than one variable, but I will assume the singular at present for the sake of this discussion.) In other words, we may feel confident in our knowledge of the scope of the field. But traditional conceptualizations can become quickly outdated as a field advances. Most fields are in a constant state of evolution, and there are usually new alternatives and options that have been developed very recently—new theoretical conceptions, new challenges to the status quo, new approaches to handling measurement problems. As the evaluator for an intervention, one must stay current with the field. It is always a challenge to try to stay aware of what we don't yet know—that is, turning our *unknown unknowns* into, at least, *known unknowns* (Pawson et al., 2011).

Identify the Alternatives

To the extent possible, try to familiarize yourself with a wide range of previous evaluations. Those can be a big part of finding alternative ways to assign meaning to a construct. Some of these evaluations will appear in the published literature, but many of them may only be available in unpublished reports or on the web.

Consult With Your Primary Stakeholders

Your stakeholders are the ones who have to live with the program. They may be more invested in the program than you are, and some of them may have decision-making capability that can decide the fate of the program. Therefore, it is best if they can be on board with all of your choices about the evaluation, including those highlighted in the other chapters of this book. If they don't understand your decisions concerning variable choice, it will be that much harder for them to be your allies in this decision process.

Make Sure Your Choices Are Logically Defensible

In keeping with House's perspective that evaluation is a process of argument (see Chapter 3), the choices that the evaluator makes in the specification of variables are part of the process of making the evaluation comprehensible and defensible. Expect that at some point in your conversations with program stakeholders, you will be required to defend those choices.

Thus, if you choose a variable that happens to be one of several alternatives, all of which may seem to you to be reasonably equivalent to the underlying construct, be prepared to explain why the one you chose is the superior choice. This could be for reasons of theory (e.g., the variable is more directly reflective of the construct) or for reasons of logistics (e.g., it is more straightforward to measure than other options which may require additional resource or time commitments). Presumably there is some reason for your choice, and you should be prepared to make the case for it.

Chapter Summary

- The variables to be included in an evaluation study must be identified and defined to ensure that they accurately represent their underlying constructs. This translation process needs to be conducted with attention to maintaining understanding and consensus among the evaluation's critical stakeholders.

- Several kinds of variables may be included in the evaluation study:

  - Variables that represent exposure to the intervention.

  - Outcome variables, which represent the characteristics that the intervention has been designed to influence.

  - Mediating variables that may be part of the hypothesized outcome chain between intervention exposure and outcome variable change.

  - Moderator variables, which influence who will be impacted by the intervention.

  - Demographic variables.

  - Variables that may reflect potential undesired effects of the intervention.

- The process of conceptualizing variables and arriving at measures to be used in the evaluation is presented as a series of four steps:

  - Identify the target constructs to be examined in the evaluation. In discussions between the evaluator and stakeholders, these target constructs are often expressed colloquially in nontechnical, everyday language. The evaluator should ensure that there is consensus regarding the general meaning of the constructs.

  - Identify one or more variable that will be used to represent each construct. These variables need to be stated with more precision than the constructs themselves, in order to facilitate decisions about interpretation and measurement.

  - Choose the measurement strategy (or strategies) that will be used for each variable. "Measurement strategy" refers to the information source, the format of the instrumentation, and the data collection activity.

  - Select or develop the measurement instruments that will be used in the evaluation. Any given measure will have limitations, and the use of more than one measure may be warranted in the case of variables that are particularly important for the evaluation.

- In this translation process, the multiple decisions that link the original constructs to the measures eventually chosen to represent them must be made with attention to construct validity.

- For reasons of logistics or feasibility, it may sometimes be necessary to use proxy variables in place of variables that would represent the target construct more directly. For example, if an evaluation needs to be conducted on a very short timeline, a short-term outcome might be selected to represent a longer-term outcome of greater interest. In such cases, there must be confidence that the proxy variable is adequately correlated with one or more variables that would represent the target construct.

- When the translation process goes awry, variables may be selected that are not strongly reflective of the underlying construct of interest. These errors may be due to any number of reasons including convenience, mistaken organizational or administrative decisions, changes in conceptualization from research to practice, and the evolution in the understanding of concepts over time.

Questions for Reflection—Chapter 5

1. Figure 5.2 takes a general construct—"healthy eating"—and demonstrates how it can be expressed using any of a variety of variables. Consider a construct from a field with which you are familiar, such as health care, education, political science, psychology, economics, etc.

   - Suggest how it could be operationalized into one or more measurable variables.

   - Do you think it would require multiple variables to represent the construct adequately? If so, identify those variables.

2. In a program or policy context with which you are familiar, what are some long-term outcomes that would probably require too long a timeframe to include in an evaluation study with a one-year timeline?

   - For each of these long-term outcomes, identify one or more shorter-term outcomes that could possibly be substituted as proxy outcomes.

   - How strong is the evidence base for using these proxies as suitable substitutes? What could be done to make the evidence base stronger than it is at present?

3. In your own field of expertise, identify one or more constructs whose definition or interpretation has changed over the years. How did that process of evolution change attempts to measure the construct?

Measurement Strategies and Measurement Instruments

This chapter discusses the last two steps of the four-step process for developing evaluation measures, which was introduced in Chapter 5. By *measurement strategies* I refer to the broad range of approaches to operationalizing a variable. These approaches dictate, to a large degree, the format of the data that will represent the variable of interest, as well as the range of options for examining and analyzing those data. Once the strategies are decided upon, the actual *measures* must be developed or selected.

My aim in this chapter is not to provide a comprehensive treatment of the measurement process in evaluation, but rather to discuss some of the major measurement-related choice points and challenges, from the perspective of construct validity. These considerations revolve around questions such as these:

- What is the nature of the information that our measures are providing us?

- Is the information accurate and clear? Can we be confident that it reflects a true state of affairs?

The answers to these questions lie on a continuum rather than being binary or discrete. In many respects the answers are also ultimately unknowable. What we can do is plan as well as we can and try to anticipate and minimize the effects of those elements that may interfere with valid inference about our constructs.

Measurement and Validity

Measurement and Campbell's Validity Typology

Shadish et al. (2002) proposed a unitary definition of validity ("the approximate truth of an inference," p. 34), but, as discussed in Chapter 3, they identified four distinct categories. The measurement process is most directly related to *construct* validity, but it affects all four of the validity types. Table 6.1 provides a summary of these relationships.

TABLE 6.1 ● How Measurement May Affect Each of the Validity Categories

Validity Type	Conceptual Focus	How Measurement Affects This Type of Validity
Internal	Whether a relationship between variables is causal	Measurement processes are involved in several of the validity threats identified by Campbell. Consider, for example, a difference between the mean scores on a pretest and a posttest, used to evaluate the delivery of a program. A difference in the mean scores might be caused not by the presumed causal relationship between program and outcome scores, but by factors such as the following:
		• *Instrumentation*: A difference in the measurement process, such as:
		• the actual measures (e.g., alternate forms that are not truly equivalent)
		• the measurement procedures (e.g., different amounts of testing time inadvertently allotted at pretest and posttest)
		• the scoring processes (e.g., inconsistent raters inadvertently score the posttests more leniently, or more strictly, than the pretests).

TABLE 6.1 ● *(Continued)*		
Validity Type	**Conceptual Focus**	**How Measurement Affects This Type of Validity**
		● *Testing*: Posttest scores are boosted because the program participants have taken the pretest, rather than due to the effects of the program itself.
External	Whether a hypothesized causal relationship can be generalized to other settings, populations, times, measures, and versions of the treatment	Constructs can be measured in different ways, and when the results of one evaluation are being applied to a different program setting, the relevance of the findings will depend, in part, on the comparability of the measurement procedures used in the two settings.
Statistical Conclusion	Whether, and how, two or more variables covary (are statistically related)	The ability to detect a statistical relationship between variables, and to estimate its strength, depends on the adequacy of the study's measures. The reliability of measures is directly related to statistical power. Measures with low reliability decrease power. (See, e.g., Meyer, 2010.)
Construct	The extent to which generalizations can be made about the constructs that are operationalized in a research or evaluation study	The higher-order constructs addressed in our program theory, as well as in the more general theories on which our program is based, are represented by our choice of measures. The accuracy and validity of our conclusions about these constructs depend on the adequacy of the measures and the measurement process.

Auxiliary Measurement Theories

The relationship between constructs and the measures that represent them was described by Blalock (1982), who postulated how substantive theories across the social sciences are linked to the measurement processes that are used to test those theories. Applying these measurement processes in order to subject a theory to a real-world test, he reasoned, will always necessitate a set of assumptions which, taken together, comprise what he called an *auxiliary measurement theory*. This auxiliary theory, in essence, makes the case for why the selected measure is a valid way to represent the construct (see also Edwards & Bagozzi, 2000).

> [T]he process of measurement requires a set of theoretical assumptions, many of which must remain untested in any given piece of research... [The] auxiliary theory will usually contain a number of causal assumptions connecting theoretically defined concepts and their measured indicators, and therefore such causal models can be conceptualized in much the same way that causal models among substantive variables can be constructed. (Blalock, 1982, pp. 25–26)

Blalock was referring to theories in the social science disciplines, but it seems reasonable that the same relationships between theory and measurement will apply in the case of the program theories that guide evaluation studies.

Blalock also wrote that being aware of the assumptions underlying the measurement of a theoretical concept—that is, a construct—enables us to make judgments about the appropriateness of generalizing across studies that use different measurement approaches for the same construct. Thus, for example, suppose we are trying to compare the effectiveness of two programs that both aim to promote the growth of, say, *civic engagement* in youth. If we already have an extant evaluation study for each program, but those studies have used different measures of the core construct, civic engagement, how should we approach the task of using those evaluations to compare their respective programs? Must we abandon the evaluations due to their disparate measures? If not, what principles should guide our interpretation process? How should we determine our level of confidence in our conclusions?

In Blalock's model, an auxiliary measurement theory does not correspond directly to the substantive theory as a whole, but rather to the constructs that comprise that theory; that is, each construct has its own measurement theory. From a pragmatic perspective, the significance of recognizing and accounting for these measurement theories is that they call attention to the unavoidable assumptions that underlie the representation of any construct through a specific measurement strategy and a specific measure. Thus, it could be said that the measurement theories reflect the construct validity of any specific measurement process—although Blalock himself did not use the term "construct validity" in his discussion.

It may be helpful to provide some illustrations of these measurement-related assumptions:

- Providing the correct answer to a problem on a test will be accepted as evidence that the test-taker had the skills or knowledge necessary to produce that answer. Is that assumption justified? Is it possible that the student had a different way of arriving at the answer, such as taking an educated guess on a poorly constructed multiple-choice item?

- Asking students directly what their grades were in a number of courses will be accepted as a truthful and accurate representation of those grades. Among the assumptions required by this particular strategy are that (1) the students can accurately remember their grades and (2) they are being truthful in their report—even though it could be argued that it is self-protective for the students to inflate whichever of their grades may be poor.

This last example demonstrates that some measurement assumptions can be challenged. But first they have to be acknowledged and recognized as assumptions. We will discuss some of these assumptions in more detail later in this chapter.

The Reliability of Measures

The *reliability* of a measurement is an assessment of its precision, consistency, or replicability. Reliability is generally viewed as a component of validity, since replicability is a prerequisite for the accurate interpretation of a score. But in distinguishing between the two, "reliability is conceived in more narrowly statistical terms than is validity" (Haertel, 2006, p. 65). That is, validity is concerned with identifying and understanding all of the potential factors that can affect the proper interpretation of scores, including the theory that links the score to its underlying construct and the nature of phenomena that interfere with that relationship. By contrast, reliability is generally concerned with the estimation of the degree of consistency that characterizes a set of scores.

Most formal definitions of reliability rely on classical test theory, which assumes that the variable we are trying to measure—whether through the use of single items, multiitem scales, or any other kind of measurement procedure—has a hypothetical true score for a given individual at a given point in time. The score that we obtain will always consist of some combination of the true score and other factors, which are grouped collectively under the term *error*. Reliability, then, is considered to be the proportion of variance in the measurement that can be attributed to the true score of the variable (DeVellis, 2017). In more practical terms, reliability is also interpreted as the correlation between different replications of the measurement (assuming a single individual and time point). It is expressed as a coefficient that can take values between 0 and 1.

What we refer to as "consistency" of measurement can take different forms (Braverman, 2019). We may be referring to the consistency of scores across different administrations of an instrument, different versions of an instrument, different raters assigning scores to a behavior or work sample, or the set of questions that make up a scale. Several of the major categories of reliability, as applied to quantitative forms of data, can be described as follows:

- *Internal consistency* refers to the concurrence of items that make up a scale. For example, in a 10-item scale that measures attitude toward school, each item should correlate positively with the others and contribute toward the overall score. It is presumed that all of the items are observable indicators of the underlying construct. The concept of internal consistency is usually assessed with the statistic Cronbach's alpha. Attention to internal consistency is typically applied in the scale development process, to produce the strongest scale from a group of candidate items.

- *Alternate forms reliability* refers to consistency across what are considered to be equivalent forms of a measure. The use of alternate forms may be desirable to control practice or memory effects when an instrument will be administered more than once, such as in a prepost design. In such cases, it is critical to have confidence that the two forms are truly interchangeable. This form of reliability is measured by the correlation of the two measures.

- *Interrater reliability.* This form is relevant for scores produced by the judgments of raters. For example, ratings can be used to assign global scores for writing proficiency, public speaking skills, or figure skating performance. In order for the scores to be meaningful reflections of whatever is being judged, there should ideally be minimal variation between raters. Indexes of interrater reliability include Cohen's kappa (which reflects the extent of exact agreement for binary judgments) and Cronbach's alpha (which allows for gradations of agreement).

- *Test–retest reliability* refers to the consistency of scores across different testing occasions. It is usually measured by the correlation between the sets of scores at the two occasions. This form of reliability is most appropriate for the measurement of constructs that are expected to be relatively stable, as might be true for some academic skills over very short time intervals.

Our expectation of consistency is tied to our understanding of the variable being measured and the circumstances under which we would expect scores to be equivalent. For example, if we are assessing the reliability of a physical scale to measure people's weight, we would expect scores to be identical if taken within several minutes of each other, assuming that no eating or drinking has taken place. However, we would have no expectation of identical scores for weight measurements taken one week apart, since a difference between those scores could easily be the result of an actual change in weight rather than measurement error. Almost all social, psychological, and physiological variables tend to lose stability over time, although the rate and form of that change will vary greatly depending on the variable. For example, a measure of *food insecurity* (Barrett, 2010) can be expected to be more stable than the level of *hunger*, which will fluctuate over a matter of hours. Thus the proper interpretation of reliability requires an understanding of the expectations of replicability or, in Blalock's terms, the application of a measurement theory that links the measurement procedure to the underlying construct.

More detailed practical treatments of reliability are provided by Meyer (2010), Bandalos (2018), Price (2017), DeVellis (2017), and other measurement texts.

Identifying Your Measurement Strategies

Considerations in Selecting a Strategy

For any given variable the available choices for measurement strategy depend, first and foremost, on the nature of the variable, which will dictate and limit the variety of ways that measurement can take place. Creative thinking can sometimes reveal unexpected measurement possibilities. It can be helpful for the evaluation team to make sure they are considering all the potential options before they move to making a definitive choice. Once they do move to the task of choosing the strategy, that choice will depend on factors such as the following:

- *The conceptual link of the strategy to the underlying construct and variable.* Considerations of construct validity—the match of construct with measure—may be significant in the comparison of different measures, which should be a critical factor in decision-making.

- *Considerations about potential bias associated with each strategy.* If one strategy (e.g., self-report) is considered to be associated with substantial bias, the evaluation team may decide it is worth the added expense to use a competing measurement alternative.

- *Prior validation studies for particular measures.* There may be a strong tradition of validation studies in the existing literature for some constructs and variables, and this information can inform the decisions about measurement. For other variables, the evaluation team may be entering new territory.

- *Credibility in the eyes of primary stakeholders.* In some cases, one strategy may be perceived as more rigorous than its alternative and therefore preferable, for example, behavioral observation versus self-report. The primary stakeholders need to be satisfied with the quality of the data, and this may be a deciding factor in the decision. Alternatively, the evaluators could try to convince these stakeholders that the less rigorous—but also less expensive—option is fully adequate. If so, this may pose a risk because credibility of the data will be a crucial factor in determining the ultimate usefulness—and actual use—of the evaluation.

- *The timeline available for data collection.* Strategies may vary considerably in the time required to implement them. For example, one option may involve group measurement while another requires individual measurement. Although the accuracy may be much better with the individual option, it might simply not be feasible. This factor will also depend on the sample size, since smaller samples may make individual measurement more feasible.

- *Expense of applying the strategy.* All measurements involve expense but the difference between options can sometimes be substantial. For example, analysis of biological samples, e.g., to assess substance use or aspects of health status, will typically entail high costs.

- *Balancing priorities and the overall resources available for the evaluation.* If one strategy is more expensive but is desirable for other reasons, the affordability of the option will run up against the overall evaluation project budget. It may be feasible to apply the expensive strategy if other activities that involve expense can be curtailed.

- *The importance of the variable: is it worth the added effort and resources?* This will involve trade-offs with other aspects of the evaluation, such as data collection for other variables.

- *What has been used in the field before.* If there is a long tradition for how to measure a particular outcome that tradition may be influential in the decision about how to measure the target variable. This will be particularly true if the evaluators or the stakeholders wish to make the evaluation convincing to a particular outside audience. It will also be a consideration if there is intent to publish the results. The measurement choices must be defensible in light of prior research practice, either by using similar strategies or by being able to justify the use of a different strategy.

- *What has been used in prior evaluations of this intervention (or similar interventions).* The evaluators and stakeholders may consider it important to compare the results from this study with results from prior studies. For example, the evaluation may be covering a revision of the intervention, in which case the ability to apply historical comparisons with prior versions will be critical.

- *Acceptability to the participants who will be supplying the measurements.* A measure may be desirable in several respects but if its acceptability is low, that can be a fatal flaw in the logistics of its use. For example, some measurement strategies are unacceptable because they are viewed as privacy invasions (e.g., consent for online tracking) or because they tend to generate feelings of aversion (e.g., requests for biological samples).

Some strategies will present singular types of challenges. For example, for a long-term follow-up several months after intervention delivery, we may wish to get participants together and survey them in a group setting at a single time. But that strategy may present problems related to participants' ability to travel to the site or their availability at one particular time. Thus, there will certainly be some level of nonattendance. If the nonattendance is expected to be substantial, the feasibility of that strategy could be compared with other options, each with its own drawbacks.

Using Multiple Strategies for the Same Construct

If a variable is particularly important to the evaluation, or has troubling levels of bias associated with one or more strategies for measuring it, the evaluation team may decide to measure it using two different strategies, an approach known as triangulation. Using this approach, the weaknesses of the individual strategies, considered on their own, can be counterbalanced.

For example, cigarette smoking can be measured both by self-report and by biochemical measurement. The latter strategy involves measuring the levels of nicotine metabolites present in bodily fluids such as saliva or urine, or by measuring carbon monoxide levels in expired breath. However, both self-report and biochemical measurement have significant shortcomings. Self-report is subject to underreporting, especially in certain populations such as people with smoking-related diseases (Gorber et al., 2009). Biochemical measurement, on the other hand, is invasive, logistically awkward to collect, and very expensive to analyze. In addition, the biochemical substances' half-lives within the body mean that they are only able to detect tobacco use within a period of, at most, several days, so this would not be a valid strategy to measure whether smoking has occurred in, say, the past month. Thus the patterns of strength and weakness for these two strategies are highly disparate. Generally, biochemical measurement, when used at all, is administered with only a random subsample of study participants as a validity check to assess potential underreporting in the self-report data.

Thus, the choice of measurement strategy for each variable can be a high-stakes decision for the evaluation. If a variable is assessed through only one measure—as is the case for most variables—the evaluators will not necessarily know if the choice was a good one, since they will probably not know the degree of bias that exists in those scores. A stark illustration of the stakes that may be at play with this choice, also involving the example of tobacco, is described in Case Study 6.1.

CASE STUDY 6.1 A COMPARISON OF STRATEGIES FOR MEASURING SCHOOL-BASED CIGARETTE AND ALCOHOL USE

Sussman and Stacy (1994) conducted a convergent validity study involving 20 continuation high schools in California. The researchers were interested in measuring two variables, school-level use of cigarettes and of alcohol, and they compared different strategies for doing so. For cigarette use, the five strategies were (a) students' self-reports of their own use, with their responses aggregated to form school-level averages, (b) students' estimates of school-level prevalence (that is, their estimates of use by other students), (c) staff estimates of school-level prevalence by students, (d) naturalistic observations of smoking at locations near the school, and (e) tobacco trash evidence observed at selected sites, such as parking lots and sports fields. For alcohol, four strategies were used, including all of the above except (d), naturalistic observation of drinking near the school. All three of the strategies that involved reports from students and staff (a through c above) used interviews with samples of selected respondents. For the sample of 20 schools, bivariate correlations were calculated for all possible pairs of measures of the same variable. Thus, the comparisons produced 16 separate correlations: 10 possible pairs of the five smoking measures and six possible pairs of the four alcohol measures.

The study found that the correlations between these variables diverged to a remarkable degree, ranging between .01 and .54 for cigarette use and between .09 and .63 for alcohol use. The findings are noteworthy for the overall low levels of these correlations, and perhaps most particularly, the fact that none of the correlations was very strong, considering that each of them compared

(Continued)

measurement strategies intended to assess the same institutional-level variable. The highest correlation (.63) was between student estimates and staff estimates of alcohol use prevalence, but even these two measures shared only 40% of their variance (obtained by squaring the correlation coefficient). As a bottom line, evaluators would want to know which of the different strategies were more and less accurate. That question could not be answered since, as is typically the case in validation studies, there was no criterion yardstick known to be objectively correct against which all the measures could be compared. All that was learned was that the measurements disagreed to a sizable extent.

Once you have decided on your measurement strategy, the final step in the measurement development model is to determine what the actual measure(s) will be. We turn to that topic next.

Identifying Your Specific Measures

The decision to use a particular measurement strategy—a way to get at the variable of interest—does not fully identify the instrument or measure that will actually be used. Most of our discussion in this section will involve measures that require human response, most often responses to survey questions in written, interview, or online modalities, or test performance. For each such variable to be measured in the evaluation, the evaluation team will need to decide whether to develop a new measure or try to find an existing one that fits the bill. If the variable represents a well-known construct that has been explored in previous research—such as locus of control, parenting style, and so on—it will probably be reasonable to first look for an accepted measure with a known history of use. Sometimes it may be possible to adapt existing measures for the specific purposes of the current evaluation. The evaluators may also be able to use a measure that has been used in a prior evaluation of the current intervention. The continuation of use of a prior instrument can provide valuable comparative information, provided that the instrument has maintained its appropriateness for the current context.

Other variables may be unique to the intervention, in which case the evaluation team will need to develop new measures for them.

Single Item or Scale?

One of the first questions you should consider is whether the measurement of the variable requires a series of items or can be accomplished with a single item. Single-item measures are much more efficient but are commonly prone to higher levels of error or inconsistency, which could occur because of respondents' misinterpretation of the particular wording, carelessness in responding, and so on. A well-established principle of measurement is that adding items to a scale will yield greater stability of scores, assuming high levels of item quality (e.g., DeVellis, 2017). The strength of this scale length effect declines as the number of items increases, so that the improvement in reliability of 21 compared to 20 items is much more modest than the improvement of five compared to four. One can appreciate, then, that this is particularly relevant in the case of a single item.

Not only do we know that single-item measures are more prone to error, but the opportunity to assess reliability afforded by single-item measures is constricted as well. Whereas the reliability of a set of items can be assessed through various methods of analyzing the item intercorrelations, reliability testing of a single item can only be considered in terms of its consistency over time through a test–retest framework or a validity assessment through its agreement with an external criterion such as an alternate form of the question (DeVellis, 2017).

However, in addition to the consideration of response stability, you will need to consider what makes sense for the variable at hand. It would probably not make sense to use more than one question to measure simple demographic characteristics such as the respondent's age, ethnicity, or level of education. These and other demographic variables are typically measured with only one question.

The use of multiple items to measure a variable does not always mean that those items are being formed into a scale, to produce a single score on a single variable. Sometimes the variable and its associated construct are multidimensional, and information is desired about the components. An example is gender, for which our contemporary understanding has eclipsed what was once considered to be a simple dichotomous variable (discussed in Chapter 5). In some evaluation circumstances, it may be reasonable to ask about both gender identity and biological sex—two separate constructs that are often conflated under the more general construct of gender (Bittner & Goodyear-Grant, 2017; Glick et al., 2018). If the understanding of respondents' gender at this level of detail is an important part of your evaluation study, then the use of these two items, or other items, will be appropriate. However, it should not be done routinely because gender can be a sensitive topic, perceived as invasive of privacy. The need for specific kinds of gender-relevant information with respect to answering the evaluation study's guiding questions should be considered in each case.

In addition to demographic variables, the issue of single item versus scale might be relevant for other kinds of variable as well, including behaviors, attitudes, opinions, beliefs, skills, or personal history. For example, a relatively simple and straightforward variable such as satisfaction with services can potentially be encapsulated into one question, or represented through several questions that address components of the phenomenon being measured (e.g., delivery of a conference). Similarly, more complicated variables such as food insecurity, level of daily exercise, or adolescents' college intentions can potentially be captured with a single question but might be usefully addressed with multiple questions.

When you are considering this issue, several relevant considerations for the decision are the following:

- Does it make logical sense to ask this question in multiple ways?

- How important is this variable?

- Does the variable have subcomponents for which information is desired?

- What is the amount of time required of respondents by the overall measurement process? Is managing overall time an important consideration?

- How has the measurement of this variable been handled in previous evaluation studies and research settings?

Whatever your choice on this issue with regard to a particular variable, you will probably need to decide whether to use a measure that has been used before or to develop your own. For single-item measures, it may be possible to use an item wording that is taken from a larger scale or survey, e.g., a survey administered by a government agency. This is the general topic that we turn to next.

Consistency Across Studies When Doing Replications

Case Study 6.2 describes an evaluation setting in which a follow-up population survey on a university campus was conducted after a period of five years to examine change over time. However, decisions had to be made with respect to maintaining the exact wording of a critical question or updating it to reflect changed circumstances.

CASE STUDY 6.2 REPEATING VERSUS REVISING QUESTIONS IN A REPLICATION STUDY

In 2013 I was part of a research team that conducted an online survey of students, faculty, and staff at my university campus to evaluate the first year of the campus's smoke-free policy, which had gone into effect nine months earlier. The policy prohibited both smoking and vaping (e-cigarette use) in all indoor and outdoor locations on campus. One of the primary aims of the study

(Continued)

(Continued)

was to gauge support for a smoke-free campus. To assess this support we used the Likert-type item, "Our campus should be 100% smoke-free," providing seven response options including a neutral point. Survey results showed that support was high, with 72% of students and 77% of faculty and staff expressing agreement (that is, selecting scale points 5 through 7), as opposed to being neutral or opposed. We prepared a final report that we shared with the campus community, including administrators, faculty, and others. We also published an analysis of the predictors of support for the research community (Braverman et al., 2015).

In 2018 I was part of a new team that conducted a follow-up online survey, in part to examine whether policy support had changed (Braverman et al., 2021). Most of the procedures and much of the survey content closely followed the 2013 version. But our analyses of the 2013 survey led to one feature of question content that we wanted to change: this time, we wanted the smoke-free campus support question to refer explicitly to the policy itself. We developed a new wording that stated: "I support the current policy that makes the OSU campus 100% smoke-free." One could argue that the two wordings, old and new, covered the same content and were functionally identical. That may in fact be true for all or most respondents. But we also reasoned that such an assumption of equivalence might not be justified. For example, some respondents may have unpredictable reactions to the idea of setting policies to influence behavior, and this framing context could influence the responses of at least some participants. Thus, we figured, if we wish to measure support for the policy, it probably makes most sense to be explicit about it.

But with this desired change we faced a conundrum. Although the new wording was closer to what we specifically wanted to ask, we would thereby lose the ability to compare responses with those from 2013. Without this comparison we couldn't examine how support might have changed—up, down, or unchanged—with the policy having been in place for five years. Therefore, we had to decide which option was more essential to what we wanted to learn: changing the item wording to refer explicitly to policy support or allowing for comparability over time?

We finally decided to include both wordings in the survey. The cost of this option was that we added slightly to the overall survey length and ran the risk of respondents becoming frustrated because of a perception of redundancy. But we decided that the different kinds of value to be gained from each of the wordings made the repetition worthwhile.

An important difference between the two items was in the response scale options. The new item was given five response points, from "Strongly Disagree" to "Strongly Agree," with a middle point labeled "Neutral or unsure."

As an added complication, the environmental context of tobacco use had changed radically in the intervening five years. The phenomenon of e-cigarettes and vaping had exploded onto the scene. So we also judged it inadequate to use the exact original wording because respondents might be

(Continued)

left to wonder whether vaping is included in the phrase "100% smoke-free." Since vaping is generally considered as distinct from smoking, it might be ambiguous as to whether "smoke-free" includes the aerosol produced by e-cigarettes. So we expanded the wording of the original question to read: "Our campus should be 100% smoke-free, including cigarettes, other smoking products, and vaping products." As with the decision to include both questions, the decision to make this revision was a matter of trade-offs: we ultimately decided that the clarity to be gained from the new wording was the overriding consideration. In this case, one cost for making this change was that interpretation of our findings would be somewhat more complicated, but we felt that this was the best alternative.

Results from the survey revealed that policy support had increased somewhat since 2013, and more to the current point, we were pleased that the two wordings provided very similar results. Using the new wording, support levels were 75.2% from students and 83.9% from faculty/staff. Using the original, slightly revised wording those levels were 73.9% from students and 84.7% from faculty and staff. The two wordings yielded percentages that differed by only 1.3 percentage points for students and 0.8 percentage points for faculty/staff. The correlation of the two items was .844 for students and .631 for faculty/staff.

From a measurement perspective, our conclusion with this endeavor was that responses seem to be robust with regard to these changes in wording. Believing that one's campus "should be smoke-free" is very similar to expressing support for a policy that makes the campus smoke-free. That information will be valuable going forward.

Using Extant Measures

There are several reasons why it may be advantageous for you to identify and use an extant measure that closely fits the requirements of your current study. First, it can save considerable time and effort (although the search process can be time-consuming). Second, it can increase comparability with prior studies, which can increase the value of your own study in promoting learning, both about your own intervention and what is known in the field as a whole.

When you have identified a measure that might be a good candidate for inclusion in your study, some essential considerations are the following:

- Is the measure fully relevant for your needs?

- If it is partially, but not fully, relevant, is it permissible and practical for you to adapt it so that it becomes more relevant?

- Is the focus of the measure appropriate for your purposes? That is, if the variable being measured is at all complex, does the candidate measure emphasize the elements of the variable that are consistent with your needs? For example, some self-esteem measures emphasize that variable's relevance in school settings, social settings, or more globally (Mecca et al., 1989).

- Is the measure compatible with contemporary research and evaluation practice?

- Does the measure involve a cost that is acceptable for your project?

- Is the measure under copyright protection, and will your use of it require permission from the copyright holder?

Existing measures can sometimes be difficult to locate, depending on the nature of the construct, but there are many internet-based resources that can be of invaluable assistance. For relatively mainstream constructs that have been the focus of prior work, repositories of measures may exist that are curated by government agencies, foundations, nonprofit organizations, universities, research centers, or other organizations. For example, if you wish to find measures of food insecurity, you could examine websites maintained by the US Department of Agriculture, the Food and Nutrition Technical Assistance (FANTA) project of the US Agency for International Development, the University of California's Global Food Initiative, and other agencies and organizations.

For psychological constructs, an excellent resource can be the Mental Measurements Yearbook (MMY), maintained by the Buros Center at the University of Nebraska (https://buros.org/mental-measurements-yearbook). The MMY classifies instruments into 18 categories and provides reviews and critiques of individual instruments.

In many other cases, you can locate measures through the research literature. Finding articles that use instruments similar to what you are looking for can be informative, and contacting the researchers can frequently result in their sharing their instruments, providing background information, and permitting your use of the instruments.

When you have located a measure, it will often be the case that it looks promising for your purposes but you would like to make some adjustments or adaptations, such as changing some wordings, dropping some items, and so on. If done well, these adaptations can be helpful or even necessary, but the process involves some caveats. First, you must determine whether you are free to make those changes. Second, there may be important considerations with respect to validity. The items in the scale may have been arranged for a specific purpose after a careful process of scale development and testing. Thus you should be deliberate regarding any changes you would like to make. Whether or not you do make edits, you should pilot test the instrument for use in your own setting.

With respect to the use of existing scales for your evaluation, Johnson and Morgan (2016) discuss the importance of avoiding both plagiarism and copyright infringement. Plagiarism is the presentation of others' work as your own. Typically, conceptions of plagiarism involve the use of text rather than a measurement scale, but in some cases it may be necessary to attribute a scale to its original author. With regard to copyright infringement, if a measure is copyrighted you will need to seek permission to use it. You can contact the copyright owner, e.g., often the researcher, to initiate this discussion. Johnson and Morgan note that the American Psychological Association has taken the position that permissions might be needed even for the use of individual items from scales and tests.

Validity considerations when using extant measures. For those variables in your evaluation for which you use an extant measure, you cannot assume that validity has been established for the purposes of your own study. As discussed in Chapter 2, validity is not a quality that travels with an instrument across times and settings. It is not a permanent feature, once established and then enduring. Researchers and evaluators, in their reports and publications, sometimes make the error of describing an instrument's validity as having been demonstrated at some prior time, with the implication that this is an issue that has been resolved. It is true that prior studies can provide a certain level of evidence in support of construct validity claims for a measure, but you should seek to demonstrate it for your own population and your own study. For example, a content review by expert colleagues can help to establish that the content of a scale is appropriate for the judgments you wish to make from its scores. Other forms of validity evidence can be explored as well, including factor analysis on the data you have collected, to ensure that the latent variable structure in your sample is similar to the structure that has been found in prior studies.

Developing Your Own Measures

You may find that the existing measures you examine for potential use are too long, too old, a poor match for your purposes, or otherwise inappropriate. In addition, you may have variables that are unique to your evaluation study and for which measures do not currently exist. In these cases you will need to develop your own measures.

In the following sections I will discuss some of the important considerations in the development of scales, surveys, tests, and other measures, highlighting the ways that the process intersects with issues of construct validity. More information about the process of developing questions, scales, surveys, and questionnaires can be found in texts by Dillman et al. (2014), DeVellis (2017), and Johnson and Morgan (2016).

Pilot testing and refining your measurement protocol. Conducting a pilot or field test should be considered an essential step in the development of your measure. This usually involves administering the questionnaire, test, or other measure to a small group of participants who are selected to be as similar as possible to your population of interest. Going through the planned measurement process can provide you with procedural information about the adequacy of instructions, the time needed, the costs of implementation, and the range of participant responses to the process. The field test will also produce a data set that can be examined for aspects of data quality such as patterns of nonresponse and the adequacy of response distributions for each item or question. A series of smaller, noncomprehensive pilot tests, focusing on specific aspects of either instrument content or administration procedure, may be helpful as well.

In addition to the field test, other methods for testing questionnaires and other measures are also available (Dillman et al., 2014; Presser, Couper, et al., 2004; Presser, Rothgeb, et al., 2004). These can include:

- *Reviews by experts.* Getting an experienced evaluator or other type of expert to review your draft instrument, and procedural plan will generally be an important and productive source of feedback. A single review may be inadequate if different kinds of expertise are called for. Dillman et al. (2014) recommend that the individuals who are recruited to review a draft include content experts, questionnaire design experts, and experts in the anticipated analytic procedures. They note:

  It would be quite unusual for a single person to have the ability to identify all of the potential problems with questions and a questionnaire....Many studies fail to achieve their objectives because surveyors limit this phase of pretesting only to colleagues down the hallway who are experts in some aspect of survey construction or, at the other extreme, to people who are members of the study population. But questionnaires fail for many reasons, and having a systematic approach to obtaining feedback from a variety of knowledgeable people...is essential (Dillman et al., 2014, p. 243).

- *Cognitive interviewing.* This procedure, which became common in the 1990s, involves asking a potential respondent to read through an instrument and provide a think-aloud protocol to each of the items. Through this procedure the evaluator can seek to assess the ways that questions are interpreted, the thinking processes that are generated by the questions, and the ways that responses are formulated. The process is time-consuming and requires intensive one-on-one administration, so the number of interviews will usually be small. Several variations exist regarding the way that the researcher leads the participant through the interview process (Presser, Couper, et al., 2004; Willson & Miller, 2014).

- *Split-sample experiments.* These experiments are formal procedures that typically are used to provide guidance for large-scale studies. They can be used to compare variations in question wording, question placement, or questionnaire administration, including many of the issues that are discussed in the next section. In such an experiment, a sample of participants can be randomly divided into subgroups that each receives one of the variations under consideration. Experimental investigations of questionnaire options or other measurement-related considerations can be conducted with a relatively small sample in advance of the full study, or they can be incorporated into a more general pilot test. They can also be built into the full study, either to balance out the unknown effects of alternative options or to provide guidance for future cycles in the case of ongoing projects.

Measures Not Based on Human Response

Electronic and mechanical measures. Some variables can be measured through the use of an electronic or mechanical instrument. In such cases one should specify the protocol for using the instrument. For example, as mentioned in Chapter 5, for measuring weight one will need to decide whether it is important to always do the weighing at the same time of day, or before a meal, and so on. As far as the actual scale to be used for those measurements, consideration should be given to the possible variations across instruments. If the evaluation team is confident that each of several scales under consideration would provide equivalent scores, then this choice is not a concern with respect to validity.

Some instruments are expensive, and a trade-off may need to be made between precision and cost. The evaluation team should be able to identify the desired level of precision, and thus the balance between instrument quality and instrument cost will be a practical matter (Braverman, 2013).

Government or institutional records; community statistics. Target outcomes of a policy intervention may be community-level variables such as hospital utilization rates, arrest records, or new cases of a disease or other health condition. The potential sources for these records depend on the nature of the variable.

The use of an institutional statistic carries with it a characteristic set of potential biases and assumptions. One potential concern is the completeness of the data. For example, many cases of illness go unreported, and government agency records on a reported illness may not be fully accurate as measures of the actual incidence or prevalence of that condition. Nevertheless, it may be the best type of information available, despite these limitations. The assumptions required with the use of such statistics to serve as indicators of variables of interest need to be identified and examined.

Anticipating Potential Sources of Bias and Error

As described earlier, in classical test theory an observed score is theorized to be a combination of the respondent's *true score*, for that variable at that point in time, and *error*. The error term is a complex summation of all of the factors that lead to a distortion from the true score. But in general, error is divided into two types: random error and systematic error, or bias. Bias occurs when a measurement, to some degree, reflects influences that lead it to deviate from the true score in a consistent fashion across the units being measured. For example, if a mechanical scale is consistently high or low in the weight it provides, perhaps by two or three ounces, the scale is biased. Similarly, if a set of survey items that is meant to measure people's typical alcohol intake tends to consistently provide an underestimate of their alcohol use, that measure is biased as well.

By definition, the expected value of random error is zero, which means that hypothetically, over an infinite (or at least extremely large) number of measurements, the deviations from the true score that are caused by random error would balance out. But for any single measurement, random error will operate to make the observed score different from the true score to an unknowable degree. In designing and using measures, random error cannot be eliminated, but our goals are to identify the extent of it and to minimize it, to the degree possible.

With regard to systematic error or bias, there will be numerous potential sources that contribute to bias in a set of observed scores. We seek to identify these sources and, as with random error, to estimate the extent of their influence on the scores. But in contrast to how we deal with random error, we seek to eliminate bias wherever possible. That may be feasible with some forms of bias, though certainly not all. It can be challenging to assess where bias exists, to estimate the extent of it, and to determine how to deal with it in the most efficient way.

Bias as a failure of the measurement assumptions. For any specific measurement strategy and measure, the auxiliary measurement theory that links them to an underlying construct of interest provides a set of propositions that justifies their use as a valid representation of the construct. In that sense, the existence of bias may be seen as a breakdown in the adequacy of that theory.

Bias doesn't need to apply to all respondents in order for it to present a problem. Some forms of bias associated with a measure may apply to all respondents, e.g., a poor way of wording a question that leads to a particular kind of misinterpretation that was unintended by the evaluator. But in other cases, a particular form of bias may affect only a subset of respondents. For example, consider a survey question that asks students to self-report their school grades. Students may be tempted to give an answer that makes them look good, a phenomenon known as a *social desirability* response set. But it is reasonable to expect that those students who have received poor grades will be disproportionately affected by this impulse, while those who have received good grades will be inclined to report them accurately. This circumstance will be likely to inflate the lower end of the distribution of reported grades, raise the overall mean of the set of student grades, and obfuscate the meaning of reported scores in the lower and middle sections of the distribution of scores. Thus, this phenomenon will constitute a significant concern for the overall measurement strategy of self-reported grades, causing problems for the interpretation and use of those scores.

A note from my personal experience: When working with a team on a survey development project, I will occasionally hear a student or other team member argue in defense of a particular option for question wording by saying something to the effect of, "I think that most respondents will understand what we're saying here." Hearing that justification predictably launches me into educator mode, leading me to explain that even if most respondents do indeed understand, if some subset of respondents *don't* understand what we're saying, that is still a threat to construct validity and a problem requiring remediation.

Dealing with bias. For any specific measure, it is important to think actively and creatively about what the potential sources of bias may be. In that way you can try to identify and correct those biases. For any particular forms of bias that cannot be fully eliminated, at least by identifying them and trying to determine their influence, you may be able to estimate the extent to which they are problematic for your data set. You can then try to account for those issues in your interpretation of findings. For example, if you are aware that a particular variable, such as a self-reported health behavior, is probably overreported by many of your respondents, incorporating that knowledge into your interpretations and conclusions will increase the accuracy and usefulness of those findings. In addition, awareness of probable biases in your data set could be a reason for you to limit the confidence you can place in the conclusions that are drawn from the data.

The following sections illustrate some of the complexities of measurement and some of the ways that evaluators might be misled due to methodological aspects of their measurement decisions.

Asking About Sensitive Subject Matter

A source of bias that frequently occurs in surveys is the misreporting of information by respondents due to sensitive question content. This can result when respondents perceive the question to be embarrassing, invasive, or threatening. Question topics that fall within this category can include sexual behaviors, health conditions, income, alcohol or drug use, voting history, personal prejudices, illegal activity, cheating (e.g., in school or on taxes), and many others. A good deal of research has been devoted to understanding this form of bias, predicting its occurrence, and developing strategies for dealing with it.

Tourangeau et al. (2000) proposed that the concept of sensitivity rests on at least three distinct dimensions. First, the behaviors or opinions being asked about may be subject to social norms. The respondent may be reluctant to admit to having violated those norms and thus may be motivated to provide the socially desirable response. Second, a question may be perceived by respondents as invasive of their privacy and thus inherently offensive. Finally, the question may arouse respondents' anxieties about the possible disclosure of their responses to third parties. Each of these dimensions may lead respondents to intentionally overstate desirable behaviors and opinions, and to understate behaviors and opinions that they perceive to be socially undesirable or unacceptable. The fact that these tendencies influence responses in a similar direction for a given question makes this misreporting a problem of systematic error, i.e., bias. As a related issue, encountering sensitive questions may lead some respondents to decline to provide any answer at all, or even to abandon the survey, thus increasing nonresponse at the level of the individual item or the full study.

It is in the nature of perceived norms and social desirability that bias due to misreporting will be unequally distributed across respondents, being heavier among those whose answers would represent the undesirable side of the spectrum. For example, in the case of alcohol use, misreporting may be a more significant problem among heavier drinkers, and their underreporting will make them appear to be light or moderate drinkers. The validity implications of this shift are that heavier drinkers will be more difficult to distinguish, attenuating relationships with other variables. The overall mean of the variable will be affected as well—shifting down in the case of alcohol use, reflecting lower use overall.

The perception of certain question content as sensitive or threatening may vary for different segments of a population, depending on the topic. The age of respondents may play a role if the perceived norms for a behavior are age-dependent. For example, questions about tobacco use are perceived as threatening by adolescents, but much less so by adults (Tourangeau et al., 2000). Therefore, one would anticipate that response bias due to underreporting of tobacco use may be a heightened concern in surveys of adolescents.

Survey researchers have recommended several strategies to reduce misreporting due to sensitive question content:

- Before you include a question that you expect will be sensitive, make sure that you really need the information and you know how you will use it. For example, questions about demographic information such as race, gender, income, and marital status are often included by rote and may seem routine from the evaluator's point of view. There are often important reasons for collecting demographics, such as to demonstrate that a program is serving a representative cross-section of the larger community. But some demographics can be perceived differently by respondents, who might not see the relationship of that personal information to the larger subject of the survey. If you don't need the information, leave it out. And if you do need the information, it can be helpful to communicate to respondents, in the survey instructions, what purpose it will serve.

- Make the survey anonymous if possible. Respondents will be more likely to provide accurate answers to sensitive questions when they are confident that they can't be identified. When anonymity is not possible, try to ensure that the confidentiality of responses will be strictly protected, and communicate that to respondents. This will involve a measure of trust on respondents' part because they must take you at your word about the treatment of their data.

- Be attentive to the format of the requested response and the structure of response categories. For questions on income, Dillman et al. (2014) suggest presenting broad categories rather than asking for an exact amount. When asking about gender identity, an extended list of options may be viewed as intrusive (e.g., *woman, man, transgender male, transgender female, gender fluid, genderqueer, agender, gender questioning, unsure*), raising a concern about why all that detail is needed. Conversely, however, a set of options that collapses together categories that are clearly disparate (e.g., *woman, man, other*) may be viewed as inappropriate as well (Glick et al., 2018). The detail requested should match the information needed.

- Try to word questions in a way that reduces the salience and importance of social norms and expectations. That is, try to make every possible answer to a sensitive question socially acceptable, to the degree possible. For example, Tourangeau and Yan (2007) describe a technique they call "forgiving wording," which conveys a priori acceptance of the problematic level of response. They illustrate this with a question on parenting:

> Even the calmest parents get angry at their children sometimes. Did your children do anything in the past seven days to make you yourself angry? (Tourangeau & Yan, 2007, p. 874)

- If possible, use a survey mode that does not involve interaction with an interviewer. Social desirability processes have been found to operate more strongly in the presence of another person, even if that person is a stranger (Tourangeau & Yan, 2007). Therefore, respondents will answer more honestly when a survey is self-administered, that is, in web or paper-and-pencil format, rather than administered by an in-person or telephone interviewer.

- Place sensitive questions near the end of the questionnaire (Dillman et al., 2014). This minimizes any disruptive effect on respondents' answers to other questions in the survey and also reduces the likelihood that respondents may decide not to participate in the survey upon encountering the questions.

In addition to these general recommendations, several formal procedures have been developed that provide statistical estimates of the extent of bias in responses to sensitive questions. Three of these procedures have been summarized by Rosenfeld et al. (2016). The *randomized response* technique operates by introducing a degree of uncertainty on the researcher's part into the question that the individual respondent has actually answered. Two others—the *list experiment* and the *endorsement experiment*—involve subdividing the responding sample into two groups, manipulating the information presented to the groups (one of which receives the sensitive content), and using the difference in responses between the groups to derive a statistical estimate of the extent of bias. These techniques are complex in both the required logistics and the statistical analyses, and they add to the time required for the survey. They are not commonly used in evaluation studies but may be of interest in certain evaluation contexts.

Overly Restricted Response Range: Ceiling and Floor Effects

For any given sample of respondents and variable being measured, the measure should allow for the full range of variability to be expressed. A *ceiling effect* may be operating when a large proportion of scores are bunched near the top of the range of possible scores. More variability would be introduced into the distribution if the measure allowed for higher scores on the variable. For knowledge or skill tests, ceiling effects suggest that the test is too easy.

When the variable being measured does not involve right and wrong answers, you may wish to expand the range of response options, primarily for the purpose of increasing variability. Case Study 6.3 provides an example.

CASE STUDY 6.3 DEALING WITH THE POSSIBILITY OF CEILING EFFECTS ON A SINGLE SURVEY ITEM

Sometimes the distribution of responses to a survey item will be naturally unbalanced. When my colleagues and I evaluated the campus smoke-free policy that had been enacted at my university nine months before (Braverman et al., 2015), we expected support for a smoke-free campus to be generally high. We knew from the research literature that these policies tend to be popular and furthermore that their popularity tends to increase after they have been enacted.

We measured support for the smoke-free campus with the item,

Our campus should be 100% smoke-free.

In anticipation that support might be high, we wanted to provide the opportunity for variability in the responses to this question. Therefore, we used a large response range, with seven options:

Strongly Disagree   Disagree   Slightly Disagree   Neither Agree nor Disagree   Slightly Agree   Agree   Strongly Agree

We conducted the survey with two campus populations: (1) students and (2) faculty and staff. The distributions of responses were as follows:

	Students (N = 5,690)	Faculty and Staff (N = 2,051)
Strongly Agree	54.6%	56.1%
Agree	12.8	15.2
Slightly Agree	5.3	5.9
Neither Agree nor Disagree	6.2	6.1
Slightly Disagree	3.7	3.7
Disagree	6.0	5.9
Strongly Disagree	11.5	7.1
TOTAL	**100.0%**	**100.0%**

(Continued)

(Continued)

The results confirmed our expectations about strong popular support for a smoke-free campus. In both the student and faculty/staff samples, more than half of the respondents selected the highest option, "Strongly Agree." Further, about 73% of students and 77% of faculty/staff selected one of the three "agree" options.

This pattern of scores, clustered at the top of the scale, is indicative of a strong ceiling effect. The clustering may have been even more pronounced had we included only five responses, the more common format for Likert-type items. The extended number of options probably did provide an additional degree of variability between the respondents, which was helpful for the analyses.

However, our use of seven options did not contribute toward making the distribution of scores closer to normal. The distributions for both samples can be described as bimodal. At the lower end, the percentages of respondents who selected any of the three "disagree" options were small (21.2% of students and 16.7% of faculty/staff), but within those categories the largest proportion of respondents selected the most extreme option ("Strongly Disagree"). And in both samples, only slightly more than 6% of respondents were neutral.

It is also noteworthy that the distributions within the two samples were strikingly similar. The replication of this pattern strengthened our confidence in the accuracy and stability of these scores, and the validity of our conclusions about the opinions within the campus community about a smoke-free campus.

A comparable situation exists when scores for a measured variable are bunched at the bottom of the distribution, which is known as a *floor effect*. If that pattern occurs with a test, one can conclude that, overall, the test is too difficult for that group of respondents: an easier test would have revealed the differences in ability that probably exist among those test-takers whose scores are all near zero. For variables that don't involve right and wrong answers, the problem is that there is greater variability at the bottom end that is not permitted to be expressed by the question, scale, or other measurement procedure.

A caveat must be noted here: The clustering of scores at the top or bottom of a distribution will suggest that ceiling and/or floor effects may exist, but one should not automatically presume that the measure is deficient and needs to be revised in order to allow further room for variation. One case of this potential exception occurs with ratio scaling: a count variable—e.g., number of hours of exercise in the past week—may wind up with many scores of zero. Despite the accumulation of scores at the bottom of the permissible range, there is no possibility of lower scores, since a count score cannot descend into negative territory. Furthermore, depending on the group being measured—e.g., consider a group of older, out-of-shape adults embarking on an exercise program—a score of zero may in fact be accurate for many of those individuals, and a clustering of scores near the bottom might make perfect sense.

Another example in which an aggregation of scores at one end of a distribution—this time the top end—is not necessarily a problem involves criterion-referenced testing. Consider a knowledge test that is designed, not with the goal of producing maximum variation of scores, but rather to represent a body of knowledge that students in a certain grade are expected to master. In that case, it may be fully appropriate for most or all of the students to score near the top of the potential range. Indeed, that may be the desired outcome, and potentially quite plausible if the teaching has been of high quality.

Thus, the determination of whether ceiling and/or floor effects exist in a set of scores is largely dependent on the prior expectation for the shape of the distribution. If the expectation is that the distribution of scores should be roughly normal—with the majority of scores being bunched together in the middle of the range and the frequencies tailing off in each direction as scores become more extreme—then the suspicion of a restricted range problem may be warranted. In addition, pilot testing an assortment of possibilities for the structure of the response options will also shed light on the extent to which this may be a problem.

In all cases of restricted range, information is lost that could otherwise be informative with regard to understanding the variable of interest: a group of respondents is scored as equivalent on the variable, or nearly so, when in fact the respondents may differ from each other considerably. The reliability of the measure will be reduced, and the validity of conclusions will suffer as a result. In addition, certain statistical tests may be compromised if they rely on assumptions that the variable's distribution is normal in character.

Memory Demands

One element of a question's cognitive load is the demand placed on the respondent's memory. Dillman et al. (2014) noted that

> ...surveyors should consider three recall problems. First, memory tends to fade over time. Second, individual episodes or occurrences of regular and mundane events are generally not precisely remembered....And third, people usually do not categorize information by precise month or year. Given these limitations, respondents are unlikely to be able to accurately report how many days they drove more than 1 mile during the past 6 months. But they can probably very accurately report how many days they drove their car during the past week or drove more than 200 miles at a time in the past 3 months. (p. 98)

The upshot with respect to writing good items is that accommodations must be made for common limitations of memory. Dillman et al. (2014) and Tourangeau et al. (2000) provide additional recommendations.

Incomplete Understanding of the Question

Respondents may have difficulty understanding a question due to unwieldy syntax, vague or unfamiliar terminology, an unclear logical basis to the question, or other problems. Case Study 6.4 describes a study that demonstrated that many respondents will answer questions whether or not they understand what is being asked. In that specific case, the problem was that respondents were unfamiliar with the question's central concept.

CASE STUDY 6.4   RESPONDENTS' TENDENCIES TO ANSWER QUESTIONS THEY DON'T UNDERSTAND

In his text on the varieties of survey error, Robert Groves (1989) described a classic study (Ferber, 1956) demonstrating that respondents will answer questions about various phenomena even if they do not understand what is being asked. Survey interview respondents were asked for their attitudes about several political issues: minimum hourly wages, guaranteed annual wage, government bond yields, and fair trade laws. The response options were *For*, *Against*, *Neutral*, or *Don't Know*. Following the attitudinal question they were asked to define the term in their own words, and those qualitative definitions were coded by judges as basically correct or incorrect. Thus, this process created three categories with regard to each respondent's understanding of the construct: correct definition, incorrect definition, or admitted ignorance. The researcher then calculated the proportion of respondents in each of these three categories who expressed an attitude about the construct.

The study found that respondents who had provided a correct versus incorrect definition were almost equally likely to express an attitude. Furthermore, among the respondents who admitted ignorance of the construct, the proportion who expressed an attitude varied between 14.1% and 82.7% across the four questions, depending on the subject. For example, with regard to *guaranteed annual wage*, an attitude about the concept (for, against, or neutral) was offered by 90.6% of the respondents who defined it correctly and 83.6% of those who defined it incorrectly. Furthermore, an attitude was expressed by 47.0% of the respondents—nearly half of the sample—who said in the later question that *they didn't know what the term meant*, even though "Don't know" was an explicit response option available to them.

One takeaway from this study is that however you ask a question, you will probably get an answer from the majority of respondents—and unless you also take specific measures to assess their comprehension, you will never know whether they fully understood the question they were answering. Groves (1989) summarized the phenomenon this way: "...respondents interpret the interview rules to require them to answer each question, not merely

(Continued)

to answer the questions they view as completely unambiguous. For the most part, they will follow these rules." (p. 457)

It is possible that the expectations and pressures felt internally by respondents to provide an answer varies according to the survey mode, e.g., face-to-face interview versus telephone versus paper-and-pencil versus web survey. Nevertheless, the phenomenon has been widely demonstrated. Accordingly, do what you can to make your questions as comprehensible as possible, and do not assume *a priori* that the mere provision of a response implies a meaningful item of information from the respondent.

A second takeaway is that this study provides a vivid example of the valuable information that can be gained from conducting a pilot test in advance of your evaluation or research study.

You should try to ensure that the question is likely to be understood by all respondents. Going further, Dillman et al. (2014) recommend using wordings that are as simple and commonplace as possible. They illustrate this point with the following suggestions regarding word choice (p. 188):

- *work* instead of *employment*

- *your answers* instead of *your responses*

- *people who live here* instead of *occupants of this household*.

Dealing with double negatives in survey questions is also a problem, because they create confusions of syntax. Converse and Presser (1986) provide an example in which respondents are asked to state whether they agree or disagree with the following statement:

Teachers should not be required to supervise students in the halls, the lunchroom, and school parking lots.

Converse and Presser explain: "One may Agree that teachers should not be required to do this kind of duty outside of the classroom. But the Disagree side gets tangled, for it means, 'I do not think that teachers should not be required to supervise students outside of their classrooms'—that is, teachers should be required" (p. 13). This wording places a burden on respondents' comprehension due to confusing syntax for *one* of the response categories.

Question Wording, Context, and Framing Effects

A great deal of research has demonstrated that people's responses to a question may be influenced by the use of specific words and the context within which the question is asked. *Framing effects* are factors that affect responses to a question due to contextual or surrounding information, which can include instructions, word choice, the amount and type of information provided, and the formatting of response options (Bruine de Bruin, 2011; Chong & Druckman, 2007). One may perhaps not be surprised that measurements of attitudes, opinions, and beliefs are highly susceptible to these contextual effects, but they have also been found to operate for questions that focus on presumably more objective content such as behavioral self-reports (Schwarz, 1999; Schwarz & Oyserman, 2001).

A few examples can be helpful in illustrating the range of potential framing effects.

Wording choices. Unintended meanings may be associated with particular word choices. Some words will carry connotative meaning beyond their straightforward definition—baggage, if you will—that can sway some respondents' answers in a certain direction. Thus, respondents can be expected to respond differently if they are asked whether they favor "increasing government revenues" versus "increasing taxes" for some specified purpose (Clark & Schober, 1992).

One of the most famous examples of word choice effects is what has come to be known as the "forbid/allow asymmetry" (Holleman, 2006). Consider two forms of what might seem to be the same question:

- Do you think the government should forbid the use of mobile phones while driving?

- Do you think the government should allow the use of mobile phones while driving?

At first glance it appears that these two forms, though worded in opposite directions, are equivalent in meaning. Respondents who answer Yes to the first version (yes, mobile phones should be forbidden) should logically answer No to the second version (no, they should not be allowed). But many studies have shown that this apparent symmetry does not completely hold, and the two word forms do not in fact produce mirror-image results. Over a series of experiments involving dichotomous forbid/allow questions on multiple topics with multiple populations, Holleman (2006) found that respondents are more apt to answer "no, do not allow" (which constituted 44% of all responses) than they are to answer "yes, forbid" (37% of all responses; difference tested with chi-square, $p < 0.001$). Holleman attributed this asymmetry to several factors relating to respondents' interpretation of the terms. Most notably, despite the ostensible semantic equivalence, "yes, forbid" is judged, whether consciously or not, to be a more extreme position than "no, do not allow," which leads respondents to choose it less often.

The particular example of choosing between terms such as *forbid* and *allow* (as well as other terms such as *prohibit, ban, permit,* etc., which have not been systematically examined) can be directly relevant in the evaluation of regulatory policies. Administrators and other stakeholders will be keenly interested in community perceptions about existing or proposed regulations governing, e.g., helmet use requirements, the use of alcohol or tobacco, or the sales of sugary beverages within schools. The levels of support within the affected community (such as an organization, school district, city, or county) will constitute one component of perceived policy success, and word choices that might nudge the expressed support levels in either direction by a few percentage points may turn out to be consequential for decision-making.

Another example of framing effects due to word choice is presented in Case Study 6.5.

CASE STUDY 6.5   THE INFLUENCE OF LABELING EFFECTS ON SURVEY RESPONSES: OPINION POLLS ABOUT US NATIONAL HEALTH POLICY

National health care policy is a complex, politically charged subject and a frequent focus of public opinion polls. Numerous studies have found that differences in how questions are worded and framed can create variability in the apparent levels of public opinion about the topic.

The Affordable Care Act. The Patient Protection and Affordable Care Act (ACA), often referred to informally as "ObamaCare," was signed into law in 2010 and its major provisions had come into force by 2014. Holl et al. (2018) published an analysis of 376 national opinion surveys conducted between 2010 and 2016 by news organizations, polling firms, and universities. They found several notable variations in how the law was typically presented in survey questions, and conducted a regression analysis to examine which types of variation resulted in significant changes in approval levels. The way that the law was identified in the question—which might be "the Affordable Care Act," "Obamacare," or "the health care law"—did not result in significant differences in support, but one of the factors that did affect support was whether the response alternatives included an option stating that the law should be repealed (or repealed and replaced). If that terminology was included, as opposed to simply asking about one's level of support or approval, the responses tended to be significantly more supportive of the ACA, by about nine percentage points on average. Holl et al. (2018) hypothesized that the effect may have been due to the activation of a phenomenon called *loss aversion*, in which respondents tend to express reluctance to reverse or change a present state of affairs.

Medicare for All. The national health insurance system established by the ACA was based on private insurance. In the run-up to the US presidential election of 2020, one of the most heavily debated topics was whether the ACA

(Continued)

(Continued)

should be replaced by a national health care system similar to Medicare, in which the federal government played a more central role and introduced public insurance options. A multiplicity of proposals, especially from the candidates vying for the Democratic Party nomination, focused on either retaining and/or expanding the ACA, or instituting a national system that included public insurance and deemphasized or eliminated private insurance. Those latter approaches went by a variety of names that included *single-payer, universal health coverage*, and *Medicare-for-all*. Political opponents of the concept sometimes referred to it with the term *socialized medicine*.

The support of the American public for different options regarding national health insurance policy was a subject of intense interest in the political process. The topic was complicated, with a large variety of potential options, and numerous national surveys attempted to assess public opinions. In this political environment, the Kaiser Family Foundation (2019) conducted a national survey in 2019 that directly compared a number of terms commonly used in the surveys. They found that question terminology had a substantial effect on support levels. The survey asked respondents for their reactions to several different terms, with the following results:

Term Used to Describe a National Health Plan	Percent of Respondents Who Reported That Their Reaction Was...		
	Positive (%)	Negative (%)	No Opinion (%)
Medicare-for-all	63	31	6
Universal health coverage	63	34	3
National health plan	59	36	5
Single-payer health insurance system	49	32	19
Socialized medicine	46	44	11

Thus, the level of public support varied between a low of 46% and a high of 63%, a difference of 17 percentage points, depending on the terminology used. The tendency of respondents to decline to offer an opinion, based on the question's terminology, varied as well: only 3% of respondents reported that they had no opinion regarding *Universal health coverage*, while the No Opinion figure climbed to 19% for *Single-payer health insurance system*.

Source: Kaiser Family Foundation Health Tracking Poll. (2019). https://www.kff.org/slideshow/public-opinion-on-single-payer-national-health-plans-and-expanding-access-to-medicare-coverage/

The formatting of response alternatives. A fundamental choice that evaluators and researchers must make in designing questionnaires is whether the response format should be open or closed. In an open format, respondents are given only the question and are free to shape their response in their own words. In a closed format, they are given options from which they must select. Most often, the closed format is used, primarily for reasons of logistics and efficiency. Open responses must be individually coded. This requires much more time for the analysis process, and in light of available resources it is usually not feasible in evaluation studies with large sample sizes. The coding process also introduces greater potential for problems of reliability regarding consistency between coders, even when methodological protections are put into place.

Nevertheless, the two types of format can produce very different responses. Schwarz (1999) describes a study on parental values in which parents were asked what they consider to be "the most important thing for children to prepare them for life." When potential responses were presented in a closed format using a list of options, 61.5% of parents selected the option, "To think for themselves." Yet when the question was asked with an open format, only 4.6% of parents spontaneously provided a response that was coded as an expression of this same idea.

For questions that involve self-reports of behavior—a common component of many program evaluations—variations in the list of presented options can also produce large differences in response. In a study involving self-reports on daily TV viewing in Germany described by Schwarz (1999), 16.2% of respondents reported that they viewed TV for more than two and a half hours a day when that figure was the *highest* of six options (a "low-frequency" scale that ranged from "Up to ½ hour" to "More than 2½ hours"). However, when two and a half hours was the cutoff for the *lowest* of six options (a "high-frequency" scale ranging from "Up to 2½ hours" to "More than 4½ hours"), the comparable figure was 37.5%. That is, respondents were more than twice as likely to place themselves in that range, probably because the available options in the high-frequency case implicitly suggested that "more than 2½ hours" is a customary and reasonable amount of daily viewing (Schwarz & Oyserman, 2001).

In accounting for the substantial differences that can occur due to the framing of response alternatives, survey researchers refer to the cognitive aspects of the response task (Tourangeau et al., 2000). Respondents use all of the information contained in the survey question as clues about the subject's larger context and the questioner's intent. In the example of behavioral frequency questions, the provision of response options, which are open for inspection before answering, can be interpreted as defining what levels of behavior define the population at large. In selecting their answer, respondents may be influenced to some degree by social desirability concerns, e.g., wanting to appear typical rather than extreme. But they might also be using the information in an attempt to map their indistinct sense of behavioral frequency, e.g., heavy or light, onto the available alternatives. Evaluators must take these possibilities into account when drawing conclusions about the validity and accuracy of findings.

Providing examples within the question. Evaluators may sometimes be tempted to include a few examples in a question that asks respondents about their experience with a broad category such as type of food, type of exercise, type of screen time, or type of health care provider. The rationale is that those examples can help to stimulate memory as well as clarify the intended meaning of what is being asked. In addition to lengthening the question, providing examples raises the issue of how the specific examples might affect the response, and thus the choice may come with potential costs as well as benefits.

Tourangeau et al. (2014) reported a series of experiments in which they asked respondents about their frequency of consuming different kinds of foods: dairy, poultry, vegetables, grain, and wine. Among other findings, results showed that respondents reported higher consumption when the examples tended to be foods that are frequently consumed but somewhat atypical (e.g., butter, cream, sour cream) rather than very typical (milk, cheese, yogurt) or very unusual (sheep cheese, goat's milk). The researchers reasoned that the frequent but atypical examples resulted in higher reported consumption levels because they represented foods that respondents would be relatively unlikely to recall spontaneously. The bottom line is that the provision of examples represents a framing feature for which the effects may be difficult to anticipate.

The nonneutrality of questions and the impermanence of attitudes. These examples illustrate a few of the ways that framing effects can operate. One should assume that framing effects might always be present in some form when asking a question. Clark and Schober (1992) recommended that we should seek to understand and control these effects, rather than aiming to eliminate them:

> It is futile to search for neutral questions. They don't exist. Every question carries presuppositions, so every question establishes a perspective. So for each question we must ask: Is the perspective taken really the one from which we want the respondent to answer? If the answer is yes – if we can justify the perspective – then we can also justify the question. (p. 30)

Compounding the challenges of question quality is the inherent precariousness of the psychological phenomena we are trying to tap. Chong and Druckman (2007) wrote that "despite [the] ideal of firm, full, articulate opinions,... citizens have been found to have low-quality opinions, if they have opinions at all. In the public opinion literature, high-quality opinions are usually defined as being stable, consistent, informed, and connected to abstract principles and values. The general conclusion among scholars is that such opinions are rare in the mass public" (p 103).

From the perspective of cognitive psychology, Tourangeau et al. (2000) describe why this state of affairs may exist:

> [A]ttitude judgments are temporary constructions....They may rest on long-standing evaluations and beliefs about a topic, but the judgments themselves must often be created in response to a question, sometimes quite quickly. Moreover, the judgments called for by attitude questions are rarely absolute but are typically made in relation to some standard, generally an implicit one. It is hardly surprising, then, that attitude judgments turn out to be quite context-dependent. As survey researchers have demonstrated repeatedly, the same question often produces quite different answers, depending on the context. (p. 197)

These insights, stemming from the fields of political science and psychology, are very relevant for what we try to do as evaluators. While attitudes, opinions, intentions, and beliefs are not typically the endpoint outcomes in our evaluation models, those constructs frequently appear as mediators in our program theories and explicit short-term outcomes in our logic models, hypothesized to be intermediate influences and determinants of program participants' postintervention behaviors. The uncertainties represented by framing effects and other threats to validity operate, to some degree, every time we try to measure a variable by asking someone a question.

Controlling framing effects. There are several ways that evaluators and researchers can try to take account of framing effects for measurement strategies that involve survey methods.

- If possible, try to ascertain what differences in response may result from potential variations in the question format. This might be done by direct experimentation (of a formal or informal nature) as well as by reference to the research literature on the topic. When variations can be identified based on different framing options, you can use that information to estimate a confidence interval for the potential variability of response, bounded by the highest and lowest levels obtained. Overall, we can have more confidence in the stability and validity of responses when they display relatively limited variability across experimental manipulations.

- Seek to replicate your procedures and results. Replications of findings will go a long way toward establishing the degree of stability of response for measured variables. These replications could result from investigations of your own, instances from previous evaluation practice, and findings reported in the relevant research literature.

- The recommendations for pilot testing your instrument, discussed earlier in this chapter, can apply to addressing concerns about potential framing effects. Conducting a small number of cognitive interviews (Dillman et al., 2014; Presser, Rothgeb, et al., 2004) can shed light on how respondents interpret particular features of question wording, sequence, or other framing effects.

- To assess, and possibly counterbalance, different kinds of framing effects, Converse and Presser (1986) recommend that you may wish to include multiple questions on the same topic. While this strategy creates redundancy with regard to the focus of the questions, it can provide insight into the stability of responses across variations in presentation, as well as suggest upper and lower estimates for those variations. The potential benefit of using multiple questions must be weighed against the increased length of the instrument. I used this approach in my campus tobacco policy evaluation study, to measure attitudes toward a smoke-free campus policy, as described in Case Study 6.2. Converse and Presser note that the different questions can be combined into a scale or analyzed independently and compared; each of those approaches has its own advantages.

Effects of Question Order and Placement

In a study on bullying, researchers in Virginia examined high school students' self-reports of having been bullied, using results from a statewide school climate survey (Huang & Cornell, 2015). Two *general* bullying victimization questions were worded, "I have been bullied at school in the past month" and "I have been bullied at school this year." In addition, four *specific* bullying questions asked students whether they had been bullied in the past year in specific categories: physical, verbal, social, and cyberbullying. On all questions, four response options ranged from "Never" to "More than once per week." In a randomized experiment involving 9,585 students in 60 schools, half of the students received the two general bullying victimization questions first, followed by the four specific questions. The other half of the sample received questions in the reverse order: specific questions followed by general questions.

The results showed a powerful effect for which set of questions was presented first. When seeing the specific questions first, students were more likely to report victimization (having been bullied) at least once in the past year, on the general questions as well as on all four of the specific questions. The increases in students' reports of victimization ranged from 29% to 76% across the questions.

The mechanisms underlying these significant order effects were not clear, but the researchers proposed several hypotheses. First, the specific bullying questions may have produced a *priming* effect on memory, helping students to better recall their experiences of having been bullied and making those experiences more accessible in memory for the later questions. Second, students may have been guided by a desire to appear consistent. In the group that saw the general questions first, those who underreported their victimization—saying that they had *not* been bullied—may have been reluctant to contradict themselves when they later encountered the specific questions, even when those questions sparked memories of specific events.

The researchers concluded: "To place this in context, the question order effect for general bullying victimization can be more than twice as large as the effect of interventions designed to reduce bullying" (Huang & Cornell, 2015, p. 1490). In other words, this measurement artifact may have been more impactful for the apparent results than the effect of the actual program itself. Clearly, this particular form of bias—i.e., *systematic error*, as defined earlier—has the potential to be highly consequential for evaluations of interventions aimed at reducing the incidence and impact of bullying in schools.

Decades of research have shown that question order—the question's overall positioning within the questionnaire, especially with respect to the items that immediately precede it—can profoundly influence respondents' answers to a survey question (Dillman et al., 2014; Tourangeau et al., 2000). Dillman et al. (2014, ch. 7) have identified several potential causes for these effects, which can operate in different ways and which they group into the general categories of *contrast* effects and *assimilation* effects. Consider two questions presented in sequence. A contrast effect will cause respondents' answers on the later question to diverge (that is, become more different) from their answers to the earlier question. An assimilation effect will cause answers to the later question to become more similar to the answers to the earlier one. "Both of these types of effects become increasingly likely to occur when the questions are closer to one another, both in terms of topic and physical proximity on the page or screen" (Dillman et al., 2014, p. 234).

Furthermore, for both of these types of effects, the underlying mechanism may be based on either:

- **cognition**, for example, the earlier question's stimulating effect on memory (as described above) or the way that the respondent interprets the question, or

- **norms**, that is, tendencies to present oneself in certain ways, such as agreeable, fair, conventional, and so on.

Dillman et al. (2014) provide a full typology, but a few examples of specific kinds of effects can be found in Table 6.2.

TABLE 6.2 ● A Sampling of Types of Question Order Effects and How They Operate

When Question A precedes Question B, a *question order effect* can change respondents' answers to Question B to some degree, compared to Question B being presented by itself. This may be due to any of these specific effects.

Effect	Based on	Typical Direction	Description
Priming	Cognition	Assimilation (Question B answer will tend toward similarity with Question A answer)	Question A calls relevant information to mind, such as autobiographical memories, which the respondent accesses in answering Question B.
Appearing moderate	Norms	Contrast (Question B answer will tend toward divergence from Question A answer)	Having answered Question A in a certain way, the respondent changes direction for Question B so as not to appear extreme.
Norm of even-handedness	Norms	Assimilation	The respondent just expressed an opinion that situation A should be handled a certain way. Confronted now with situation B, It's only fair that similar rules be applied.
Anchoring	Cognition	Can be either direction	The respondent's answer to Question A sets a standard, or *anchor*, to which the answer to Question B is calibrated. For example, both A and B might involve one's attitude toward a series of policy alternatives.

Based on Dillman et al. (2014).

Chapter Summary

- This chapter covers the final two steps of the four-step process for developing measures: determining a measurement strategy and deciding on measures. A *measurement strategy* refers to the range of approaches to operationalizing a variable.

- An *auxiliary measurement theory*, discussed by Hubert Blalock, is a set of assumptions that makes the case for why a particular measure is a valid way to represent a target construct. Among other uses, this theory enables us to make judgments about the comparability of different measurement approaches and different measures for representing a specific construct.

- The reliability of a measurement is an assessment of its precision, consistency, or replicability. It is generally viewed as one component of validity, which is more broadly concerned with all of the factors—in addition to consistency—that can affect the interpretation of scores.

- Several categories of reliability exist, which differ according to the type of consistency that is being examined. Some of these categories include internal consistency reliability, alternative forms reliability, interrater reliability, and test-retest reliability. Our expectations about reliability, i.e., the consistency of a measure's scores, is tied to our understanding of the circumstances under which we would expect scores to be equivalent.

- The choice of which measurement strategy to use for measuring a given variable is typically based on a number of considerations, which include methods used in prior validation studies, considerations about potential biases associated with different strategies, credibility in the eyes of stakeholders, the timeline available for data collection, the expense associated with different strategies and the overall resources of the project, and other factors.

- All measurements involve some degree of error, but it is difficult to assess the extent of that error. Two distinct types of measurement error are random error and systematic error, i.e., bias. Random error cannot be eliminated but we can attempt to assess it and minimize it to the degree possible. We can also attempt to identify and eliminate bias whenever possible. Even though error exists in our measures, it will be useful for us to understand its extent and to incorporate it into our interpretations of scores.

- In identifying a measure to be used in the evaluation study, the evaluator may be able to use an existing measure or may need to develop a new measure. Whichever approach is used, the evaluator should anticipate potential sources of bias and error. Bias and error may be particular concerns in certain circumstances, which include the use of questions that ask about sensitive subject matter, questions that require significant memory demands, overly restricted response ranges, question wording and framing effects, and other situations.

Questions for Reflection—Chapter 6

1. The validity of a measure refers to the use of its scores for a particular purpose. Why is the reliability of a measure considered to be an intrinsic component of its validity?

2. As discussed in this chapter, being able to measure a variable using a single questionnaire item is fast and efficient, but it might not be reliable or accurate. Consider a program or policy intervention that you are familiar with.

   - Identify some potential outcome variables that measure behaviors, beliefs, or attitudes. Which of these, in your judgment, can reasonably be measured with a single item? Which cannot?

   - Which of the variables could potentially be measured using *either* a single item or multiple items, and how would you decide between those options?

3. Select one or more of those outcome variables. If you needed to develop your own measure for them, how would you go about doing so?

   - How would you examine the reliability and validity of the scores?

4. What are framing effects, and what potential biases do they pose for your measurement plans?

   - Suppose you are developing a series of questions to measure attitudes relating to an intervention or its outcomes. What are some variables that might be particularly susceptible to framing effects?

   - In your planning process, how would you go about examining the potential existence of those effects?

Evaluation Design

Once you have defined the intervention for the purpose of your evaluation study, identified your primary constructs and variables and devised your measures, you can turn your attention to the formal design of the study. This includes the choice of study conditions, the assignment of individual participants (or other units) to those conditions, the number and timing of planned measurements, and the sequencing of those measurements in relation to intervention delivery. The design is the plan for collecting and producing the data that will be analyzed and interpreted.

This chapter discusses the components of research design with a view toward understanding what makes the study stronger or weaker with respect to the validity of its conclusions. That is, how can we plan our evaluation study so as to adequately answer our primary evaluation questions and best understand the intervention and its effects[1]

The Function of Evaluation Design

Schwandt (2015) describes three general types of questions into which a study's guiding evaluation questions can be classified. *Descriptive* questions ask about a current state of affairs, such as the characteristics of a target

---

[1]The literature on experimental and quasi-experimental design goes beyond the evaluation discipline to focus on research studies in general. In this chapter, I do not draw a sharp distinction between the terms "evaluation design" and "research design." The primary difference between the two lies in the questions that are being investigated, and in particular the evaluation study's primary focus on studying the effects of interventions.

audience or details about how a program is being implemented. *Normative* questions "invite comparison of what is actually being done in a program to an agreed-upon or required way of doing things" (p. 72). Such questions generate evaluations that are oriented toward program accountability or ensuring that the program is meeting predetermined standards. Neither descriptive nor normative questions typically require hypotheses about causality or comparisons between conditions. Finally, *explanatory* questions ask "whether observed outcomes are attributable to a program or policy" (p. 72). These are the program effectiveness and program impact questions, which hinge on an evaluation's ability to demonstrate a causal relationship between the program and the measured outcome variables, that is, whether the delivery of the intervention causes change in participants' status on the outcome variables of interest.

Estimating the Counterfactual Condition

The ideal way to demonstrate a causal relationship between a program and its outcomes requires a flight of fancy involving alternate realities. As Lipsey (1993) and Reichardt (2019) have described, this hypothetical ideal would be to compare the outcome status of individuals after they experienced the program with the outcome status that they would have had at the same point in time if the program had never happened. Unfortunately that logical ideal is logically impossible. For program participants, their outcome status in the hypothetical no-program condition is known as the *counterfactual*, which can be labeled more colloquially as a *no-treatment expectation*. Since the true counterfactual is impossible to establish, the fundamental goal of every program impact study is to approximate the counterfactual condition as accurately and convincingly as possible. This attempt to achieve an appropriate comparator is the principle underlying program impact designs. Most often, this comparator takes the form of another group that is configured, in varying ways, to be reasonably similar to the treatment group. Other types of impact studies create comparator conditions that are based on comparing the same group at different points in time, rather than comparing different groups.

Research designs are typically depicted and classified using a diagrammatic system and nomenclature popularized by Campbell and Stanley (1966), which is still in wide use. Exhibit 7.1 illustrates the use of this notational system to portray a number of common designs. Case Study 7.1 provides one example of how this system was slightly revised and pictorially enhanced, while maintaining the essential elements, to communicate an evaluation study's design in a report to stakeholders.

EXHIBIT 7.1 STANDARD DESCRIPTIVE NOTATION FOR IMPACT EVALUATION DESIGNS

The standard notation for identifying impact designs was popularized by Campbell and Stanley (1966) and is still in wide use. In the following examples, time moves from left to right and the notation is as follows:

- R signifies that the groups were created by randomized assignment.
- NR signifies that the groups were created by a method other than randomized assignment.
- X signifies the delivery of the intervention.
- O represents an observation or measurement point.
- A dotted line between the groups indicates that the groups should be considered non-equivalent, which is true for all cases in which randomization was not used. In the absence of a line, as in (1), the groups can be considered equivalent at the study's start.

(1) A 2-group, pretest-posttest randomized experimental study:

$$R \quad O_1 \quad X \quad O_2$$
$$R \quad O_1 \quad \quad O_2$$

(2) A 2-group, pretest-posttest nonequivalent comparison group study:

$$NR \quad O_1 \quad X \quad O_2$$
$$NR \quad O_1 \quad \quad O_2$$

(3) A single-group pretest-posttest design with two pretests:

$$O_1 \quad O_2 \quad X \quad O_3$$

(4) **A cohort comparison group design** (e.g., comparing the achievement test scores of last year's third graders with this year's third graders to assess the effectiveness of a new curriculum that was introduced this year):

$$NR \quad O_1$$
$$NR \quad \quad X \quad O_2$$

Further elaboration of these and other designs is provided by Peck (2020), Reichardt (2019), and Shadish et al. (2002).

CASE STUDY 7.1   VARIATIONS ON THE STANDARD NOTATION FOR PURPOSES OF PRESENTATION AND ILLUSTRATION

The following diagram was used in an evaluation report to university campus stakeholders about an on-campus program called *Learning in Communities* (*LinC*). The program was aimed at boosting the campus engagement and academic success of first-year college students. The diagram follows basic Campbell and Stanley notation, but is enhanced by illustrations that describe the measurement procedures. At posttest, the measurement procedure needed to change to an online survey because classes had ended and it was not possible to gather students together to administer an in-person questionnaire.

Design of the LinC comparison group evaluation

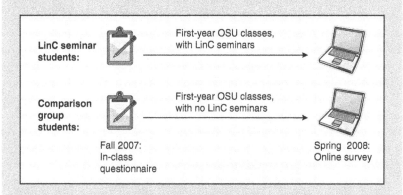

Source: Braverman, M. T., & Gray, L. (2008). *Executive Summary, Program Evaluation, College of Health and Human Sciences LinC–Learn 1st-year seminars, 2007–08.* Oregon State University.

A comprehensive evaluation study that includes a number of different outcome variables can encompass more than one specific design, if some of the observation points apply to only some of the outcomes. For example, some target outcomes may be hypothesized to require a relatively longer time period for measurable change to occur, in which case the post-program measurement of those outcomes should be delayed. Thus, the evaluation research plan for a weight reduction program will measure certain variables at the program's immediate conclusion, such as dietary plans and behavioral intentions, but actual weight might not be measured until some number of weeks or even months have passed. In these cases the specific pattern of O's depicted in the design may vary, depending on the particular outcome being addressed. This illustrates why a clear and comprehensive program theory, which identifies time expectancies for short- and long-term outcomes and the mediating processes that link those outcomes together, is a prerequisite for creating useful and valid evaluation research designs.

The next section identifies the elements of evaluation design, including the study participants, study conditions, assignment procedure, measurement plan, and critical comparisons.

Significant Elements of Impact Evaluation Design

All of the following elements of study design play a role in aligning the study with its guiding evaluation questions, and ultimately in optimizing the validity of conclusions.

Study Participants (or Other Units): Who and How Many?

In the majority of evaluations, the study units that are the targets of the intervention, and on which measurements are made, are people, either as individuals or in groups. Because most evaluations involve people as the units of interest, for ease of reference I use the term *participants* in this discussion. But the units can certainly be other kinds of entities as well, particularly in time series studies and policy evaluations that focus on organizations or communities. For example, quarterly time periods were the units in an evaluation that assessed the impact of a 1984 Florida statute on statewide pedestrian fatality rates (Porter et al., 2018). The legislation established a statewide "Complete Streets" policy for transportation planning, requiring specific accommodations for bicycles and pedestrians in the design of roads and facilities. Using an interrupted time-series design that incorporated 39 quarters preadoption and 117 quarters postadoption, the researchers concluded that the legislation caused a reduction in fatalities, estimating that more than 3,500 lives were saved.

Worksites were the study units in an RCT evaluation of *HealthLinks*, an employer-focused intervention that aimed to facilitate the implementation of evidence-based health programming for employees in small, low-wage worksites (Hannon et al., 2019). In a randomized trial in King County, Washington, 68 worksites were divided into three study conditions: the standard HealthLinks intervention, an expanded version, and a delayed control condition in which the sites did not receive HealthLinks during the study period but received it afterward. The primary outcome was a measure of intervention implementation at each site.

Depending on the specific evaluation setting, the evaluation team may have either no choice, a few limited options, or a great deal of choice over who the study's participants will be. For example, when an evaluator is called in to assess a local program taking place at a single site, the participants are often a preexisting group that comes intact with the program itself, e.g., children attending an ongoing afterschool site. In such cases no discretion over the selection of study participants will be possible. Conversely, consider a curriculum that has undergone initial development and is considered ready for field-testing, and for which there are no preexisting groups standing by and available for curriculum delivery. In such cases the evaluation team may need to seek out partner organizations, such as school districts or health clinics, with access to target population members. In collaborating with other organizations to gain access to participants, the evaluators will typically have some control over the choice of organizational partners, but once selected, they may need to give up control of decision-making with regard to who actually participates, in deference to the partners' contingencies. Collaborating with school districts, for example, generally means that unit selection will take place at the level of intact groups—classes or schools—rather than individuals. The district administrators will often be the primary drivers with regard to inviting, negotiating, and selecting the units that ultimately participate.

In still other kinds of intervention settings, the participants may need to be individually recruited, especially when the intervention targets a specific population with distinct characteristics. For example, the evaluation of a smoking cessation program may need to recruit smokers individually, and may require potential participants to meet certain eligibility criteria such as their amount of current smoking, number of years smoking, expressed motivation to quit, or past history in trying to quit.

When the evaluators have a choice in the procedures for identifying and recruiting study participants, they must ensure that the sample is compatible with the characteristics of the intervention's hypothetical target audience. Ideally, all of the study participants will be eligible targets, that is, they will meet the specified target audience criteria. That is easy to ensure when recruitment takes place individually, but it may be problematic or impossible when recruitment involves intact groups that include small proportions of ineligibles. In those cases it may be possible to apply adjustments later during data analysis, such as excluding ineligible study participants from the analysis, even though they participated in the intervention delivery and data collection.

As an alternative scenario in the recruitment of study participants, it may occur that everyone in the sample is eligible but the sample as a whole represents only a restricted portion of the range of eligibility criteria. For example, if the intervention being evaluated is a nonopioid behavioral pain management program and the evaluation team partners with a veterans' organization to recruit potential participants, there may be a degree of similarity among the participating veterans in the kinds of characteristic injuries causing their chronic pain, which, taken as a whole, might not represent the full array of health conditions for which the intervention is targeted.

Sample attrition. An evaluation's final participating sample is shaped not only by the recruitment and selection processes that take place before the study begins but also by attrition in various forms. Thus, some proportion of participants who contributed data at the initial measurement will be absent at later measurements due to illness, low motivation, or other reasons. Beyond absences for measurement, some participants may abandon the program itself before it is completed. A different form of study loss is survey nonresponse. Policy evaluations that incorporate population surveys (e.g., Braverman et al., 2015) always encounter some degree of nonresponse, which creates inconsistency between the original target sample and the obtained sample. The potential biasing effects of attrition must be addressed in the data analysis and interpretation of findings.

Sample size. In addition to who the study participants are, the size of the sample is an essential consideration in evaluation design. As we describe later in this chapter, sample size is a major determinant of the study's statistical power, that is, its capacity to detect a true intervention effect for a given outcome measure (Lipsey & Hurley, 2009). As sample size increases, so does the statistical power of a data analysis.

Another reason that sample size is an important planning consideration is that it has logistical implications for the management of the evaluation. Increasing sample size is accompanied by increasing demands on many parts of the evaluation including data collection procedures, data management, and communications. Thus a larger sample size frequently implies an increased need for financial resources and staff time. On the positive side, however, larger sample size will also produce greater stability in outcome measurement (hence its beneficial effect on statistical power) and greater opportunity for studying important subgroups within the overall sample.

Choice of Study Conditions

As described earlier, evaluation questions that focus on program effectiveness require comparing the outcome status of people who experienced the program with some facsimile of what their outcome status would be if the program had not occurred. This is the basis for setting up multiple study conditions. The evaluation questions will provide guidance for deciding on the number of study conditions and their defining characteristics. Separate considerations apply to the study conditions that represent the intervention and the comparison.

Study conditions involving the intervention. A straightforward impact evaluation that looks at the program as a single whole entity will generally involve just one *program* condition. This is probably the most common case in evaluation practice. Sometimes, however, the evaluation questions will suggest the need to examine program variations, such as the inclusion or exclusion of different intervention components or the use of different strategies for delivery. Conducting those comparisons will generally require that the design incorporates multiple program conditions to reflect those features of interest.

Study conditions created for purposes of control or comparison.[2] When a comparison condition is included, the evaluators need to determine what exact state of affairs will be represented by that condition. This decision reflects the conceptual link to the evaluation question and, thus, to the evaluation study's relevance and validity. As we discuss later in this chapter, alternative comparison conditions might easily result in different estimates of program effectiveness. The evaluation questions, if adequately formulated, will provide essential guidance for deciding on the nature of the comparison condition(s). Some standard possibilities are these (see, e.g., Peck, 2020):

- *Standard business as usual:* Study participants in the comparison condition will receive whatever services or programs currently exist. Thus the new program is being compared against the status quo. For example, an agency may be testing out a new service delivery approach to replace its current services. *Business as usual* may refer to a standard educational curriculum, health care delivery approach, jobs training program, and so on.

- *Alternate intervention:* If the evaluation question calls for two treatments to be compared against each other, comparison participants will receive an alternate treatment that, like the first treatment, may be untested or new. In this case the designation of which condition is the "treatment" group and which is the "comparison" group might not be relevant.

- *Nothing at all:* The comparison condition will consist of no programs or services—relative to the outcomes under study—being delivered to participants.

To be clear, not all impact evaluations involve multiple conditions. For example, a single-group pre-post design sets up a simple comparison of participants' posttest status versus their pretest status, as a way of answering the question about program effectiveness. This is not considered a strong

---

[2]A note on terminology: There are several conventions that have been used regarding the use of the terms *control* and *comparison*. I use the convention that a *control group* is one created through a randomization process, whereas a *comparison group* is one that is already intact when included in the study, such as a classroom, or that is created for the study by any other means.

design with regard to internal validity, as we shall shortly discuss, but for pragmatic reasons, in many real-life situations a single-group study might be the only design choice that is reasonably available.

The interrupted time-series (ITS) is another type of quasi-experimental design that can address causal questions using just a single group. The ITS employs measurements at numerous time points to provide the basis for the comparisons that allow inferences about causality (Reichardt, 2019).

Assignment of Participants to Conditions

Having decided upon the study conditions, a pivotal consideration is the way that participants will be assigned to those conditions. This forms a primary basis of the distinction between experimental, quasi-experimental, and nonexperimental designs. An *experimental* design uses a randomization procedure to make the assignments. Randomized assignment allows the evaluator to consider the groups equivalent at the outset of the study. A *quasi-experimental* design does not entail randomization but uses other means to assess and approximate the equivalence of the groups. Other kinds of designs are deemed to be *nonexperimental* or *descriptive*.

Number and Timing of Observation Points

A simple configuration of an evaluation design may call for measurement to take place at one point in time (after delivery of the intervention) or, more commonly, at two points (before and after). But there are many occasions when the number of observation points will be expanded from this basic model. The additional observations may include multiple pretests, multiple posttests, or observations during the course of intervention delivery. As with other design decisions, the choices about configuring observation points depend primarily on the information needs, as reflected in the evaluation questions. In addition, including extra observation points may be important for addressing particular validity threats, as we shall discuss shortly.

Multiple pretests. It is not very common for a design to specify multiple pretest observations before beginning the delivery of the intervention, but this design feature may be advisable in some circumstances, such as when there is interest in ascertaining the natural patterns of change of the target outcome within the population. Multiple pretests can be particularly valuable in a one-group pre-post design. If a one-group design includes only one pretest, the effects of the intervention will be confounded with (that is, inseparable from, with regard to inferring causality) whatever changes might have occurred naturally in the outcome variable over the same time period, e.g., due to maturation if one is studying children. As a remedy, including two or more pretest measurements can serve to establish a baseline pattern of outcome change, which may then be shown to be disrupted or altered when the intervention is introduced. In particular, if multiple pretests show a pattern of relative stability in the target outcome prior to introducing the intervention, this can strengthen the argument for using pretest status as the counterfactual estimate for what would have been observed in the absence of the intervention.

This use of two pretests reflects the same basic logic as the one-group interrupted time-series design, which applies it with far greater sophistication: to see if a prior pattern can be detected that is disrupted by the intervention (Reichardt, 2019).

Multiple posttests. More than one posttest measurement will be needed if the evaluation questions call for an understanding of the intervention's impact over multiple time periods. Most commonly, there may be concerns about whether, and how quickly, a program's measurable effects will fade over time. To address this question, the evaluators may decide to measure outcomes immediately following the program's completion and then again after some time period has passed, even up to several years. Indeed, a program's lasting impact after the passage of a year or longer will often be the timeframe of greatest interest to funding organizations that expressly seek to create long-term change in target populations.

Critical Comparisons Between the Conditions

In addition to specifying the points in the timeline at which measurements will be made on different groups, an evaluation research design should also indicate the ways that those measurement points will be combined, contrasted, and compared to produce the data analyses that address the primary evaluation questions. Boruch (1997) calls this the *core analysis*, and he describes how it can be differentiated from the full range of data analyses that may be conducted: "...the comparisons among treatments that are regarded as important for decisions ought to be specified as part of the experiment's design. This specification helps to ensure that the objectives of the study are met in a core analysis. It also ensures that exploratory analyses (fishing expeditions) are identified as such and that the findings from these are marked for deeper examination in later stages of research" (p. 202).

The early identification of the critical comparisons is important because most designs, if sufficiently complex, will present options for how the analysis can be conducted. As an example, consider the two-group pretest-posttest randomized design, illustrated in Case Study 7.1 as design 1. This design identifies four observations, a pre and a post for each of the two groups. The goal is to compare the groups on the outcome variable, and even with this basic design the core analysis can take different forms. It could consist of a simple comparison between the groups' mean posttest scores at O_2. Alternatively, the core analysis could be planned as a direct comparison of the pre-to-post gains ($O_2 - O_1$) in the two groups. Finally, the core analysis could utilize an analysis of covariance framework, which compares posttest scores in a regression model that represents group membership by a binary variable and includes pretest scores as a covariate. The first of these options (comparing only the O_2 scores) is not advisable because it doesn't make use of the information contained in the pretest scores. But both of the latter two alternatives are tenable options, though they might return different results.

With more complex designs that include more groups and more measurement points, the number of possible approaches will quickly expand, making the choice of analysis a consequential decision. Evaluators can, and should, be flexible in their approach to data analysis, but they should also be explicit about the way they intend to utilize the design's unique features to answer their primary evaluation questions.

Evaluation Designs and Validity Theory

As discussed in Chapter 3, the four-part Campbellian validity model that identifies internal, external, construct, and statistical conclusion validity as attributes of the research process (Shadish et al., 2002) is dominant in the evaluation literature, particularly with regard to the design of impact studies (e.g., Chen et al., 2011). Therefore it will be useful to review how the Campbellian model maps onto the points discussed in this chapter.

Internal Validity

Shadish et al. (2002) defined internal validity as the accuracy of "inferences about whether observed covariation between A and B reflects a causal relationship from A to B in the form in which the variables were manipulated or measured" (p. 53). Two points can be highlighted from this definition. First, internal validity is a characteristic that applies to the exact situation at hand in the study as conducted. That is, are our conclusions about treatment effects justified with respect to the way this treatment was delivered in this single instance, with these participants, in this setting, with these measures?

The second point is that internal validity is exclusively about the causal aspect of the relationship. Thus, in an impact evaluation, internal validity focuses on the specific questions about the program's impact.

Shadish et al. also note that in order to make a convincing argument for causality, three characteristics must be demonstrated:

- The presumed cause must precede the presumed effect in time.

- The cause variable (e.g., the binary 1–0 determination of whether an individual did or did not receive the program) and the effect variable must indeed covary. That is, program participants must have a different outcome status, on average, than program nonparticipants.

- Plausible explanations for the relationship, *other than* the causal explanation between program and outcome, must be ruled out.

The first two propositions are, for the most part, matters of fact, even if they may sometimes be difficult to establish. By contrast, the third proposition is primarily a matter of logical analysis and argument rather than of fact. Effective research design is largely about trying to present that argument convincingly.

Plausible rival hypotheses, as described in Chapter 3, are potential alternative explanations for a pattern of obtained results that are sufficiently reasonable that they cannot be easily dismissed as false. Since these hypotheses cast doubt on the accuracy of the causality claim, Campbell and Stanley (1966) referred to them as *threats to internal validity*. Campbell and Stanley introduced a typology of these threats, which has since been expanded by other theorists (see, e.g., Reichardt, 2019; Shadish et al., 2002). Table 7.1 lists several of the best known. Each of these threats should be viewed as a family of potential hypothetical explanations that can be grouped together thematically. Not all of these threats will be applicable to

TABLE 7.1 ● Threats to Internal Validity in Designs for Impact Evaluation

Threat	Description	Example
History	Changes in outcome scores due to external events that occur during the time that an intervention is being delivered.	For an intervention intended to teach driving safety, a driving-related tragedy that occurs in a community may temporarily heighten students' sensitivity to driving safety and produce safer driving behavior, for reasons unrelated to the program.
Maturation	Outcome changes due to changes in participants that occur over the time period in question. In a literal sense of the term, children naturally gain proficiency in many domains as they get older	A 12-week educational program for young children may show gains in language and counting skills, which in reality are attributable to children's maturation through their

TABLE 7.1 ● (Continued)		
Threat	**Description**	**Example**
	and experience the world. More broadly, this also refers to any changes internal to the participant, including temporary changes such as fatigue or boredom.	family experiences at home rather than to the program.
Testing	The effect that having taken a test or other measure one time may have on scores the next time it is taken. This can occur with achievement tests, for which familiarity with the question characteristics can lead to higher scores on the second testing. Testing effects can also occur with attitude scales, e.g., if the first administration results in greater sensitization to the scale's subject matter.	An out-of-school training course for a standardized college entry test for high school students may administer a practice test at the beginning and end of the course. But if the course is ineffective, students' gains from pre to post may be no larger than the gains of students who simply took the test twice.
Instrumentation	Changes due to differences and inconsistencies in how an outcome is measured, either across time from pre to post or across participants within or across groups. This threat should not be confused with *testing*, which refers simply to the fact that measurement takes place more than once, even when measures are identical.	Instrumentation effect due to different measures: ● Supposedly equivalent forms of an achievement test are used pre and post, but in reality the test at pre is easier than the test at post (or vice-versa). Due to inconsistent scoring: ● Different raters divide up a set of work samples and apply different interpretations. ● A single rater grows more strict or generous when going through a stack of writing samples.

(Continued)

TABLE 7.1 • *(Continued)*

Threat	Description	Example
Selection	Treatment groups are different from each other on one or more characteristics at the very start of the study and this difference is the cause of group differences, rather than the treatment itself. Randomization is the only strategy for assigning units to conditions that creates groups that can be considered equivalent (within the limits of statistical random variation). When intact groups are used in an evaluation study, they must be assumed *not* to be equivalent, which gives rise to the theory of quasi-experimentation.	A middle school develops an experimental track for teaching seventh-grade algebra, and populates it with students who volunteer for the program. At the end of the year, those students score higher on end-of-year math tests than students in the traditional classes. However, those students had superior math skills at the outset and were highly motivated to learn math. These characteristics were the cause of the new class's superior outcome scores, rather than the new program's instructional effectiveness.
Attrition	Changes in group scores that occur because participants or units drop out of the study. Any loss of participation impacts the precision of outcome estimates, but some theorists maintain that only *differential* attrition—patterns of participant loss that vary across the conditions—poses a threat to a study's internal validity.	A clinic delivering smoking cessation services tests out a new program utilizing nicotine replacement therapy against its standard behaviorally based program. More than half the participants in the new program drop out because they find the nicotine product physically uncomfortable, while dropout from the traditional program is 10%. An evaluation conducted on program completers several weeks postprogram finds the cessation rates to be 80% in the new program and 30% in the traditional program. However, the

TABLE 7.1 ● *(Continued)*

Threat	Description	Example
		new program's apparent success is inflated by not considering the people who abandoned the program before its conclusion.
Regression to the mean	The tendency for initially extreme scores to be less extreme upon a second measurement. Regression to the mean comes into play when units are selected into the program on the basis of their extreme scores. It can occur for several reasons. First, problems often naturally resolve to some extent, a phenomenon exacerbated if the treatment is sought out at a time when the problem is at its most severe. Second, extreme scores are, to some degree, the product of random error that will not occur in the same combination upon a second testing.	Regression based on low scores: An elementary school uses a standardized reading skills test to select low-achieving students into a reading supplementation program. If those selection test scores are later used to represent the students' pretest status on reading, that estimate is unrealistically low. An immediate second testing would result in a slightly higher overall mean score for the group of selected students due to the redistribution of random statistical error.
Ambiguous temporal precedence	If one's status on *variable A* (e.g., experiencing or not experiencing an intervention) is a cause of one's status on *variable B* (e.g., one or more outcomes), it follows logically that variable A must precede variable B in time. If there is uncertainty about which preceded the other, there will be uncertainty about which of the two variables represents the cause and which the effect (Shadish et al., 2002). This is one reason why correlational relationships are considered inadequate to demonstrate causality.	A cross-sectional study finds an association between the practice of yoga and lower levels of biological markers of stress in a sample of study participants. It would not be justified to conclude from these findings that practicing yoga results in lower stress levels because, among other reasons, the stress levels of participants may have preceded their uptake of yoga.

(Continued)

TABLE 7.1 • *(Continued)*		
Threat	**Description**	**Example**
Cyclical changes	Outcome scores may be affected by cycles that occur regularly within a day, week, or annual season. A *weekly* cycle may influence scores because of differences in people's motivation or attention on, e.g., testing occurring on a Friday versus a Monday. A *seasonal* cycle could affect the levels of outcome scores that vary according to the time of year.	A university policy prohibiting smoking in all campus locations, including outdoors, takes effect in October. An observational count of butts and other cigarette trash is conducted in September before the policy takes effect and the following February. The evaluation finds that tobacco trash has declined significantly and concludes that the policy has reduced smoking prevalence. However, this reduction may be due to a general reduction in people's time outside in cold weather. Because of seasonal cycles affecting people's time outdoors, a stronger test would be to assess tobacco trash in September, a full year later.

every evaluation study or intervention setting. For any given study and pattern of results, critical analysis is required to determine just how plausible each of these hypotheses may be.

As we have described, a control or comparison group is the most common design strategy for creating an estimate of the counterfactual condition, i.e., the no-treatment expectation. The control group's value lies in its effectiveness in allowing the internal validity threats to be ruled out. The logic goes like this: Consider, for example, that the treatment group shows a desired pre-to-post change in the outcome variable following program delivery, and we must consider whether that change might be due to history, maturation, or some other rival hypothesis rather than, or in addition to, the program itself. Based on the setup of the study, these rival hypotheses are operating in both groups, and thus if one or more of them are the actual cause of the change, that same level of change will be observed in both groups rather than just the treatment group. If similar change is not observed, we can rule out the hypotheses as potential explanations. Ideally, in the spirit of the counterfactual, the treatment group and control group are equally susceptible to the effects of all rival hypotheses and the *only* difference between the groups will be that the former has experienced the program while the latter has not. In reality, every study's design is fallible to some degree. That fallibility is embodied in the inability to convincingly rule out one or more of the internal validity threats.

In summary, internal validity is the component of the Campbellian validity model that is most broadly implicated when designing an impact evaluation study, and in fact serves as a driver for most of those design decisions.

External Validity

By contrast, an evaluation study's guiding questions do not typically include consideration of the alternative populations and settings to which the study's causal conclusions can be generalized, which is the domain of external validity. In most cases, external validity considerations are applied after the fact, when we have understood what happened in the present study and we turn our attention to considering how widely relevant those results are for other settings. Cronbach et al. (1980, p. 7) defined external validity as "the validity of inferences that go beyond the data," which suggests that making judgments about external validity does not directly involve processes of statistical data analysis. Shadish et al. (2002) concurred, writing that "judgments about the external validity of a causal relationship cannot be reduced to statistical terms" (p. 91).

Generalization—the assessment of relevance across variations in participants, settings, outcomes, or treatments—is often an ad hoc process. A district-level educational administrator may review a curriculum evaluation study that was conducted in a different part of the country and try to determine if the curriculum is worth trying in her local schools by intuitively comparing the study's participants and setting with those of her own district. A drug prevention counselor may look at an evaluation of a drug program that was conducted some years ago and try to decide whether circumstances have changed so much that the program and its results now have very little applicability to the current setting. Program staff and evaluators have to grapple with these questions themselves, and they may also find themselves fielding similar questions from stakeholders: *This other study found a certain pattern of results; what does that mean for us?*

In addition to comparing the features and contexts of disparate local sites, generalization can take the form of drawing implications from the study sample to the larger population from which the sample has been drawn, provided that an appropriate sampling procedure has been applied.

Thus external validity is related to evaluation study design with regard to the way that participants or program sites are selected into the study. The formal sampling of participants from a larger population is relatively unusual in impact studies, but in some cases, particularly large evaluation studies, random sampling can indeed be an option. In that case the study sample can be considered representative of the larger population and the generalization of findings can be done with much more confidence, even though the evaluator will still need to take account of factors that degrade the sample's representativeness over the course of the study such as nonresponse and attrition (Shadish et al., 2002). Similarly, for large-scale evaluations of multisite programs, random sampling of sites for inclusion in the study will allow generalization of the causal conclusions to the entire population of program sites.

Construct Validity

Construct validity relates to the constructs embedded in the evaluation questions, the operationalization of those constructs into the particulars of the study, and, finally, the representation of the constructs in the assessment of what has been learned from the study. As has been described in earlier chapters, the study's constructs pertain to the intervention, study participants, settings, and outcomes.

Construct validity comes into play because of the need for close correspondence between the constructs and the study's specifics. There are several ways in which that correspondence can be weakened, which are characterized as *threats to construct validity*. For example, the treatment that is actually delivered needs to be an appropriate exemplar of the treatment as understood by stakeholders prior to the study. This is not a sure thing, even in the case of a well-established program. Treatment delivery can become degraded due to inadequate instructor preparation, unforeseen local events, or other factors.

Design decisions may also affect the construct defining the study's participants. Consider what may be a fairly common scenario: a school-based intervention has been designed for grades 4–6, but the evaluators may find that the partnering school district can only make its fourth-grade classes available. This grade restriction will result in important limitations for any subsequent conclusions about program impact. Blanket statements of effectiveness for the intervention's full target population are no longer an option because the characteristics of the study sample are not fully consistent with those of the target population. Consideration of the gap between the knowledge desired and the particulars of the study setting will inform the decision about whether to proceed. If the evaluation does proceed, its guiding questions will need to be modified to reflect the limited realities of what can be learned.

A more dramatic example is the experience of *Un Buen Comienzo*, an intensive preschool program that was evaluated in a cluster-randomized experimental design in several municipalities near Santiago, Chile in 2008–2011 (Moreno et al., 2011). The study design included three over-lapping cohorts that were each followed for two years. In February 2010, midway through the second cohort and shortly before the launch of the third, the region experienced a major earthquake. After taking time to assess and contain the damage, the educators and researchers needed to decide how to proceed with their study. They conferred with the host school districts, local governments, funding organizations, and other partners. They finally decided that the *internal validity* of the study had not been compromised because all schools in both conditions had experienced the same disruption, and thus they continued the study. They recognized, however, that the study's *external validity* had been significantly compromised by the unique nature of the earthquake's disruptive effect. For our current purposes, the point is that several aspects of *construct validity* were also compromised. First, the intervention *setting* took on unique features due to the rarity of this historical event. Second, one could infer that the representativeness of the *participants* was compromised, since, e.g., 19%–23% of families experienced symptoms of increased anxiety and impaired family income. Third, careful examination was required to determine whether the intervention itself had undergone significant disruption and adaptation mid-study. The authors assessed that the intervention was not changed to a substantial degree, but the possibility was present and, in the end, it was a judgment call. Overall, the experience of the earthquake altered the conditions of the study, and although the ability to draw valid causal conclusions—i.e., internal validity—was retained, the ultimate utility of the study, in terms of its applicability to other settings, may have been compromised.

Statistical Conclusion Validity

Statistical conclusion validity is concerned with two specific kinds of inferences (Shadish et al., 2002, p. 42). The first is whether there is covariation between "the presumed cause and effect," that is, between the intervention and the target outcome. The second is the strength of that relationship.

In many respects, statistical conclusion validity is less relevant to the study's design than it is to the data analyses that come later, following data collection (which is the topic of Chapter 8). The existence and the strength of a relationship are established through data analyses that incorporate significance testing and effect size estimation. But there are also design elements that can influence the study's ability to detect the existence and strength of a program effect. One such element is the size of the study sample, which is directly related to the statistical power of the analysis.

Another is the timing of posttest measurement. We consider both of these elements in the next section.

What Makes a Design Strong?

In the big picture, the qualities that make a design strong are those that enable the study to answer the evaluation questions accurately and comprehensively. More specifically, we consider several particular characteristics: aligning study constructs with the evaluation questions, minimizing validity threats, meeting assumptions, ensuring adequate statistical power, incorporating transparency to protect against deliberate bias, and making optimal use of time and resources.

Alignment of the Design With the Evaluation Questions

The evaluation questions, if drafted appropriately, provide the roadmap for the information that is needed from the study and for which it has been initiated. The validity of the study, as we have defined it, is to a large degree dependent on this correspondence between the evaluation questions and the information to be gained. As discussed in previous chapters, this process of alignment includes the particulars of the treatment realization, the choice of variables, and the operationalization of those variables into specific measurement strategies and instruments. In addition, specific components of evaluation design can be shaped and selected so as to answer the evaluation questions most convincingly.

Several examples of this alignment can be considered. First, if the study involves a comparison condition, one major decision involves the choice of that comparator, which will establish the no-treatment expectation against which the intervention will be compared. Earlier in this chapter, we identified three distinct options for configuring the comparison condition: (1) standard business as usual, i.e., the current set of programming or other services that are being offered to the target population; (2) an alternate intervention, such that two or more interventions are being directly compared; or (3) nothing at all, i.e., an absence of programming. One reason this choice is consequential is that these options can be expected to produce differing levels of change on the outcome variables for the comparison group, which in turn will result in differing estimates of impact for the intervention being evaluated. The first two options involve some alternate form of intervention which, if effective to any degree, should provide some level of benefit. This would then result in a smaller difference between the groups and a smaller estimate of impact. The third option—no programming—provides no benefit, and thus might be expected to result in the largest estimate of impact when compared to the intervention. An evaluator with a vested interest in the results may be tempted to adopt this third option so as to maximize the difference between treatment and control, regardless of the information that is most needed from the evaluation. However, a carefully worded evaluation question should be able to identify which of the options for the control condition is most relevant. Sometimes a no-treatment control will be fully appropriate, and other times not.

House (2008) notes that this manipulation occurs frequently in drug studies for the sole purpose of inflating estimates of impact: "Drug companies insist on using placebos against which to compare new drugs. In other words, the comparison of a new drug is against no treatment, not against other treatment drugs in use. Because 77% of new drugs are slight variations of those already on the market, many new drugs would not look more effective than the old drugs in head-to-head trials" (p. 417).

A second design-related element that may be pertinent to the evaluation questions is the choice of *who* the participants are (The number of participants is a separate factor, to be discussed shortly). For example, selecting a study sample whose characteristics make them a subsample of the actual target population of interest will limit the usefulness of the study's results.

A third design element that may need to be aligned with the evaluation questions is the timing of posttest measurement. For example, for programs aimed at boosting academic skills or behavioral intentions, it may be reasonable to expect that effects will probably be strongest at the program's immediate conclusion and then gradually fade thereafter (although this pattern is certainly not universally true). The evaluators might reasonably be interested in measuring program impact when it is expected to be at its strongest, but this decision must also align with the question of what kind of timeframe is most important to stakeholders. For example, a quickly fading effect might not be highly valued. If stakeholders are most interested in whether a program effect can be detected after one year, a study that omits this time frame will likely be considered inadequate. Indeed, the rate of decline may itself be of interest for stakeholders and evaluators, which would suggest a series of posttest measurements. Given the inherent instability of effect strength, properly worded evaluation questions will provide guidance as to what period of time, post-program, is considered most essential for documenting the arc of the program's effectiveness. Furthermore, a study may be unnecessarily disadvantaged if the post-program measurement is scheduled purely on the basis of convenience or logistics, rather than being guided by the evaluation questions or program theory.

Answering the Evaluation Questions With High Confidence: Minimizing Threats to Validity

A methodologically rigorous evaluation study will allow for a high level of confidence in the conclusions. With respect specifically to design elements, much of this confidence is linked to the ability to minimize threats to internal validity, i.e., plausible alternative explanations for the observed pattern of results.

This chapter has described what some of those threats might potentially be. But their identification cannot be reduced to an automatic cookbook process. The task is not simply to go down a list such as that of Table 7.1, or longer lists in other sources (most definitively in Shadish et al., 2002), and check them off in sequence. Those lists are only heuristic guideposts. The criterion of plausibility requires that each individual program context be examined critically to decide what might be reasonable alternatives that can threaten the straightforward causal conclusion that the intervention produced the observed effect. Many potentially plausible rival hypotheses might not be captured by the standard lists.

The evaluator may occasionally find it useful to introduce a very specific element into the design, intended to counter the plausibility of a single anticipated alternative explanation, sometimes taking up considerable resources to do so. For example, with a pre-post nonequivalent groups design involving two conditions, interpretation may be enhanced by using two or more pretests, which can assess whether the groups were experiencing differential rates of change before the delivery of the intervention to the treatment group. If the groups do indeed have differential rates of change, this would be masked by using a single pretest, especially if the scores are roughly equivalent on that pretest. A single-pretest design would be unable to rule this out. Therefore the new design element, multiple pretests, could serve to rule out this internal validity threat, known as selection-maturation interaction.

To illustrate this, suppose that the outcome pattern illustrated in Figure 7.1(a) is obtained: the participants in the program condition score modestly higher at pretest but substantially higher at posttest. Stated differently, both groups improve from pre to post but the program group improves more. This pattern is vulnerable to the threat of selection-maturation because it is consistent with the possibility that the program group participants have, collectively, greater aptitude in whatever skill is being taught and measured. Thus, the argument could be made that they were higher to begin with and continued to excel over time, resulting in an ever-expanding gap, such as the one obtained. It is reasonable to presume that this could be a common pattern that will be found between a higher-skill group and a lower-skill group. However, if the design includes two or more pretests, and a widening differential does *not* appear prior to the introduction of the intervention, as illustrated in Figure 7.1(b), the plausibility of this particular hypothesis is reduced.

As this example illustrates, considerable foresight may be needed to anticipate the most relevant validity threats and introduce design elements that can test them and rule them out.

FIGURE 7.1 ● Design Options for Examining a Potential Selection-Maturation Interaction Effect

(a) Single pretest.

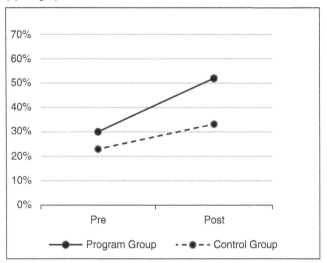

(b) Addition of a second pretest. Scores for Pre 2 and Post are identical to Fig. 1a.

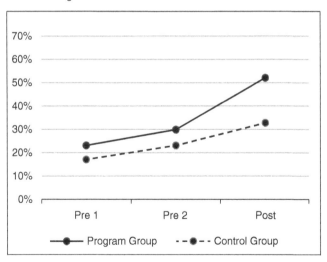

Meeting Assumptions

As we saw in Chapter 6, our measurement strategies and instruments carry certain assumptions. For example, if the study utilizes self-report, the evaluator assumes that the respondents have the requisite information needed to answer the questions posed, and that they are motivated to do so honestly. Thus the information generated will not be marked by inaccurate answers due to, e.g., the respondent's desire for positive self-presentation or other factors. A well-resourced evaluation may have the option of introducing multiple measures to explicitly examine the soundness of this assumption, but that case is the exception rather than the rule. In most instances the evaluator will not know if these assumptions are sound for a particular study.

In addition, the creation of experimental subgroups using random assignment produces an assumption that those groups are equivalent to each other, within certain known limits based on statistical random error. If these groups are kept intact throughout the course of the study, this assumption is seen as justified and the groups are treated as if they were equal prior to the introduction of the intervention. But if the groupings break down to any extent due to attrition or participant noncompliance, the degree to which the initial equivalence is maintained becomes a concern and may introduce the requirement for analytic adjustments (Reichardt, 2019). Furthermore, even groups created by random assignment will vary to some degree based on random error, which is the reason that statistical power increases, and confidence intervals decrease in width, with increasing sample size. There is an inverse relationship between sample size and the standard errors of sample statistics. Indeed, one of the great benefits of random assignment is that even though the procedure does not entirely eliminate differences between the groups, the likely scope of those differences for *all* characteristics, both measured and unmeasured, can be estimated. That is not the case for any other methods of grouping participants.

Statistical procedures carry with them a more explicit set of assumptions. Parametric analyses such as t-tests, ANOVA and linear regression are based on the assumptions that the variables are distributed normally and that responses are independent of each other. In many cases these statistical assumptions are violated to varying degrees, and a great deal of study has been applied to determining the degree to which various analytic procedures are robust to those violations (Maxwell et al., 2018).

Adequate Statistical Power

The power of a statistical analysis is defined as the probability that the analysis will detect a program effect or other significant finding, such as a difference between groups, when that program effect does indeed exist in the population(s) being studied. Identification of this probability involves the specification of a target effect size of interest, usually expressed in standard deviation units. For example, in a study comparing intervention and control groups, one might calculate that the analysis has power of .70 to detect a difference between the groups (that is, to return a statistically significant result) if the true difference between the populations is .25 standard deviation or larger. That is, if the population difference between program and control conditions really is at least one quarter of a standard deviation, it is expected that this analysis will result in a statistically significant finding in 70% of all potential samples, despite the presence of random sampling error. A power analysis can be calculated for a single target effect size of greatest interest, or it can display a range of probabilities associated with a range of hypothetical effect sizes. To be clear, note that "detecting a program effect" means only that the analysis will show that the groups are not equal to each other on the measured outcome variable, consistent with the logic of significance testing. It does not refer to the probability that the difference found between the groups in the study will reach the magnitude of the targeted effect size.

The reason that power is expressed as a probability is that given an infinite number of samples, the vagaries of sampling error will mean that some samples will produce estimates short of statistical significance, despite the actual presence of a true difference between the populations.[3] Given that the probability of failing to detect a true difference, known as a false negative or Type II error, is generally represented by the Greek letter β (beta), power is equal to $1 - \beta$. Type I and Type II errors are discussed in more detail in Chapter 8.

In evaluation planning, power calculations can be used to determine the sample size needed. Typically, the evaluation team will specify what they consider to be a critical effect size for the outcome variable, expressed in standardized units, and their desired probability for being able to detect an effect of that size. The sample size that will accommodate those parameters can then be calculated.

---

[3]A potentially confusing discrepancy can exist between the way that groups in a study have been formed and the populations that they are purported to represent. The groups are frequently described as representing separate populations, e.g., the population of individuals who have received the program and the population of individuals who have not. Yet in reality the study may have recruited a single sample from a single population—which in itself is often ill-defined—with the sample being split into subgroups only *after* having been recruited, in which case the suggestion of separate selection from 2 larger populations does not seem relevant or accurate. Indeed, if an evaluation consists of a newly developed program that is being delivered for the first time, there *is* no larger population of individuals, beyond the study sample, who have received the program and are represented by the sample. Thus, this convention of describing the relationship of a sample subgroup to its hypothetical larger population should be viewed as a heuristic simplification, used for the purpose of considering issues such as generalization, representativeness, and sampling bias.

Besides being dependent on the size of the true population program effect and on sample size, statistical power is also dependent on the reliability of measurement. Because a study will typically incorporate multiple analyses that focus on different outcome measures and different subgroups, power is a projected characteristic of a particular analysis rather than of the study as a whole. Both measurement reliability and sample size will vary across the statistical analyses conducted within an evaluation study, resulting in different levels of statistical power for each analysis.

Power analysis should be an important part of outcome evaluation planning but it is often neglected. Meta-analyses have found that far too many evaluation studies lack adequate statistical power—usually due to very small sample size—to produce an adequate test of program effectiveness (Lipsey & Hurley, 2009). In those cases, an intervention effect would have to be quite strong in order for the study to have a reasonable probability of detecting it, and a program effect of small to moderate size—which is frequently the case with new programs—would simply be missed. Obviously, devoting time and effort to conducting an evaluation that has low probability of detecting a true difference is a poor use of valuable resources.

Transparency and Built-in Protections Against the Possibility of Deliberate Bias

In a range of evaluation settings, the stakes can be high for certain stakeholder groups. For example, evaluations of commercially available school-based educational programs in math or reading may influence a school district's choice of which program to use, with significant implications for the financial interests of the developers of the competing programs. In many cases, program evaluations that appear on agency-developed lists of exemplary programs have been conducted by the program developers, introducing a conflict of interest that complicates the interpretation of findings (Weiss et al., 2008). In the ultra-high-stakes pharmaceutical arena, House (2008) identified numerous strategies by which the evaluations of new drugs have been manipulated to produce apparent evidence of product effectiveness (beyond the choice of control condition, which we have already discussed). Specific elements of study design will frequently provide opportunities for tipping the scales in a certain direction, and a careful attempt to protect against deliberate bias can be an important component of evaluation design.

More generally, the issue of transparency also reflects the importance of identifying the study's *core analysis* (Boruch, 1997), as described earlier. An initial commitment to a data analysis plan, based on an assessment of what will be the most logically consistent approach, will protect the evaluator from suspicions that a set of positive findings may have been arrived at through a "fishing expedition," in which the evaluator conducted multiple analyses and then chose the one that produced the most desirable result.

Optimal Use of Available Resources

In addition to the conceptual, analytical, statistical, and technical considerations, the evaluation needs to be capable of being conducted within the limits of available resources and a reasonable time frame. The time frame may be set either formally by a contract or informally by the needs of stakeholders or regular cycles such as an academic year. The decisions making up the evaluation design will be constrained by these practical considerations, which may ultimately be reflected in the number and location of intervention sites, sample sizes, sample recruitment methods, number and timing of observations, and other elements. Taking account of these considerations, the evaluator will be challenged to make choices that maximize the utility and power of the design.

Taking Account of Limitations and Weaknesses in the Evaluation Study Design

Every study has limitations, as most research texts remind us. I draw a distinction here between the concepts of a design's *limitations* and its *weaknesses*. A limitation is a restriction on the inferences that can be made from the study, and is thus a necessary feature of external validity. Given the sampling of units, outcomes, time, and settings that characterize any study, there will be limitations between those samplings and the populations of units, outcomes, time, and settings that stakeholders may be interested in. A weakness, by contrast, is any characteristic of the study that reduces the confidence with which inferences and conclusions can be drawn. For example, the existence of a plausible rival hypothesis, constituting an internal validity threat, is an important kind of design weakness. Evaluators should strive to recognize and communicate the limitations of their study design, which are unavoidable. But they should strive to anticipate and eliminate any weaknesses in the design whenever possible.

Case Study 7.2 provides an example of a study that incorporated a series of complex design decisions.

CASE STUDY 7.2 ASSESSMENT OF A REGULATION REQUIRING MENU LABELING OF CALORIE INFORMATION IN CHAIN RESTAURANTS IN NEW YORK CITY

In 2008, New York City became the first city in the United States to require restaurant chains to post calorie information on their menus. Restaurant chains that had at least 15 locations nationwide were included under the

(Continued)

(Continued)

regulations, resulting in approximately 2,600 individual restaurant sites in the city. Researchers at New York City's Department of Health and Mental Hygiene designed a study to assess the impact of this new regulation, in the form of customers' awareness of the calorie information labels and their use of that information in making their purchase decisions (Dumanovsky et al., 2010).

This could be considered a high-stakes evaluation study. It was focused on a wide-reaching regulation that affected thousands of business establishments, and it provided information on a landmark, previously untested regulation that, if successful, could serve as a model for other cities. Thus the implementation of the regulation and the evidence of its impacts were likely being closely watched by multiple stakeholder groups including health officials, policy administrators, and industry advocates.

Consider the complex challenges facing the researchers. For example, with regard to sampling, how were they going to select locations, times of day, and actual customers to represent the millions of purchase transactions that take place each day in New York City's fast food restaurants? Here is how they structured their study.

- *Locations:* The researchers chose to include in their sample the 17 chains that had the most locations in the city. Two of those chains were later deemed ineligible for the regulation, resulting in 15 chains. Those chains represented approximately 75% of the roughly 2,600 affected restaurant sites in New York City. For each of the chains, the researchers randomly sampled three locations in the city, for a total of 45 observation sites.

- *Design:* The study used a single-group pre-post design, using the same locations at both time periods rather than drawing independent samples each time.

- *Calendar time:* City officials phased in the enforcement of the regulation. The regulation took effect on March 31, 2008, but the city did not begin to issue violations until May, and full enforcement, including fines for violators, became effective on July 18. Against this backdrop, the study collected pretest data over a 3-week period in March–April 2008, approximately 3 months before enforcement began. Similarly, posttest data were collected over a 3-week period in September–October 2008, approximately 3 months following the onset of enforcement.

- *Time of day:* The researchers distinguished between what they called "fast-food chains" ($n = 11$) and "coffee and ice-cream chains" ($n = 4$). Data collection for fast-food chains took place on weekdays between 12:00 and 2:00 p.m. Data collection for coffee and ice cream chains took place on weekdays between 2:00 and 4:00 p.m. The article did not state the reasons for this timing decision.

- *Data collection strategy and participants:* The researchers used 3-person teams to collect data at each site. The teams approached customers exiting the restaurants and asked them to participate in a brief survey. The

(Continued)

questions were administered via oral interview. The teams collected data for two hours or until they had completed 50 surveys at the target location. Respondents were compensated with a $2 city MetroCard that was good for one public transit ride.

- *Outcome variables:* Among the variables measured were these: (1) whether respondents had purchased food for themselves, (2) whether they had seen calorie information in the restaurant, (3) where they had seen it, (4) whether the calorie information affected the purchase they made, (5) their frequency of going to fast-food chains and ice coffee chains, (5) how often they considered calorie information when making food purchases.

Decision choice points

Consideration of a few key choices can serve to illustrate the relevance, importance, and consequences of the decisions that go into creating any evaluation research design. Inherent in this analysis is the nature of the information trade-offs that occur in the design process. The final decisions prioritize certain domains of information while deemphasizing others. They also may protect the study against some validity threats while leaving it vulnerable to other threats. These trade-offs will influence the value of the study and its alignment with stakeholders' original information needs. Thus, the trade-offs will also influence different aspects of the study's validity. Four of these decision choice points are considered here; the list could easily be expanded.

Selection of locations. The researchers stratified the restaurant locations by chain, so that the 15 chains were equally represented among the selected locations. Why didn't they stratify by a different variable, such as geographic location within the city, approximate volume of sales, or neighborhood income level? Each of these variables, and numerous others, could provide valuable insights into customers' attention to posted calorie information, including the identification of important moderator variables that may account for differences in consumer behavior and policy effectiveness across sites. Alternatively, since the 15 chains represented approximately 75% of all restaurant locations affected by the regulation, why didn't they select a simple random sample from the full population of locations, so that each affected location had an equal chance of selection into the study? These alternative procedures might or might not be preferable to the procedure selected; the point is that whatever choice is made should be supported by a reason. The authors noted that they elected to stratify by chain because of their interest in assessing how consumer outcomes might vary across the chains. This justification seems reasonable because, among other considerations, the city health department would be interested in learning how chains differ in their compliance with the new regulations, due to its responsibility for enforcement.

Selection of times of day. The times of day selected for the 11 "fast-food chains"—noon to 2:00 p.m. on weekdays—ensured that the data would reflect lunchtime business. Since customer traffic would be especially high during that time period, there may conceivably be a time-of-day effect, in which customers are motivated to complete their transactions quickly in consideration of their

(Continued)

(Continued)

short lunch hour as well as the line of customers behind them. Consequently, they may be less likely to notice, or less interested in examining, the posted calorie information. This validity threat, which focuses on patterns that occur predictably over the course of a day, could be placed in the category of *cyclical changes*, described earlier. If such a possibility were deemed to be a plausible hypothesis in terms of its effect on customer behavior, this could constitute a weakness of the study's ability to determine the overall size of the policy's treatment effect. At a minimum, it could be seen as constituting a *limitation* of the study's conclusions, in that the findings reflect a specific and nonrepresentative sampling of the day and week. Although the reason for this choice is not discussed in the article, it may have been made in an effort to maximize the time efficiency of the teams in completing their surveys, since there were some sites that fell short of the targeted 50 surveys within the allotted two hours. If so, this would be an example of how the available resources for an evaluation study can affect decisions about study design.

Selection of individuals to interview. Based on information provided in the article, the data collection teams were not given instructions on which customers to approach from among those exiting the restaurant. With heavy traffic flows during the lunchtime period, there was probably considerable choice available for this decision. Without explicit guidance, data collectors may be inclined to select whom to approach based on a large number of variables that may bias the sample of respondents. For example, it may be tempting to approach individuals who are alone rather than in a group, who are walking relatively slowly, who appear to give nonverbal cues signifying friendliness, who are similar to members of the study team in ethnicity or age, and so on. Variables that influence participant selection by the study team could well be associated with the outcome behaviors that are being measured. For example, someone perceived as in a hurry on leaving the restaurant may also have been in a hurry inside, and thus less likely to read and consider the calorie information. These confounding variables produce a strong possibility of bias in the measurement and estimation of the outcome variables because potential respondents' outcome status is confounded with their probability of selection into the study. A remedy that is sometimes used in studies involving similar street-level recruitments is to have the data collectors adhere to certain procedures that can be randomized regarding whom to approach, such as initiating a count of eligible respondents passing by and then approaching the *nth* individual, with *n* varying according to a predetermined sequence (e.g., Johnson et al., 2006).

Single-group pre-post design. In this type of design, the counterfactual condition is represented by the pretest. As described earlier, the pretest provides a poor representation of the counterfactual condition because it is usually likely that some change in the outcome state would occur even in the absence of any intervention. But research theorists also acknowledge that in some circumstances the single-group pre-post design can provide useful information, and it may be a reasonable choice if a comparison condition would be exceedingly difficult to arrange (Reichardt, 2019; Shadish et al.,

(Continued)

2002]. In this policy evaluation setting, it seems that incorporating multiple conditions to produce a no-treatment estimate, i.e., counterfactual, would be exceedingly challenging. All eligible establishments in New York City needed to comply with the regulation, and thus it was not an option to set up a comparison condition within the city. Going outside the city to locate other communities to produce a comparison condition would present enormous practical challenges, since the city's Department of Health would not have jurisdiction in other locales, and there would also be significant interpretive problems in making a case for the comparability of any city (or cities) with New York City. Thus it seems reasonable to conclude that the single-group design was the only realistic option for this policy evaluation (although the authors did not go into this argument in their article). The cost of this circumstance is that it cannot be strongly claimed that the pre to post changes observed in this study reflect whatever true differences existed between the two time periods. Nevertheless the study provides substantial value in establishing that there was indeed a change in customer behavior after (compared to before) the policy went into effect, even though the precise extent of that change cannot be fully known from these data.

Source: Dumanovsky, T., Huang, C. Y., Bassett, M. T., & Silver, L. D. (2010). Consumer awareness of fast-food calorie information in New York City after implementation of a menu labeling regulation. *American Journal of Public Health, 100*(12), 2520–2525. doi:10.2105/AJPH.2010.191908

Chapter Summary

- A primary function of an impact evaluation design is to estimate the counterfactual condition relating to the causal relationship between a program and its potential outcomes. The counterfactual—also known as the no-treatment expectation—is an estimate of what the program participants' status on the outcome variables would have been if they had not experienced the program. Once a group of participants has gone through the program, the true counterfactual for those individuals is impossible to know, so every evaluation design uses its own approach for generating an estimate. For example, a control group approach uses a group of individuals who are judged to be very similar to the program participants and who do not receive the program.

- The significant elements of an impact evaluation design include the following:

- The study participants (or other units). In most evaluation studies the study units will be individual people, but they may also be groups, communities, time points, or other entities. This design element includes who the participants are, how they have been selected, and the sample size.

- The choice of study conditions. For example, there may be one or more intervention conditions and one or more comparison conditions. The characteristics of these conditions should be specified.

- Assignment of participants to condition. A randomization process or other procedure may be used to assign study participants to the various conditions, or the study may use intact groups.

- Number and timing of observation points. For example, there may be multiple pretests and/or multiple posttests. The length of time between observations will be an important consideration as well, and should be determined based on identifying the time frames that will provide the most useful information about outcomes.

- Critical comparisons between the conditions. The design should specify how the various measurements involving different groups and different time points will be compared.

- The four kinds of validity that are identified in the Campbellian validity model provide a useful road map for examining the design of an evaluation study. Of those subtypes, *internal validity* is the most directly affected by elements of the evaluation design. It is concerned with the strength of conclusions about causality, and the way that the study design has estimated the counterfactual condition has strong implications for the degree of confidence with which conclusions about causality can be drawn from the study. *Construct validity* is also affected by design decisions with regard to identifying the study participants and the ways that the intervention, outcomes, and settings have been operationalized. *Statistical conclusion validity* will be affected by the study's sample size, e.g., being weakened by an inadequately sized sample. Finally, *external validity* is less directly tied to the particulars of the study design, because it involves processes of generalization that usually take place after the study has been completed.

- The qualities that produce a strong evaluation design are those that will enable the study to answer the evaluation questions accurately and comprehensively. These qualities include:

- Aligning the design with the evaluation questions.

- Minimizing threats to internal validity—that is, conclusions about causality between the program and its effects—by being able to rule out plausible rival hypotheses that might otherwise account for the obtained pattern of results.

- Meeting assumptions that are inherent in the measurement and analysis strategies.

- Maintaining adequate statistical power.

- Incorporating transparency and protections against bias.

- Making optimal use of available resources.

Questions for Reflection—Chapter 7

1. In a comparative design for an outcome evaluation, what are different types of control (or comparison) conditions?

    - How do those options drive the conclusions that can be drawn from the study analysis?

2. Consider an intervention that you are familiar with and that could be the focus of an outcome evaluation.

    - In this particular case, could it be helpful to include more than one control condition? What would those multiple control conditions be?

3. Suppose you were evaluating your selected intervention using a one-group pretest-posttest design. As described in this chapter, that design is vulnerable to numerous validity threats, of which several of the most common are listed in Table 7.1.

    - If you were using that design and given the specific features of your intervention, are any of the threats in Table 7.1 not particularly relevant for your evaluation?

    - Can you identify some validity threats that are not listed in the table but which might be a concern for this particular evaluation?

4. Describe an outcome evaluation scenario from your experience for which multiple pretests and/or posttests would be particularly valuable.

    - What specific kinds of information could they add to your interpretation of results?

8

Data Analysis

Once you have your data "in the can," you must make sense of it all.[1] The start of this process can be an overwhelming feeling. In this chapter I will explore several themes related to the data analysis process. One of my goals is to highlight the occasions in the analysis process that allow—and sometimes even demand—creative and opportunistic decision-making. Data analysis benefits from processes of imagination, originality, and insight. Our guiding concern is to find ways to make sense out of the data, to find underlying patterns and threads of continuity.

Are those underlying patterns in the data already there waiting to be discovered, or do we create them by developing a convincing narrative? The answer to that question harkens back to our underlying philosophies of science and inquiry, and by extension, our philosophy of evaluation. Recall my anecdote in the preface about the three baseball umpires. Are the pitches already balls and strikes, or are they nothing at all until the umpire calls them? How much of what we describe in our analyses is the real world located in the proverbial "out there," and how much of it is our construction?

This is one place where philosophy questions take on actual meat and bones. And this is where the concept of validity takes front and center stage. Validity, in House's (1980) sense, is our guiding principle: we strive to ensure, to the degree possible, that our conclusions can be defended as accurate, fair, and coherent.

---

[1]I speak here of data analysis as a distinct, separate stage that unambiguously follows data collection. In fact, that is an oversimplification. Data analysis can sometimes be ongoing while data collection is occurring as well. And new, unanticipated questions—hypotheses, inconsistencies, ambiguities, and/or creative flights of fancy—may arise during data analysis that send the evaluator back to the field to collect more data.

Data Analysis and Evaluation Validity

As described in Chapter 7, the evaluation design—a series of critical deci-sions including *what* data will be collected, *when* and *from whom* it will be collected, how the units will be *assigned to condition* (if relevant), and what general *comparisons* will be made (Boruch, 1997; Lipsey, 1993)—is devel-oped as a way to answer the evaluation questions most effectively and with best use of resources. The design provides an essential set of guideposts for the data analyses. But it would be a mistake to conclude that all data analysis decisions are derivable from the design. In fact, the data analyses themselves are a creative part of the evaluation process. There are multiple ways of answering questions, which sometimes do not become apparent until after the data have been collected. And there are multiple surprises that occur during data collection.

Further, there are usually disruptions in the planned process that make the data set somewhat different from the way it had been originally envi-sioned. There might be fewer or more participants at the outset than you had expected; participant attrition over the course of the intervention may have changed the sample from the way it looked at the start of the evalu-ation study; the timing of data collection might have been thrown off by unexpected events or contingencies during program delivery; some pro-gram sites might have been found to be deficient in program delivery; and so on. These disruptions will often require adjustments in the data analysis process in order to maintain the logic of your analysis in the best possible way.

In addition, a critical part of data analysis is to ask, and try to answer, new questions that follow from the originally anticipated analyses. It may turn out that certain participant subgroups were particularly affected or unaffected by the program; the same might be said for participants at particular sites; or a mediating variable may appear that didn't seem important when the program theory was first constructed. These events will require a string of analyses in order to plumb the data set to uncover the secrets that can be gleaned from it.

Thus the data analyst needs to be skeptical, critical, and alert to follow these rabbit trails to their logical ends. Sometimes the surprises and unex-pected directions are the most productive parts of a study.

Some ways of dividing up the data also tell a story that is clearer and more compelling than other approaches. These decisions bear on the val-idity of your analytical conclusions, calling to mind House's (1980) dictum that an evaluation should be coherent—that is, should tell a good story—as a component of its validity.

On the other hand, reanalyzing your data to see how things turn out can sometimes turn into fishing, that is, manipulating your analyses to try to show impressive results when, in fact, it would be more accurate and fair to show weak effects or no effects. The objectivity and integrity of the data analyst can be tested during this phase. These issues are covered in this chapter.

Of the four validity types delineated by Shadish et al. (2002) and discussed in Chapter 3, the most relevant for the purposes of this chapter is statistical conclusion validity, which refers explicitly to relationships among variables. Internal validity comes into play as well, since a thorough data analysis will be able to shed light on relationships involving causality.

Statistical Conclusion Validity

As Shadish et al. (2002) describe it, statistical conclusion validity may seem to have a limited scope. It refers to (1) the correctness of our conclusions about whether or not the variables in our analysis covary and (2) the strength of that covariation. It does not address whether we have correctly established that the covariation is due to a causal relationship between intervention and outcome status. In a logical sense, the determination of covariation precedes any inferences about potential causality: let's first figure out *if* there is a relationship, and then try to determine what accounts for it.

Type I and Type II errors. One key to statistical conclusion validity is an understanding of the types of errors to which statistical analysis is prone. A Type I error is a false positive: concluding that there is a relationship when in fact there is not. Conversely, a Type II error is a false negative: failing to catch a relationship that truly exists. Table 8.1 provides an illustration, using a bivariate case. In this context there are two kinds of conclusions that can be drawn about the possibility of covariation: either the variables are associated with each other or they are not.[2] And each of these conclusions can be either correct or incorrect, which leads to a 2 x 2 matrix. If we have concluded that there *is* an association, the only kind of error we are in danger of making is Type I. If we have concluded that there is no association, the kind of error we are at risk for is Type II.

---

[2]Our use of the terms *covariation, correlation,* and *association* can be used interchangeably to refer to a relationship between variables, and they can apply to variables with different kinds of scaling. If two variables are continuous (or treated as such), the covariation could take the form of a correlation coefficient. If one variable is categorical and the other continuous, the covariation can take the form of a comparison of group means, tested with a t-test or analysis of variance (e.g., members in group A score higher on the outcome, on average, than members of Group B). And if both are categorical, it can take the form of a chi-square association (e.g., those in the lowest (or highest) category on variable A are likely to also be in the lowest (or highest) category on variable B).

TABLE 8.1 ● Type I and Type II Errors		
Our Conclusion: **A Statistical Relationship Between the Variables...**	**Our Conclusion is...**	
	...Correct	**...Incorrect**
...Does exist (reject the null hypothesis)	Identification of program effect	Type I error
...Does not exist (do not reject the null hypothesis)	Identification of lack of program effect	Type II error

A Type I error results from claiming that a statistical association exists when it does not. Its probability is represented by the alpha (α) level of the statistical test. A Type II error results from claiming that no relationship exists when it really does. Its probability is represented by beta (β). Thus the probability of making a correct claim is represented by $1 - \beta$, which is the statistical power of the test.

Of the two types of error, the likelihood of Type I is easier and more straightforward to account for in a comparative design, because we expressly set that probability, alpha (α), in our evaluation design before we analyze the data. For example, if we choose to conduct our statistical analysis with alpha set at 0.05, we accept a probability that we will be wrong exactly 5% of the time *if indeed the association is zero in the population from which the samples are drawn*. Type II is more complicated because if the association is other than zero, we cannot estimate our probability of being wrong unless we specify what that population association actually is—and there is a vast number of possibilities. The probability of detecting a difference that truly exists, and thus avoiding a Type II error, is conditional on the potential values of that true difference. (See also Chapter 7.) A report will sometimes state something to the effect of: "Statistical power to detect a difference between the groups of .25 standard deviation was estimated to be .70." But to be more comprehensive, power analyses are often represented in graphic form, in order to include a range of values for the potential true population difference rather than a single point estimate (e.g., Lipsey & Hurley, 2009).

Note that the presence of either of these "errors" does not imply that a mistake was made by the data analyst. Rather, they occur because of anomalies in the sample (or samples) that we have analyzed. For example, in comparing two samples, Type I errors will occur because the samples are unusual with respect to the populations they are drawn from: in this hypothetical case the populations do not differ on the variable being measured, but by an unfortunate stroke of luck the samples suggest otherwise.[3] Similarly, Type II errors can also occur because of an unusual instance of sampling, in which the samples display equivalence, or close to it, despite the fact (again, hypothetical) that the populations are truly different. However, in addition to the vagaries of sampling, the probability of Type II errors also depends on design features that are under the control of the evaluator, including sample size and the reliability of measures, both of which affect our ability to detect the underlying relationship through the noise of random error. That is, we may miss identifying an association between variables if our sample is too small or our measures inadequate.

It is in the nature of statistical analysis that we will never know if we are correct in our conclusion about the presence or absence of covariation in the populations of interest because the samples are our *only* source of information about the populations they represent. Paradoxically, therefore, whether we have in fact committed a Type I or Type II error is not a matter that affects the *validity* of our conclusion about covariation. Rather, that validity is based on the strength of the logic with which we have set up the rules that guide our decision, whatever the decision turns out to be.

Internal Validity

Once we have concluded that there is covariation between our independent variable (e.g., assigned group, consisting of two possibilities: program condition or control condition) and our outcome variable, we face the task of deciding whether it is the status on the independent variable that has influenced the status of the outcome. This is the question of causality, and it is not a statistical process but rather one of logical analysis. As Shadish et al. (2002) describe, we must identify, and then determine whether we can reasonably rule out, any plausible rival hypotheses that may account for the covariation. The term "rival," of course, refers to a hypothesis that might reasonably compete with our hypothesis of interest, that the covariation was due to participation in the intervention. If we can rule these out, leaving only our hypothesis of interest still standing as a plausible possibility, then we will be justified in making the inference about causality.

---

[3]The research literature can sometimes be confusing with regard to whether we are dealing with one or more samples, and one or more populations. But if a single sample has been drawn and the individuals are then assigned to, say, two conditions (at random or otherwise), researchers will sometimes say that two populations are being represented: people who have gone through the program and people who haven't.

The collection of potential rival hypotheses that Campbell and his colleagues identified, including history, maturation, selection, testing, instrumentation, etc., have been discussed in Chapter 7. The setup of the evaluation design can allow for many of these alternatives to be rejected. For example, a study that produces its different samples through a process of random assignment allows for a reasonable claim that *selection*, that is, innate sample differences that already exist when the samples are created, is *not* the reason for any differences that may be found at posttest.[4]

It is the rare and fortunate evaluation design that allows for a reasonable rejection of all potential rival hypotheses. Much more often, the features of a design can justify eliminating at least some rivals, and the more the better. When we have analyzed our data, the judgment that intervention participation has caused an increase in outcome scores is made stronger by the ability to reject these rivals. The validity of our conclusion is also strengthened as a result. Thus, validity is a dimensional concept rather than dichotomous, that is, either achieved or not achieved.

The Core Analysis

The core analysis is the fundamental set of comparisons and other analyses that you use to answer your primary, prespecified evaluation questions (Boruch, 1997). These analyses are generally anticipated at the time that you plan and design your evaluation. For example, if you plan a three-group study to compare a newly designed program against both an existing program and a control condition, your statistical comparisons will be relatively straightforward to plan beforehand, at least in the main. You will probably intend to compare the mean scores in the different groups, using all participants to obtain those scores.

You will almost certainly be interested in also conducting other analyses in which you can explore the potential effects of other variables, in order to better understand what makes your program tick. Two ways in which additional variables can affect the relationship between intervention and outcome—the presumed cause and effect—are through mediation and moderation. If you have a detailed program theory, an examination of these potential processes may be included in your core analysis as well.

---

[4]The rejection of *selection*, that is, preexisting sample differences, is actually a little more complicated than just saying that random assignment renders that hypothesis unreasonable. Even through random assignment creates samples presumed to be equivalent, those samples must stay intact through the course of the study. If attrition (dropout from the sample) occurs, as it usually does to some degree, that initial equivalence will be compromised. The statement was simplified to illustrate the larger point about rejection of rival hypotheses.

Mediators and Moderators

Mediation and moderation are two distinct types of statistical relationship, which are sometimes confused because of their unfortunate phonetic similarity. In a *mediational* relationship, an additional variable has an intermediate influence on the relationship between intervention (I) and outcome (O): the intervention will have an effect on the intermediate variable (or *mediator*), which in turn influences the outcome (Hayes, 2013). If the mediator is not successfully impacted, then neither will be the outcome. (To be comprehensive at the cost of adding complication, the relationship between I and O can also be *partially* mediated, in which case there is a direct effect of I on O *plus* the indirect mediated effect; in such cases the direct effect can show up in an analysis even when the mediated effect is absent.) In a simple case, consider a social marketing media campaign that is intended to influence a health-related behavior of members of a community. The organizers of the campaign ask local stations to air a series of public service announcements (PSAs) by radio and television. The evaluator's main interest is in determining whether the campaign results in expected levels of change by community members. But before community members can be influenced by the PSAs they need to be exposed to them. Thus it is standard in media evaluations to ascertain whether people saw (or heard) the PSAs and with what frequency. If they did see them, they may or may not have been influenced by them, but they need first to have seen them.[5] In this situation, exposure to the campaign—having seen the PSAs to some degree—is one mediating variable for the relationship between the intervention (the overall campaign) and the attainment of change in a target outcome. Indeed, "campaign exposure" is itself a construct that can be conceived in different ways, including in a multivariate framework.

In a moderating relationship, the third variable does not intervene between the presumed cause and effect, but rather reflects conditions or population characteristics under which the intervention will have differential effectiveness. Certain demographic variables such as age or gender are often found to be moderators. For example, an educational program might be found to be more effective for younger or older audience members, or different cultural or ethnic audiences. Sometimes a program may be intentionally designed to have this kind of specialized, narrow appeal, especially if alternate programs are designed for other demographic subgroups. In other cases, this targeted effect is discovered as an unwelcome surprise. When moderating effects are found, the reasons for the differential

---

[5]It may also be hypothesized by the campaign designers that direct exposure to the campaign may indeed not be essential for individuals to be affected, due to the operation of indirect influence: individuals who were exposed may change the minds of their peers as well. But we will stick to the simple case where the program theory stipulates that direct exposure is necessary for the possibility of outcome change.

effects might not be obvious, and this may be one important engine driving supplemental, post hoc analyses.

Null Hypothesis Significance Testing and p-Values

The Critique of Statistical Significance Testing

Case Study 8.1 describes an experience from my own dissertation work in which the statistical test for one of the study's primary hypotheses barely missed the cutoff for statistical significance. Given the requirements of significance testing, the null hypothesis was not rejected and the conclusion was that the educational program had not been demonstrated to be effective. The result was disappointing, but those are the rules of the game.

CASE STUDY 8.1   STATISTICAL SIGNIFICANCE TESTING: A TRUE STORY

For my dissertation study at the University of Wisconsin, I evaluated an educational program to teach film literacy skills to students in grades 4–6. The study had three program conditions: a five-session program that taught about "visual literacy" (i.e., what the camera is doing and how it affects our reactions to the content), a different five-session program that taught about how character development is expressed through film, and a control condition that received an unrelated curriculum. The primary outcomes of interest included two knowledge tests, each covering the content of one of the two film curricula. The educational sessions had been adapted from a curriculum by a local art educator, with whom I also developed the two outcome measures. Six fifth-grade and sixth-grade classes took part in the study. After obtaining consent, roughly 150 participating students were randomly assigned into six new class groupings, two of which were randomly assigned to each of the three study conditions. I taught all four of the intervention classes myself.

In my core analysis—that is, the analysis plan leading directly out of the study design—each of the two program conditions was tested against the control condition on both of these two outcome scales. The most interesting finding from these comparisons was for the visual literacy test, in which the mean score of the program group was higher than the mean score of the control group. Higher, but not quite high enough to reach statistical significance: the p value of the t-test for the group difference was .055.

As a graduate student with limited experience, I was uncertain about how to proceed with this tantalizing result.[6] I knew, of course, that according to

---

[6]And "tantalizing" is an apt adjective here to describe a p value that is a hair short of statistical significance. In Greek mythology, Tantalus's eternal punishment was to have food and drink just barely beyond his grasp.

(Continued)

the binary world of the hypothesis test, the null hypothesis (which was that the educational program does *not* affect the outcome and there is no difference in pre-post gains between the groups being compared) could not be rejected. The decision rule of hypothesis testing treats a miss by an inch the same as a miss by a mile. Thus I could not validly conclude that the difference in the two groups' mean scores signified greater knowledge on the part of students who had gone through the educational program. Yet it also seemed to me that it would be throwing away information to disregard this intriguing (for me, anyway) finding.

To help me interpret the borderline result, I looked for guidance to my dissertation committee. They were sympathetic but firm. *Not significant. Those are the breaks.* Talk about tough love. But of course they were correct. Given the hypothesis testing frame of reference under which we were working, that was the only consistent conclusion. I just needed to hear them say it.

That was the 1980s. Looking back on it now, I believe my uncertainty was not without some justification, even though the decision was correct under the expectations of the analysis procedure that we had built into the design. The more fundamental question is: What should be the proper role of the null hypothesis significance testing (NHST) paradigm in our attempts to best learn about interventions through outcome evaluation studies?

In a more general sense, however, it is reasonable to ask whether the traditional hypothesis testing framework best promotes whatever it is that we are trying to learn from our statistical analyses. Doesn't a strict statistical view that treats these decisions about intervention effects as dichotomous (yes-no, win-lose) leave out information that could be valuable and informative? Despite the nonsignificance, did this no-effects conclusion share something in common with a Type II error?[7] From a validity perspective,

---

[7]Also with the benefit of hindsight, looking back on my study now, an analysis of this type should incorporate attention to the fact that there were two classes nested within each condition, and thus this analysis should have incorporated multilevel modeling (e.g., Hox et al., 2017). That might or might not have resulted in a different pattern of statistical significance. If anything, the p value might have been higher because multilevel analyses takes account of the fact that individual scores tend to be more similar within groups than across groups for any number of reasons. Thus multilevel analyses tend to make it harder to reach statistical significance. In an analysis that ignores a potential nesting effect, the mean scores between treatment and control groups might be different due to a true difference between the conditions, but that will be bolstered by the tendency for scores within groups to be similar. In this particular case, the analysis results might not have changed much because the class groupings were formed by random assignment and they were all taught by the same teacher.

the critical question is: What is the most *valid* conclusion—in the sense of the most true, the most accurate, the most useful, and/or the most supportable—that can be drawn about the demonstrated merit of this curriculum product based on this statistical finding?

What I did not know at the time is that there is a longstanding debate about null hypothesis significance testing (NHST), which indeed may have intensified since the time I conducted my dissertation study (e.g., Cohen, 1994; Thompson, 1996; Wasserstein et al., 2019; Ziliak & McCloskey, 2008). But perhaps to be more precise than to call the current situation a *debate*, it largely consists of statisticians calling for the diminishment or elimination of the practice, while research communities, e.g., in the social sciences, largely ignore those calls. The dominance of statistical significance testing remains firmly entrenched in research and evaluation practice.

The criticisms go beyond the single issue of what to do about borderline results. One of the most basic problems, according to statisticians, is that the meaning and implications of NHST are widely misunderstood by researchers. The esteemed statistician Jacob Cohen (1994) described the confusion as follows:

> What's wrong with NHST? Well, among many other things, it does not tell us what we want to know....What we want to know is "Given these data, what is the probability that H_0 is true?" But as most of us know, what it tells us is "Given that H_0 is true, what is the probability of these (or more extreme) data?" These are not the same. (p. 997)

Cohen goes on to describe the problem as a misapplication of formal logic: in deciding whether or not to reject the null hypothesis (H_0), researchers seek to apply a decision rule that incorporates its probability of being true, given the results from the data. If that probability is low enough (with a threshold commonly set as less than five times out of a hundred, or 0.05), they will conclude that H_0 is false and reject it. Their common error is in assuming that the obtained p value represents this probability. But in reality, the statistical result has told them nothing about the probability of H_0 being true. A relationship that logically holds in terms of truth and falsehood:

> If A is true, then B is false; B has occurred; therefore A must be false.

does not hold when the reasoning becomes probabilistic:

> If A is true, then B is unlikely; B has occurred; therefore A must be unlikely to the same degree (as B occurring if A is true).

In the application of these propositions, A is H_0 and B is the statistical result. Among other points, a reason the reverse probability cannot be predicted from this type of research evidence is that the occurrence of B (e.g., the particular difference between the two samples at the calculated p value) is affected by factors other than the prevalence of B in the population, as discussed earlier with respect to statistical power. One of these factors is imperfect measurement, the effect of which is exacerbated when the phenomenon being measured is rare within the population from which the sample is drawn. Cohen (1994) gives the example of a test for schizophrenia, the incidence of which he estimates at approximately 2%. Using a simple statistical calculation, he demonstrates that even with a hypothetical test that is 95% accurate in its diagnosis, the false positives will outnumber the true positives, confusing the estimation of probabilities.

Another problem with NHST, raised by Cohen and other critics (e.g., Hayat et al., 2019; Thompson, 1996; Wasserstein et al., 2019), is that there is virtually never a completely null relationship between any two variables in a population, and thus there is little sense in conducting a test that *assumes* that a null relationship exists. "[I]n reality H_0 is *never* true in the population, as recognized by any number of prominent statisticians....That is, there will always be some differences in population parameters, although the differences may be incredibly trivial" (Thompson, 1996, p. 27). The practical consequence of this recognition is that any relationship will be found to be statistically significant if only the sample is of sufficient size. The flip side of this issue, also a problem, is that if a sample is quite small, even a meaningful treatment effect may have a p larger than .05 and thus fail to reach statistical significance; this is the problem of Type II errors and low statistical power (Lipsey, 1990; Lipsey & Hurley, 2009).

A third problem with significance testing has been noted many times: statistical significance provides no indication about the importance or meaningfulness of a result. "Don't conclude anything about scientific or practical importance based on statistical significance (or lack thereof)" (Wasserstein et al., 2019, p. 1). A statistically significant finding may be of little or no theoretical interest, and yet will often become the focus of an evaluation report because of the perception of informational value. The aforementioned sample size problem comes into play for this consideration as well: a modest correlation, say, $r = .16$, will not be statistically significant with a sample of 100 participants ($p = .11$) but will be significant with a sample of 160 ($p = .04$). Thus those two circumstances yield opposite statistical conclusions but in both cases we are still talking about a correlation of .16. What is the practical or theoretical importance of a correlation of that size between the two variables that are being examined? The presence or absence of statistical significance in a particular sample does nothing to illuminate this basic question. For example, if this result were to be found in a validation study that compares two instruments intended to measure the same construct, the level of correlation would probably be judged as grossly inadequate to justify a validity claim, regardless of a declaration of statistical significance. The importance of a finding needs to be assessed on standards other than having reached the threshold of $p < .05$. That threshold only allows us to conclude that the correlation is not $r = .00$.

Finally, we can arrive back at my original concern about NHST: the arbitrary nature of the binary cutoff in drawing conclusions about a program's effectiveness or, more generally, the nature of a relationship between variables. Critics of NHST have shared this concern. "A label of statistical significance adds nothing to what is already conveyed by the value of p; in fact, this dichotomization of p-values makes matters worse. For example, no p-value can reveal the plausibility, presence, truth, or importance of an association or an effect... Yet the dichotomization into 'significant' and 'not significant' is taken as an imprimatur of authority on these characteristics" (Wasserstein et al., 2019, p. 2).

From one perspective, the great benefit of statistical hypothesis testing and the near-universal convention of setting alpha at $p = .05$ is that it forces a particular form of objectivity upon the decision process that follows the statistical result. The conventional .05 threshold helps to remove the temptation for the researcher/evaluator to manipulate the designation of prior expectations based on obtained results. Thus it is not possible to conduct an analysis, find that $p = .07$, and claim after the fact that alpha was set at some level slightly above the value of the obtained p (e.g., .10), thus successfully achieving statistical significance.[8] It gives us all a way to draw essential conclusions without having to think too hard. Undoubtedly this is part of the reason why the convention has traditionally been valued by journal editors. In the evaluation world, the convention has also been valued by external stakeholders who have no inherent interest in that intervention's success but just want to know if it meets a standard yardstick of success or effectiveness, perhaps so that it can be compared with competing interventions to expedite a choice between available options. Jacob Cohen again: "The fact that Fisher's ideas [*establishing the rationale for hypothesis testing*] quickly became the basis for statistical inference in the behavioral sciences is not surprising—they were very attractive. They offered a deterministic scheme, mechanical and objective, independent of content, and led to clear-cut yes-no decisions." (Cohen, 1990, p. 1307)

But the price of this presumed objectivity is an artificial distortion of reality in the form of the arbitrarily dichotomous decision rule. "Significance tests and dichotomized p-values have turned many researchers into scientific snowbirds, trying to avoid dealing with uncertainty by escaping to a 'happy place' where results are either statistically significant or not. In the real world, data provide a noisy signal" (Wasserstein et al., 2019, p. 3). Furthermore, despite the imposition of a conventional standard, the true objectivity of this process is compromised and complex, far more so than

---

[8]Actually, the post hoc fudging of alpha can still occur if the researcher, for the sake of being able to claim significance after obtaining a p between .05 and .10, decides to change the test from two-tailed to one-tailed. But one-tailed hypothesis tests are, thankfully, rare these days.

we might like to admit. House (2008) provides an impressive dissection of the ways that statistical hypothesis testing can be manipulated for unethical purposes in evaluations of drug effectiveness by pharmaceutical companies.

How to reduce dependence on statistical hypothesis testing? Fortunately, critics of NHST have provided numerous suggestions for data interpretation procedures that can be used in place of it, or alongside it. These are summarized in Exhibit 8.1.

EXHIBIT 8.1 RECOMMENDATIONS FOR REDUCING THE ROLE OF STATISTICAL SIGNIFICANCE TESTS

Some scholars recommend eliminating NHST as a feature of statistical analysis, while others prefer to relegate it to a less important status in the effort to understand a set of findings. As a general rule, evaluators should understand what NHST can contribute; be careful not to overinterpret or misuse the practice; and apply other useful forms of information that can supplement what we are learning overall from the evaluation study. Here are some recommendations from statisticians about procedures that could be used alongside, or in place of, significance testing.

- **Report p-values and use them in the interpretation process, rather than relying solely on whether the .05 threshold has been met.** The p-value of a statistical test is the exact probability of the group difference under conditions of the null hypothesis and is the basis for determining statistical significance. Occasionally in an evaluation or research report, one will see a statement such as: "This difference was significant at the .05 level." without indicating what the exact p value was. This way of reporting the results of the test is unnecessarily imprecise. Knowing whether p was, for example, .048 or .015 provides useful information that is unavailable if the report just says "$p < .05$." Some statisticians suggest reporting only the p-value without the additional judgment about significance because once p is known, that judgment adds no new information and is superfluous (e.g., Hurlbert et al., 2019).

- **Give more attention to effect sizes.** What exactly is an effect size indicator? Cohen provides a succinct description of the variety of forms it can take:

  I have learned and taught that the primary product of a research inquiry is one or more measures of effect size, not p values....Effect-size measures include mean differences (raw or standardized), correlations and squared correlation of all kinds, odds ratios, kappas— whatever conveys the magnitude of the phenomenon of interest appropriate to the research context. If, for example, you are comparing groups on a variable measured in units that are well understood by your

(Continued)

(Continued)

readers (IQ points, or dollars, or number of children, or months of survival), mean differences are excellent measures of effect size. When this isn't the case, and it isn't the case more often than it is, the results can be translated into standardized mean differences (*d* values) or some measure of correlation or association. (Cohen, 1990, p. 1310)

When effect sizes are expressed in standardized format, as in the form, "the mean difference between the two groups was .25 standard deviation of the outcome variable." they can lend themselves to comparisons across different studies and different measures. For example, if a study has included the measurement of a variable through two different strategies, this comparison can be valuable for judgments about construct validity and the stability of the measurement strategies. In correlation and regression analyses, an indicator of effect size is the "variance accounted for," which is the square of the coefficient. For example, a correlation of .40 accounts for 16% of the variance of each of the two variables.

- **Utilize confidence intervals.** When reporting the effect size and its p-value, it will be informative to also report the confidence interval (CI). The CI, which incorporates information from the error variance in addition to the effect size, displays the range of values that we can claim contains the population parameter, within a designated degree of probability. The 95% confidence interval contains the information provided by the statistical significance test at $\alpha = .05$: if 0 lies *outside* the interval, the sample difference is statistically significant because by definition we are 95% certain that the true population value is one of the values within that range, which does not include 0. Conversely, if 0 lies *within* the confidence interval, the difference is not significant. What the CI adds to the information already given by the NHST is a picture of the precision of our claim. The standard 95% interval conforms to the $\alpha = .05$ significance test, but Cohen (1990) advises that it can be informative to use confidence intervals other than, or in addition to, that convention. For example, we can report both the 95% CI and an 80% CI, which will be smaller.

- **Before the statistical analysis, decide what will be a meaningful effect size, regardless of statistical significance.** Another way to incorporate thinking about effect size is to determine, before the analysis is done—and possibly before the data are collected—how different effect sizes will be interpreted in light of our expectations about the intervention. In the two-group comparison, we can consider what level of effect size (that is, difference between intervention and control groups) will be considered meaningful for our assessment of the intervention. If the sample in our evaluation study is small, we might obtain an impressive level of difference which still does not reach statistical significance. Alternatively, if we are fortunate to have a large sample for our evaluation, we may find

(Continued)

that the difference is statistically significant but still disappointing in terms of our prior expectation. This process of setting expectations can constitute a useful conversation for the evaluator to have with stakeholders during evaluation planning, and it can set the stage for productive conversations about the interpretation of results.

- **Conduct power analyses to help interpret your findings about statistical significance.** The statistical power of a test is the probability of detecting a difference when that difference truly exists in the population. Failure to detect this true difference is a Type II error (as discussed at the start of this chapter). For a specified α level and population effect size, the power of a study depends on the sample size (larger sample increases power) and the precision of the measurement instruments. Reviews of evaluation studies have revealed that evaluations are often conducted with surprisingly low power, and the studies are thereby handicapped in the information they can provide. In many, if not most, evaluation studies, power analyses are not conducted, in which case the evaluator will not be able to estimate the likelihood of having obtained statistically significant results. Introductions to the topic are provided by Lipsey (1990) and Murphy et al. (2014), among others.

- **Along with the statistical significance test, give explicit attention to the sample size and discuss the implications.** Since the power of the significance test is highly sensitive to sample size (N), the evaluator can make a point of routinely discussing the influence of N with regard to the obtained results. Thompson (1996) recommends including an "if-then" analysis: if a test is nonsignificant, this will be a calculation of how much larger the N would have needed to be in order to achieve statistical significance. Conversely, if a test *is* significant, the calculation will be a determination of the smallest value of N that would still retain statistical significance for whatever effect size was obtained (that is, the threshold N between significance and nonsignificance).

- **Pay more attention to the replicability of findings across multiple studies.** There is only so much confidence that can or should be placed in the results from a single study. If an effect size, within a reasonably small range, is consistently found in a number of evaluations, it adds substantially to our confidence about the stability of that effect, irrespective of what may have been concluded about statistical significance in a single case. Thus, replicability is one of the benchmarks underlying our confidence in results and the validity of our conclusions (Cohen, 1994; Thompson, 1996). Of course, replication studies are resource-intensive and will often not be an available option. However, an evaluation plan may sometimes incorporate a series of small individual studies in addition to, or instead of, a single large one. In addition, Thompson describes methods for conducting "internal replicability analyses," which are different ways to configure the sample in a single study to examine the stability of results across multiple analysis approaches within the same data set.

One noteworthy point of this process, consistent with the perspectives of evaluation scholars writing about validity (House, 1980; Schwandt, 2015), is that statistical reasoning takes us to a certain point—only partway—in arriving at our overall conclusion. Beyond that point, we must carry the ball further with logic, reasoning, and argumentation. An application of well-reasoned argument is necessary to determine the best, most useful judgment to be made regarding a statistical result. The statistical finding itself may be unambiguous, but its interpretation is not.

More Advanced Data Analysis Issues

There will be additional statistical considerations in data analysis that bear on the quality of those analyses. Experienced stakeholders, especially in the research community, may well ask questions about how these have been addressed. As with other validity issues, these will become more important for evaluations that are high-stakes, e.g., because the evaluations are resource-intensive, very large, or focused on a controversial intervention. Whatever level of attention you give these issues, it will be useful to be aware of them. The discussion of these topics is beyond the scope of this book, but I will mention and briefly describe them, suggest the simplest way to deal with them, and suggest resources where they can be explored further.

- **Using multilevel analysis for multiple-site evaluations.** Consider an evaluation that includes multiple sites for both the program and control conditions. If you want to examine the overall difference between program and control, it is statistically incorrect to simply compare the grand means for the two conditions without taking any account of the local site. This is because there is an expectation that scores on any variable will be more similar for people within a preexisting group (e.g., a classroom, clinic, workplace, or other type of intervention site) than people in different groups. The best way to handle this issue is to conduct your analysis using techniques of *multilevel modeling*, which incorporate information about within-group effects and can provide statistics that do not suffer from this bias (Hox et al., 2017).

  If within-group differences are not accounted for in your analysis, the significance levels will be distorted. Indeed, the usual effect is that significance will be easier to attain. As appealing as this may sound superficially for supporters of the program, the conclusions will be biased and thus invalid. And the evaluation will lose credibility with stakeholders who are familiar with this issue.

- **Dealing with missing data.** If your data set is sufficiently large, it is almost certain that there will be some proportion of missing responses to individual questions. For example, some respondents who answer all of the questions relating to outcomes and program participation might balk at some of the demographic questions and decide not to provide their age, income level, or gender identity. Similarly, they might decide to skip questions about sensitive or private behaviors (as discussed in Chapter 6). Missing data can also result from noncompletion of a questionnaire, uninterpretable responses, interviewer error, and other factors.

  The simplest way to deal with missing data is to exclude cases at the level of the individual analysis. That is, if a particular analysis, e.g., a regression model, includes a variable for which certain cases (i.e., respondents) are missing a value, those cases will be excluded from that analysis but will be included in other analyses for which their data are complete. A second option is to exclude cases completely if they are missing answers to certain critical questions. These two methods can even be used together, with different decision rules applying for different variables. But the more complex and sophisticated methods include different ways to *impute* the answers for missing data, i.e., to fill in a predicted value. One form of imputation is to fill in the overall mean for each missing score; this is a conservative approach because it reduces the variability in the data set. A more complex approach for filling in missing scores is to calculate an individualized estimate for each case based on that case's scores on the other variables in the data set. The imputation of missing scores can be particularly important for data sets that have a great deal of missing data, especially on a few key variables, because excluding cases can introduce sampling bias into the analyses. An introduction to the topic is provided by McKnight et al. (2007).

These topics are not given enough attention in many practical evaluation settings. Indeed, in many cases they are ignored, although in recent years the use of multilevel modeling techniques has become much more widely established and thus harder to disregard. The topics bear directly on the validity of data analyses because they influence the accuracy of the conclusions that can be drawn. They will be of interest to methodologically sophisticated audiences for your evaluation and are directly related to issues of credibility and the competence with which analyses were conducted. If you do not have the resources, expertise, and/or benefit of experienced colleagues to help you address these issues in your evaluation directly, you should be prepared at least to acknowledge these issues and consider the effects they may have had on your analyses and conclusions.

Post Hoc and Exploratory Analyses

Would It Be Helpful to Conduct the Analysis in Different Ways?

Your core analysis, which you design before collecting the data, is your first line of investigation. For example, if you have a pre-post control group study, your planned analysis might involve a straightforward comparison of the means of the pre-to-post difference scores. But having conducted that analysis, you might want to incorporate one or more additional variables to examine potential interactions.

Exploring the potential influences on program success. A great deal can be learned from identifying and taking account of different kinds of variables that might be related to intervention effects. For example, you could consider particular participant characteristics that can be examined as moderators of the program-outcome relationship. In a multisite evaluation, you could consider site-level characteristics of the settings or teachers. With respect to the intervention itself, it is usually advisable to include variables related to the fidelity of implementation. In an ANOVA framework, these variables can be crossed with your primary independent variable of group membership (program or control). In a regression framework, they can be included in your model as covariates.

Ad hoc Variables

Sometimes in the analysis phase of a study, evaluators make discoveries that cause them to reconfigure some aspect of the data, such as introducing new, *ad hoc* variables that they hadn't anticipated. An example is provided in Case Study 8.2.

CASE STUDY 8.2 CREATING AND USING AN AD HOC VARIABLE

In 2013 I led a research project that administered an online survey of students, faculty, and staff at my university campus (described also in Chapter 6) to evaluate the first year of the recently enacted smoke-free campus policy, which prohibited smoking and vaping everywhere on campus, including outdoors. We asked those respondents who reported being smokers if they had violated the policy in the past year, and we sought to identify smoker characteristics that may have been related to policy violation (Braverman et al., 2018).

Therefore, one of our survey questions asked, "How do you handle the urge or desire to smoke when you are on campus?" Trying to anticipate all possible responses, we supplied the following response options, in a "check

(Continued)

all that apply" format. Each of these responses was transformed into a variable that was coded 1 if checked and 0 if unchecked.

- I use nicotine gum or patches.
- I use smokeless tobacco products or e-cigarettes.
- I go off campus to smoke.
- I take a walk or engage in physical activity.
- I distract myself in other ways.
- Other (with space to write a comment).

Part of our intended analysis was to incorporate these variables into analyses predicting policy noncompliance. For example, if smokers were using nicotine replacement products, were they particularly unlikely to smoke on campus, given that they had ready access to a substitute product? If this turned out to be true, it would suggest that providing help with smoking cessation, through the office of student health services, could contribute to successful policy implementation. To address these questions in our data analysis, we tested a logistic regression model that included each of these strategies, among other covariates, as potential predictors of our dependent variable, policy violation.

The responses contained a major surprise. Of our 1182 student smoker respondents, 474—fully 40% of them—checked "Other," and of those, 444 took the trouble to write in a response. And a remarkably high percentage of those written free-response comments described some variation of the point, "I don't have urges, so I don't need to do anything to control them." Sometimes they added an admonishment along the lines of "what a silly question" (or stronger language).

We realized that we had stumbled upon a phenomenon that we probably should have anticipated. That is, we shouldn't have assumed that all smokers have urges, or at least, urges intense enough to require some kind of strategic management. Looking further at our data revealed that the respondents who provided this answer tended to be students rather than faculty or staff members. And a quick chi-square analysis also revealed that within our sample of smokers, the nondaily smokers tended to be students.

We wanted to devise a method to incorporate this new information into our analysis. In brief, we turned these qualitative data into a quantitative variable. We assigned three people on our research team to independently review all 444 written responses and code each one as either (a) a clear instance of "No strategy needed" (examples were: "I suck it up and don't smoke"; "Wait until I get home, it's not that urgent"), (b) an unrelated response, or (c) an ambiguous response (for example, "Nothing"; "I don't smoke"). Then, on all of the responses on which there was disagreement, we discussed the response and tried to come to agreement. We created a new variable, which we named *Absence of smoking urges*, to designate this

(Continued)

(Continued)

phenomenon. All of the cases were coded 1 on this new variable if the statement was clear (category *a* above) and 0 if anything else. If the coders could not come to resolution on a statement, it was coded 0. This process resulted in 268 positive cases of this variable—60% of the added written responses.

We incorporated *Absence of smoking urges* into our logistic regression to predict policy violations and it resulted in an odds ratio of 0.37. In other words, students who spontaneously described that there is nothing they need to do in order to refrain from smoking on campus had odds of violating the policy that were approximately one third the odds of student smokers who did not write in this information. It turned out to be one of the strongest predictors in our regression model.

What did this process allow us to learn and to document? From this analysis, and pulling in some additional analyses as well, we were able to surmise that students who smoke only occasionally—e.g., at weekend parties—have no problem complying with a smoke-free policy. This makes sense because these students are probably not yet addicted to tobacco. We reasoned that a policy that prohibited their smoking while on campus—in all probability a large chunk of their day, even for students who don't live on campus—could encourage them *not* to take up the habit in any more intensity. As a side note, we were able to conclude that the absence of smoking urges was not simply a proxy variable for infrequent smoking because cigarette smoking frequency was itself included in the model, so the effects of these two predictor variables were independent of each other.

For our present purposes, what this example illustrates could be described as follows:

- Our research team was surprised by the data.

- We needed to scramble and to devise an ad hoc solution to something we discovered.

- The variable we created turned out to have powerful explanatory power.

- We did not necessarily accept that the respondents were being accurate about the absence of urges—psychological response would play a huge role here—but we judged the fact of these spontaneous descriptions to be an important variable in itself.

Finally, it was important for us to realize that this new variable was an extremely crude measure of our new construct. It depended on (1) students taking the time and trouble to write something out and (2) that written free-response comment being so unambiguous as to leave no doubt about its intended meaning in the judgments of independent coders. Consider the potential number of students who may have also felt that they have no smoking urges, but responded to the question simply by leaving all the responses unchecked. Consider how many students who provided vaguely worded comments would have been included in this category if the survey had included a precise question. Thus, one could argue that this makeshift

(Continued)

variable provided a very conservative estimate of the strength of this con-struct—the self-perceived absence of urges—on students' policy violation behavior. We took the lesson. When we repeated the survey in 2018, we essentially kept the same question but added a new option: "I don't need to do anything to handle the desire to smoke or vape."

As this example illustrates, sometimes an ad hoc procedure to create new variables can add substantially to your data analysis and your under-standing of the data. It helps to be prepared to make adjustments on the fly. Admittedly, however, if you can anticipate a phenomenon, your evidence about it will be much more precise, and proper planning will save you a great deal of time and extra effort.

The Ethical Limits of Fishing

If you have experience with analyzing data sets, you are probably familiar with what are sometimes called *fishing expeditions*. Perhaps the core analysis did not find statistically significant results on the outcomes of primary interest. Well, the analyst says, let's dig deeper. There must be *something* significant within all those data. Maybe the intervention was effective for sixth graders but not fifth graders. Maybe it was effective for low achievers but not high achievers. Maybe it was effective for…. You get the idea. We are going fishing for something—anything—that we can report. All in all, a fairly disreputable and unsavory affair.

On the flip side, however, isn't this also what we call exploratory ana-lyses? And isn't it a good thing to explore our data very thoroughly, so that we understand the inner workings of our program? So is all this supple-mental activity desirable or undesirable? To summarize, when is it OK to fish and when is it not? How much fishing can one do? What are the ethical limits of data exploration?

Different scholars will have different takes on this dilemma. Indeed, researchers have described past attempts to drag respectable results out of a data set (e.g., Gorman & Huber, 2009). For my part, I think the difference lies in several essential principles. These include *transparency, rigor,* and—to use House's (1980) terminology again—*coherence.*

Transparency in interpretation. If you love data, you probably also love taking a data set and turning it inside out, in all the different ways that you can imagine. (And if you don't love data, there might be someone on your project team who does. Or you might do this activity just as well but without the same level of enthusiasm.) Putting a good face on this activity, it can be seen as thoroughness. Putting a pejorative face on it, it is fishing.

In diving deeper into the data, being transparent about your purposes and expectations is self-protective. That is part of the value of specifying your core analyses at the outset. The ways that you intend to analyze your primary evaluation questions will be specified in advance, but when you have conducted those analyses to answer those questions, further explorations can have important value. Indeed, in many cases, that is how programs get improved.

Rigor. One way that rigor comes into play is in the number of statistical tests you are conducting. If you conduct an unreasonably large number of tests until you find something that you like, those results will not be convincing. What is the definition of "unreasonably large"? That remains to be resolved with your stakeholders and attentive critics of your study.

Coherence. A guiding principle can be: does the new analysis make sense? If you are analyzing your data for differential effects across categories of an important demographic variable, one that will make sense to the evaluation stakeholders, that analysis can be well justified. The new finding will be *coherent*. In this type of scenario you are not trying to deny that your originally intended analysis may have turned out to be a disappointment. Rather, you are going further, looking under the surface, and trying to shed further light. On the other hand, if you have eventually found a significant effect for, let's say, fifth grade boys from two-parent families—but not sixth grade boys from two-parent families or any other crossings of these categories—there is indeed no coherence. If you try to argue to your stakeholders that that subgroup has meaning on its own, they will most likely see through the attempt at misrepresentation.

Analysis Decisions and Adjustments

Analysis Decisions Related to the Evaluation Measures and Scores

It frequently happens that scores are adjusted in the data analysis process. That is, the scores are originally collected in a certain format, which is changed in one or more of the analyses. This is perhaps not surprising, since scores often need to be used for a number of purposes. The formats of measures, e.g., the response scales of questions, exist beforehand and might need to be adjusted to meet the requirements of a data analysis approach. Very often, the change takes the form of simplifying the distribution of a variable's scores. For example, a question's five-point rating scale may follow a standard Likert-type format (1 = strongly disagree, 2 = disagree, 3 = neutral, 4 = agree, 5 = strongly agree), which is then reduced in the analysis phase to just two levels: *agree* (made up of responses 4 and 5) and *does not agree* (including the neutral response, made up of responses 1–3).

One common reason why this is done is to allow the measure to be used in an analysis that requires a dichotomous dependent variable, such as a binomial logistic regression. These regression results are relatively easy to communicate and absorb: a particular level of a categorical independent variable, compared to a different level of that variable, may be associated with some greater odds of the dichotomous event happening.

But there is a cost and downside for this simplicity of explanation: every time responses are combined, you are giving up information. In the example cited, the respondents who feel strongly are combined with those who feel mildly. In such cases, one should consider whether there are data analysis options that can do a better job of preserving the variability within the data set. Keeping with the regression example, an alternative approach may be ordinal logistic regression, which can take account of a larger number of potential values for the dependent variable. But this procedure is more complicated to run, to analyze, and to explain. It may also require more stringent assumptions about the distributions of variables in the data set. Thus the choice of data analysis strategy can be complex and must take account of relevant trade-offs.

Another instance of score simplification may occur if the analyst does a median split, simply creating a new variable that divides the sample into two equal segments on the variable of interest. This may happen with an independent predictor variable that is not considered to be of primary importance in the program theory, but which the analyst nevertheless wants to include. For example, a median split might be conducted on students' grade point average or annual family income. In addition, a median split or other kind of division of the sample may be conducted to create a grouping variable that will be used in a two-way analysis of variance.

Analysis Decisions Related to the Evaluation Participants

Differences in program dosage. For many kinds of programs it is likely that the amount of program exposure will vary among participants, and thus the concept of *program dosage* can become an important consideration in trying to understand a program's impact. This can be particularly relevant for an educational program consisting of a series of class sessions, in which some participants will have attended more sessions than others. Program dosage is also a relevant consideration if the treatment consists of adherence to a regimen, e.g., of exercise or diet, and participants vary in their degree of adherence. In this latter case, determining level of adherence can be a measurement challenge, but it would usually involve self-report or the use of devices such as pedometers that can track activity levels. Assuming that we can have reliable knowledge of participants' varying level of attendance or adherence, should individuals with differing program dosage levels be treated equivalently in the analysis?

In these instances multiple analysis approaches will prove useful. The conservative approach would be to treat all members within a study's treatment condition equivalently, whereas a more liberal approach could include level of program dosage as an independent variable in a separate analysis. For example, program dosage could be examined in an analysis of variance framework or included as a predictor variable in a regression analysis of outcome scores. Consideration would need to be given to the scaling of the dosage variable, but a simple classification scheme could identify, e.g., high, medium, and low exposure.

One might reasonably expect that dosage level will predict strength of program effect to at least some degree, although this may not always be the case. Thus, for example, an analysis may reveal that those who attended regularly showed an impressive gain in outcome scores while those who attended sporadically showed little change. In that case, if the proportion of frequent attendees was small, the overall mean gain of program participants might be modest. However, that overall result for the treatment sample taken as a whole would be masking the outcome that program benefit did accrue for those who attended regularly. Further, this pattern may suggest that the limited success in getting people to attend is a significant problem for the program. All of this information could prove valuable for the program staff and other stakeholders and could provide an important basis for decisions about program revision.

Participant dropout from the intervention but not the study. It may sometimes happen that program participants drop out of the intervention early on but may be available to participate in the postintervention measurement, e.g., if the evaluation study provides a monetary incentive for completing the measures. Program dropout can be viewed as the low-end level of program dosage. In such cases it is still appropriate to include these individuals in the measurement and analysis, if at all possible. Many methodologists recommend that the data analysis should incorporate an *Intention-to-Treat* (ITT) framework (Detry & Lewis, 2014), in which all originally assigned program participants are included in the analysis, even if they dropped out of the program partway through and even if they never participated at all. One of the logical arguments in support of ITT is that loss of participants may in fact be due to a deficiency of the program. Perhaps it is too dull or too long, or perhaps its particular characteristics are poorly matched with a particular subset of its intended audience. Given such limitations, so the argument goes, it would be highly misleading to ignore participants who might well have produced low scores but didn't hang around long enough to do so. Thus, attempts are made to maintain full participation in the evaluation study, even if not in the program itself, by everyone in the original program group.

The ITT analysis is the most rigorous and stringent option for the core analysis. But it is also conservative because the scores of individuals who have had little or no exposure to the program will contribute to the assessment of program effectiveness. Therefore, secondary analyses can be done in which one examines the treatment in terms of actual participation, that is, the program group consists of those who did indeed experience the program. This is an analysis approach called *Treatment-on-the-Treated* (TOT) (Rossi et al., 2019). Including both kinds of analysis will generally provide the most comprehensive picture of the relationship between intervention and outcome.

Breakdowns in group membership. For an evaluation that involves multiple groups, it may happen during the course of the study that the original assignment of group membership will break down to some extent. Students assigned to one class may be switched to a different class that is getting a different treatment. Or, if the evaluation involves applying the treatment conditions on an individual rather than group basis, the assigned treatment might not be followed in one or more individual cases. Boruch (1997) describes a randomized study in the field of criminology examining the options of arrest versus mediation in incidents involving misdemeanor offenses related to domestic disputes. The evaluators found that in several instances the police officer making a domestic call spontaneously decided to apply the action opposite to the one assigned for that case. That is, some cases that had been randomly assigned to the mediation condition resulted in arrest and vice versa. Wouldn't it be misleading, one might argue, for the analysis to follow the original study condition assignments, e.g., categorizing individuals who were not arrested as if they had been arrested?

Indeed, most methodologists contend that ITT is the most appropriate analysis approach for randomized controlled trials, in order to maintain the integrity of the randomized assignment process and to allow for internal validity of the study's conclusions. Boruch (1997) states this principle as "Analyze them as you have randomized them" (p. 203). From a practical viewpoint, one compelling justification for using ITT is that, as with the case of program nonattendance described earlier, the breakdown in assignment may well be related in some way to the implementation or the effectiveness of the intervention.

Analysis Decisions Related to Defining and Understanding the Intervention

What counts as program fidelity, and how should it be represented? As discussed in Chapter 4, *program fidelity* refers to the accuracy with which the program was presented. It is common, even expected, that in a setting involving different delivery sites and different program presenters, the sites will differ in the fidelity of delivery. In the evaluation planning stages it is important to devise techniques to be able to capture and assess program fidelity. In the analysis stage we confront the task of analyzing how the sites did and what needs to be done about it.

One way of dealing with variations in program fidelity is a *threshold* strategy: certain minimum standards are applied to all of the cases, and those cases that fall below the threshold are eliminated from the analysis.

In our evaluation of the Project 4-Health tobacco prevention education curriculum delivered through the 4-H Youth Development Program (D'Onofrio et al., 2002), introduced in Chapter 4, the program was delivered in each 4-H club by a two-person volunteer team made up of a teen and a parent. The teams received training in program delivery before the study began. They were given detailed guidance on the materials to cover in each of the five sessions and on the content they should communicate. Not surprisingly, we found that there were important differences across sites in how closely the guidance was followed. In one of our extreme cases, the adult member of the team described to the youth that with regard to health, smokeless tobacco was a preferable alternative to smoking cigarettes. This deviated sharply from one of our core messages, which was that all forms of tobacco should be avoided. Thus this was judged to be a site with low fidelity of program delivery. But how should it be handled?

After examining the audio recordings of all program sites, our evaluation team made judgments about the acceptability of the level of fidelity at the sites, and we applied a threshold strategy to these judgments. Two program sites that were below the threshold of acceptability were eliminated from the analysis.

What were the validity implications of this decision strategy? By excluding the program sites that did not meet minimum standards of program fidelity, though this number was small, we steered our analysis toward being able to draw conclusions based on *efficacy*—looking at the intervention as it *should be* delivered – rather than *effectiveness*—looking at the intervention as it was actually delivered after all proper preparations had been made. These are two different kinds of analyses. Which of the two was more relevant to our overall evaluation purposes? That is a question that must be applied to every phase of the evaluation, including design and implementation.

The Creation of New Evaluation Questions

In conducting your analyses, you need to answer (or at least attempt to do so with your data set) your primary evaluation questions, which have been designated before the study was conducted. It is also valuable to explore whatever critical questions may have been uncovered by the first pass through the data. This could involve identifying critical covariates, demographics, personal characteristics, or setting characteristics. It could involve looking for what kinds of participants the intervention did and did not work for. It could involve identifying the most important characteristics of the program setting. It could proceed from an implementation evaluation in which certain program components were identified. Some of the program components that differ across sites are identifiable before a study is conducted. For example, in the Project 4-Health evaluation just described (D'Onofrio et al., 2002), we strongly suspected that club size (number of youth members) was going to have an impact on delivery success, for the simple reason that it is more difficult to manage program delivery to a large group of 80–90 youth than a small group of 10–15 youth. In addition, some of the important program components will be discoverable only after your study has begun or been completed.

You can attempt to answer all of those questions, planned and post hoc, but no evaluation is fully comprehensive. All analyses will lead to a trail of other questions. For example, now that you have a relatively good handle on factor X, you would like to explore how X interacts with Z. The evaluation has created new questions that need to be explored and examined in future evaluation activity. If you have conducted your evaluation carefully, some of these new questions are sure to emerge.

Thus you should never assume that your evaluation will be definitive in providing the answers you need. As Cronbach (1982), Patton (2008), and other evaluation scholars have observed, our goal is to reduce uncertainty rather than to eliminate it entirely. It is true that your evaluation, if conducted in a summative framework, may be expected to answer certain critical questions that are currently uppermost in certain stakeholders' minds, but that does not rule out the possibility that the newly learned information will lead to further questions about the operation of the program. Addressing these new questions will help your understanding of the intervention to grow more comprehensive and sophisticated.

Chapter Summary

- The data analysis stage is a creative part of the evaluation process. The core analysis, which is the designated approach for answering the primary evaluation questions, should be specified at an earlier stage of planning the study. But in addition to the core analysis there will often be numerous opportunities to conduct additional analyses to answer secondary questions and newly introduced questions. In addition, the data analysis plan may need to be adapted to account for unanticipated deviations in measurement that occurred during data collection.

- Statistical conclusion validity is concerned with two kinds of inferences: whether there is covariation between the intervention and the target outcome(s), and if so, what the strength of those relationships are.

- Type I and Type II errors represent different sides of the coin with regard to drawing conclusions about whether relationships between variables exist within a population. A Type I error is a false positive, concluding that there is a relationship between variables when in fact there is none. Conversely, a Type II error is a false negative, concluding that a relationship does not exist when in fact it really does. However, neither of these "errors" implies that a mistake was made by the data analyst. Rather, they occur because of anomalies in the sample(s) from which we draw our data.

- Null hypothesis significance testing (NHST) is an approach to drawing meaning and arriving at conclusions from a data analysis. It has long been dominant in the social sciences, including the disciplinary traditions of evaluation research and the study of social interventions. However, NHST has been criticized, primarily because it is based on using an artificial cutoff point for making binary statistical decisions regarding whether a relationship exists, i.e., significant versus not significant. Several prominent statisticians have recommended ways to reduce the role of statistical significance tests in data analysis, which include giving more attention to effect sizes than to statistical significance, utilizing confidence interviews, and paying more attention to the replicability of findings across multiple studies.

- You will often need to consider a number of decisions about how to conduct your data analysis. These decisions may include:

  - What kinds of analyses to undertake.

  - Which analyses you should try in multiple ways.

  - How to address individual differences in intervention dosage.

  - How to handle the scores on your measures, e.g., through score transformations.

  - How to include your secondary variables in the analysis.

  - Which participants to keep or remove from the analyses (and why).

  - How to characterize multiple sites, and how to operationalize the ways that they differ from each other.

- Post hoc and exploratory data analyses can yield a good deal of useful information about the intervention, outcomes, and other variables that are addressed in the evaluation. However, the results of the core analysis, which was part of the evaluation plan, should also be prominently reported. In that way, you can alleviate concerns that your detailed analysis is a fishing expedition that looks for any significant results to report, in order to make the intervention look good.

Questions for Reflection—Chapter 8

1. What are the ways in which the data analysis phase of an evaluation study is related to evaluation validity?

2. Why is identifying the intended *core analysis*, as part of the evaluation planning process, important for the credibility of the evaluation?

3. What are some ways in which program dosage—the amount of the program that a participant has received—can be incorporated into the data analysis process?

    •   What is the *intent to treat* approach in data analysis? What are its strengths? Why is it considered to be a conservative approach to studying the intervention's effects?

4. As this chapter describes, the concepts underlying null hypothesis significance testing (NHST) are often misinterpreted by audiences for an evaluation.

    •   What are the strengths and weaknesses of NHST?

    •   What are some of the most common ways in which NHST is misunderstood?

    •   If you have prior experience with evaluation, how have you found that stakeholders regard the importance and relevance of statistically significant results for arriving at evaluation conclusions? How do individual stakeholders or stakeholder groups tend to differ from each other in these perspectives?

Evaluation Conclusions and Recommendations

This book is about achieving consistency and congruence between a study's evaluation questions and the conclusions that are eventually drawn to answer those questions. Thus, the processes of determining conclusions and recommendations, and communicating them, are the final steps in that sequence.

Evaluation differs from other forms of social science inquiry in that it involves making assessments about the value—the merit or worth—of its objects of study, in addition to describing and explaining those objects. An evaluation will typically produce a great deal of new information in the form of data and analyses. The evaluator must organize and interpret disparate sets of evidence and ultimately reduce and synthesize them to arrive at summary statements that answer the evaluation questions. That process of synthesis goes beyond the mere recitation of findings and is reflected in the development of conclusions that address whether the program or policy is worthwhile.

How are evaluation conclusions related to the concept of validity? Recall that Shadish et al. (2002) defined validity as "the approximate truth of an inference" (p. 34). Similarly, House (1980) writes: "As Cronbach asserts, it is not the test or the data collection procedures themselves so much as the interpretations that are valid or invalid. This is the validity of an inference. Is the inference correctly derived from the data and premises?" (p. 90). Evaluation conclusions *are* those inferences, the realizations of what has been learned from all of the previous steps making up the evaluation study. Viewed in this light, the quality of evaluation conclusions can be thought of as the acid test for all of the study's prior decisions and processes intended to optimize evaluation validity.

Evaluation conclusions provide the takeaways from the study, but in too many evaluations the conclusions appear to be superficially constructed, without evidence of real thought having gone into what the obtained results mean. For example, if results of a two-group study show that the treatment group performed better than the comparison group on outcomes A and B but not outcomes C and D, the conclusions might be nothing more than a restatement of that finding, perhaps with an overall statement such as, "Evidence of effectiveness is mixed." Here are just a few questions that a more integrated process of interpretation might take account of:

- How did the obtained effect sizes match the original expectations for those outcomes?

- How do the effect sizes compare with the evaluation's (or stakeholders') explicit standards for what would be considered important?

- How do the isolated outcome results fit together to provide a full picture?

- What should happen now with regard to this intervention?

Synthesizing the Evaluation's Results to Arrive at Conclusions

Michael Scriven proposed a general logic of evaluation that applies broadly across evaluation contexts (Schwandt, 2015; Scriven, 1994, 2012). The model consists of four major steps:

- Determining criteria of merit. These criteria are operationalized in the variables that are being measured.

- Determining standards of merit. This step involves specifying expectations about good, acceptable, or unacceptable performance on the criteria.

- Measuring performance. This step comprises the data collection and analyses.

- Synthesizing the results to produce an overall judgment.

That last step is given relatively little attention in the evaluation literature. Scriven contends that all evaluation activity must include a process of valuing, that is, a determination of the merit, worth, or significance of the thing being evaluated. Other theorists' definitions of evaluation are broader and can encompass questions that are purely descriptive, such as asking about the degree of program fidelity or levels of program attendance. Nevertheless, one could argue that even for these descriptive questions, there is virtually always an implication that some type of judgment about quality or comparison to a standard will be applied, which is what makes the information useful and actionable.

For example, an evaluation question may ask about the level of fidelity with which a program is being delivered. Perhaps several fidelity-related outcomes will be identified for measurement and some of those outcomes will be measured using multiple strategies. When the observations have been logged and the evaluation team is assessing the results, what will be the process for synthesizing that complex array of information? And what will be the basis for determining whether the fidelity is, e.g., "moderate" or "low," "marginally acceptable" or "unacceptable"?

As described in Chapter 4, Esbensen et al. (2011) tackled the issue of implementation fidelity in a multisite process evaluation of a school-based gang resistance education program for adolescents. The 13-lesson program was taught by law enforcement officers in middle-school classrooms. The evaluators' numerous dimensions of program delivery fidelity included officer preparedness, officers' time management, classroom management, coverage of program material, and other features. The measurement of these variables included both objective data (e.g., average number of minutes per class session) and observers' global judgments (e.g., ratings of students' engagement with the lesson material). In arriving at conclusions, how are these diverse, and frequently inconsistent, bodies of data to be combined? Should the conclusion take the form of a single overriding conclusion about fidelity, or a series of categorical assessments? This illustrates the challenge of synthesis, and helps us to understand what Scriven (1991) meant when he declared, in his *Evaluation Thesaurus*: "Synthesis is perhaps the key cognitive skill in evaluation" (p. 345).

This final phase of the evaluation process—synthesis and judgment—can be complicated, especially when multiple sources of data have to be consolidated and weighed, and is often overlooked as a core evaluation competency. Schwandt (2015) has observed:

> [T]he final step in the logic of evaluation is synthesis—integrating results into an overall judgment of value. This is a particularly difficult task because the processes by which synthesis judgments are made is not well understood, and there is little consensus in the field of evaluation about how to aggregate findings across multiple criteria or across stakeholders' differing perspectives on important criteria. Somewhat ironically for a practice concerned with making warranted judgments of value, the lack of explicit justification for a synthesis procedure continues to be regarded as the Achilles' heel of the practice. (p. 59)

Providing Recommendations

Many evaluations include recommendations for action or for further consideration. These can be distinguished from the evaluation conclusions per se. Whereas the conclusions represent the synthesis of what has been learned from the study and the judgments about the intervention's effectiveness, costs, overall value, and so forth, recommendations point to concrete decisions and actions regarding what can or should be done moving forward into the future. Michael Patton (2008) describes their inherent appeal to stakeholders: "Recommendations, when they are included in a report, draw readers' attention like bees to a flower's nectar. Many report readers will turn to recommendations before anything else. Some never read beyond the recommendations" (p. 502).

Needless to say, recommendations should lead logically out of the evaluation's conclusions. But in addition, the usefulness of recommendations—as suggestions for future action—relies on budgetary, organizational, and political contexts within which the intervention has been delivered and will be delivered in the future. Many of these factors may be external to the specifics of the evaluation study. When the evaluator is deciding about what to recommend for future courses of action, the number of relevant external elements that come into play can be daunting.

For example, let's suppose that a program has been found to be promising while nevertheless containing some areas that need significant improvement. There might or might not be time, money, and staff available to produce the revision that will improve the product. Similarly, if a program has been found to be exemplary, the prospects for expanding it to wider audiences will depend on factors outside of the program's actual merits. In these cases, the necessary information to make those determinations will typically not have been part of the evaluation itself. And if the evaluator consults with stakeholders to explore these possibilities, different stakeholders will often have contrasting perspectives on what is desirable or possible. For these reasons the evaluator is on more precarious ground when compiling recommendations than when making overall judgments about quality that are based on the collected evidence. In essence, a second data-gathering investigation is needed.

This does not mean that evaluators should refrain from offering recommendations, but the process is knotty and complex. Patton (2008, pp. 502–504) offers ten guidelines for developing and communicating useful and practical recommendations. A theme running through all of the guidelines is that the evaluator needs to communicate closely with the evaluation's primary intended users at all phases of the study—including before data are collected—to establish the parameters and expectations of the recommendation process. For example, Patton notes that different stakeholders will have their own preferences for how recommendations are to be formatted: some may prefer receiving a list of options for action, accompanied by the pros and cons for each, while others prefer that a single course of action is highlighted. He also suggests that recommendations could be organized and distinguished from each other on any of a number of bases, e.g., the degree of support from the collected evidence, the time frame required for implementation (short vs. long term), or the relevance for particular stakeholder groups such as funders, program administrators, staff, and participants.

Because recommendations are a type of inference, these considerations relate directly to validity. In this regard, House's (1980) validity model is particularly helpful. House identifies the hallmarks of validity as truth (or credibility), coherence, and justice. With regard to recommendations, *truth* is reflected in the justification and clarity with which the recommendations lead out of the conclusions. *Coherence* is reflected in the ways that recommendations are structured and communicated. And *justice* is reflected in an understanding of which stakeholder audiences will benefit from the actions and decisions inherent in the recommendations. However, the extent to which recommendations depend on factors extrinsic to the evaluation itself means that their validity may be especially hard to establish.

Framing the Problem

One aspect of the *truth* of a set of recommendations is the comprehensiveness with which the potential options for action have been compiled and considered. Have all relevant possibilities been proposed? Have any been overlooked? If a program has been found to have fallen short of its goals, what options for further action should be on the table?

House (1983) contended that the search for programmatic and policy solutions—that is, the attempt to address the question, *What needs to be done?*—is dependent on how we have framed the original problem that the intervention has been designed to address. In seeking to understand a social problem, all observers—policymakers, legislators, educators, program developers, program staff, program participants, evaluators—will frame the problem in certain ways through the use of simplifying metaphors. House noted that metaphors are necessary ingredients of human cognition, and that we naturally classify complex or unfamiliar phenomena into schemes and categories with which we are already familiar, in an attempt to better understand them. When metaphorical thinking is applied to social conditions, several challenges emerge: the relationship of metaphor to reality will always be imperfect; some metaphors will be more useful or accurate than others; and the guiding metaphors will not necessarily be consistent or compatible across observers.

The metaphor highlights which features will have greatest significance for interpreting the phenomenon, often in ways of which we are unaware

(Kaminsky, 2000). Different metaphors will highlight different features of the problem, leading in turn to selective identification of the primary options for solving it (Archibald, 2020). These options will often come to embody the recommendations offered by the evaluation. Knowing how the problem is typically addressed within the frame of the metaphor suggests the potential solutions for the problem at hand. Thus there will be constraints on the range of solutions that are proposed and some potential solutions will be missed. House (1983) provided an illustration involving urban community development:

> For example, urban renewal can be viewed in different ways. The slum can be seen as a once healthy community that has become diseased. A social planner with such an image envisions wholesale redesign and reconstruction as the cure to urban blight. However, the slum can also be viewed as a viable, low-income community, which offers its residents important social benefits. The second view obviously implies strikingly different prescriptions for improving the community. (p. 8)

As an example from the field of human development, consider the history of school-based programs that aim to promote adolescent sexual health and prevent pregnancy and sexually transmitted diseases. These programs have evolved over several generations of theory and practice. Early efforts (e.g., prior to the 1990s) characterized themselves as *prevention* programs, and focused on preventing intercourse and other sexual behaviors that carry risk of disease. These risky behaviors were considered in relation to developmental timing, and the programmatic goal was often to delay them until adulthood. By contrast, more recent programs view adolescent sexuality more comprehensively as a dimension of healthy normal development and peer relationships. In this view, a strategy that focuses solely on a goal of delaying certain behaviors ignores the fact that important development processes are being actively navigated during these years, processes that need to be considered in the theory underlying the program.

A perspective that views early sexual activity as a problem behavior needing prevention will lean toward certain approaches and emphases for both the educational program and its evaluation, while a perspective that views such activity within the frame of healthy sexual development will lean toward a different set of approaches and emphases. In this example, the competing frames—*prevention of high-risk problem behaviors* versus *healthy adolescent development*—are not incompatible with each other, which is not always the case with competing frames. But they would nevertheless imply different choices about evaluation criteria (operationalized by the choice of which outcomes to track) and standards for judging those criteria. As one illustration, a recent evaluation of a comprehensive sexual health curriculum included, as secondary outcomes, adolescents' comfort in communicating with each of their parents about sexual health (Coyle et al., 2021). I doubt that this target outcome would have been selected if the frame were one of preventing problem behaviors. And, of course, if an outcome doesn't get measured we will not be able to learn about the program's impact in influencing it.

For a policy-related example, consider the treatment of drug offenses. Historically, illicit drug use and addiction have been alternately framed as primarily a criminal justice problem or primarily a health problem (Babor et al., 2019; Pardo and Reuter, 2018). In federal drug control policy, the former concept held sway between the 1970s and 1990s, while the latter concept became more prominent in the early 2000s. A metaphor of *drug abuse as crime* will focus on punitive tools of criminal justice, such as aggressive prosecutions and mandatory minimum sentence requirements for convicted users. Conversely, a metaphor of *drug abuse as illness* will suggest policy solutions that emphasize diversion of offenders from the criminal justice system and therapeutic treatments for addiction. Relevant options suggested by this metaphor have included drug courts, medical maintenance programs (e.g., methadone or opioid substitution therapy), drug treatment programs for incarcerated addicts, and harm reduction strategies such as needle exchange programs or safe consumption sites (Babor et al., 2019; Pardo & Reuter, 2018).[1] As Reuter (2013) observed, "The idea that 'addiction is a brain disease,' promoted initially by the National Institute on Drug Abuse and now a part of federal government rhetoric generally, whatever its programmatic and conceptual weaknesses, at least has provided a basis for talking in a more therapeutic and less exclusively moralized frame about criminally active drug addicts" (p. 77).

The metaphors that serve as frames for interpreting social problems and generating potential solutions are also influenced strongly by the cultural perspectives and biases of an individual or group (Hood et al., 2015: Kirkhart, 2005). The influences of culture are ubiquitous but individuals may not be completely conscious of those influences, or of the ensuing constraints on their thinking, idea generation, and problem solving approaches. One implication is that diversity of cultural background can be a significant strength in the process of interpreting evaluation findings and generating possible follow-up actions based on those findings. An awareness and appreciation of cultural inclusivity can help diverse stakeholders to analyze a social problem in a more comprehensive way.

---

[1]Rejection of the punitive, criminal justice model of drug use has also led to emphases on decriminalization and legalization of certain drugs for recreational use, as has occurred with cannabis (e.g., Fischer et al., 2021). But this policy approach represents an alternate set of potential solutions pertaining to issues of drug use in society, which fall outside of the frame of viewing drug use in medical terms.

The Validity of Conclusions From Campbell's Validity Perspective

The Campbellian validity model can help us to examine the different ways in which the accuracy of evaluation conclusions can be either compromised or strengthened. Table 9.1 presents several characteristic kinds of errors, organized around the four validity subtypes (Shadish et al., 2002). The

---

TABLE 9.1 ● Data Interpretation Errors That Can Weaken the Validity of Evaluation Conclusions

Errors related to statistical conclusion validity

1. *Misinterpreting the meaning of a statistically significant result.*

A statistical significance test tells us only how confident we can be that the difference tested is not equal to zero. It is not an estimate of effect size, and a very low *p* value does not necessarily imply that the difference between two sets of scores (e.g., intervention and control) is large or meaningful in either a practical or a theoretical way.

2. *Cherry picking the study's results.*

Most evaluations incorporate numerous analyses, targeting multiple outcomes and different sample subgroups. "Cherry picking" is the practice of highlighting desirable results while downplaying undesirable results, in an attempt to present favorable conclusions about the overall success of the program.

3. *Ignoring the role of low statistical power when interpreting a nonsignificant result.*

Low statistical power is a problem that plagues many evaluations, and may be due to using a sample of insufficient size, using unreliable measures, or other factors. In the face of nonsignificant results an evaluator might conclude that the intervention is ineffective, which would not be justified if the study's power was low.

4. *Neglecting to account for errors in the analytical approach.*

Analytical errors may arise from incorrect applications of methodological procedures or from violation of assumptions. One example: not using multilevel modeling for nested data, such as would occur when each study condition comprises multiple school classrooms. The evaluator may or may not be aware of such errors, or may be tempted to disregard them when drawing conclusions, in the interests of presenting a stronger, simpler, and more decisive description of findings.

TABLE 9.1 ● *(Continued)*

5. *Assuming that a finding of No Significant Difference serves as strong evidence that the tested groups are equal on the outcome measured.*

A lack of statistical significance means that the null hypothesis cannot be rejected, but that is not the same as the null being proved. Making a definitive conclusion that two populations are equal because a statistical test was nonsignificant is a misinterpretation.

Errors related to internal validity

6. *Overconfidence from a weak design.*

A weak design, such as a single-group pre-post design, will sometimes be used when conditions demand it and stronger alternatives are unavailable. But those weaknesses must be recognized when drawing conclusions. If a positive result is obtained, e.g., substantial growth in an outcome between pre and post, it would not be justified to definitively attribute that result to intervention effectiveness without acknowledging the study's inability to rule out other potential explanations.

7. *Ignoring a broken-down design.*

A design may be quite strong before it is implemented but break down in various ways once the study is underway, e.g., through extensive attrition or a compromised randomization procedure. The design as planned is not necessarily equivalent to the design as implemented, and it is an error to disregard design weaknesses that have been introduced.

8. *Rigidity or overcautiousness in the analytical approaches that inform the conclusions.*

Different types of data analysis contribute different insights. Certain approaches, e.g., intention-to-treat analysis (ITT), are rigorous but can be highly conservative in some contexts, leading to very conservative conclusions about intervention effectiveness. Including alternative analysis strategies can allow for a more complete picture of the intervention to emerge.

Errors related to construct validity

9. *Misconstruing the intervention that was assessed.*

Interventions can evolve, improve, or break down between the stages of planning and implementation. When the evaluator concludes, "This intervention was effective in producing growth on Outcome X," what intervention, exactly, are we talking about? Stakeholders may come away with the belief that the intervention *as described on paper* is the one that was tested, when in fact the picture is more nuanced.

(Continued)

TABLE 9.1 ● *(Continued)*

10. *Misconstruing the outcomes that were measured.*

The correspondence between the study's specific measures and the general constructs they are intended to represent (see Chapter 5) may not be strong. Consequently, conclusions about intervention effectiveness that are worded in terms of those general constructs (e.g., "reading skills," "resilience," "vocational aspirations," "drug use") may be faulty.

11. *Misconstruing the participants in the evaluation.*

An evaluation may be conducted using a pool of participants who do not exactly match the program's intended audience, e.g., using a sample of sixth graders for the evaluation of a curriculum designed for grades 4–6. The evaluation's conclusions might ignore that limitation, and the evaluation's relevance for certain populations may be therefore mischaracterized.

Errors related to external validity

12. *Overgeneralization of the intervention's causal mechanisms.*

An evaluation study may find that an intervention was (or was not) effective with a particular sample under particular circumstances. But it would not be warranted to go on to conclude that the observed causal processes will broadly operate (or fail to operate) in all other settings (e.g., "This study shows that Intervention X works"), without careful analysis of why those results were obtained in the present case.

13. *Inadequate assessment of how differences between the study setting and a target setting might affect the operation of causal mechanisms.*

The previous point refers to conclusions that are generalized widely to a broad array of other settings. It may also happen that practitioners wish to generalize from the evaluation's setting to their own local circumstances. It would not be warranted to conclude that the same result will be automatically repeated (i.e., "What happened there will happen here") without a close comparison of the two settings. Note that this is a conclusion that would probably be drawn not by the original evaluator but rather by an external stakeholder.

subtypes are presented in order of increasing complexity with regard to generating evaluative conclusions. Statistical conclusion validity and internal validity are discussed first because they deal with judgments involving factors that are fully within the purview of the study itself. The two subtypes that deal with processes of generalization—construct validity and external validity—are presented last because they require judgments that extend beyond the specifics of the study at hand.

Both evaluators and other stakeholders are susceptible to these errors, but stakeholders will typically be more prone to them because they tend not to have the necessary specialized expertise. This highlights the importance of evaluators including primary stakeholders in the process of interpreting findings and drawing conclusions (Patton, 2008), as well as being aware of the takeaway messages that are being formed. In addition, it underscores the importance of evaluative thinking (Buckley et al., 2015) being practiced by all parties to an evaluation.

In this section we will take a closer look at several of these types of errors.

Statistical Conclusion Validity

As we have seen, this type of validity considers the accuracy of claims related to two types of questions: (1) whether a relationship between variables exists and (2) how strong that relationship is. Statistical conclusion validity is strongly tied to how well the study conclusions reflect the data analyses on which they are based. Table 9.1 lists several typical types of errors and misinterpretations that can result in an inadequate match between our statistical findings and our conclusions.

Error 1 can occur if the evaluators or stakeholders misinterpret the basic meaning of a statistical test of the difference between two mean scores: whether or not that difference is zero. Obtaining a p value of .001, compared to, say, .045, does not mean that the group difference is larger in the first case than in the second. Rather, it only means we can be more confident that the difference being tested really is not zero. The p value is, of course, sensitive to the size of the difference between sample groups, but it is also highly influenced by sample size and the control of error variance. Thus, as discussed in Chapter 8, the question of how much the groups differ from each other should be addressed with an estimate of effect size rather than—or in addition to—significance level.

A related and very common misinterpretation (though not strictly under the umbrella of statistical conclusion validity because it involves a judgment about the intervention's value) occurs if stakeholders consider statistical significance to be *the* essential indicator of intervention success (see Chapter 8). An intervention effect, even though we may be confident it is not zero, may still be quite small and not necessarily worth the investment of a new and complex intervention. Effect size must play a role in this judgment too.

Most of the errors identified in Table 9.1 can be attributed to a lack of thoroughness or understanding, but a few of them may result from deliberate decisions. An example of the latter variety is Error 2, "cherry picking," in which multiple analyses are conducted but the results are presented selectively in order to put the intervention in the best possible light. For stakeholders who have a commitment to a program, it will be very tempting to focus on only the most positive findings from a comprehensive evaluation and downplay the others. Of course, this creates a misleading and unbalanced view of what the study has found. It is incumbent on the evaluator to ensure that a comprehensive and objective picture is being presented.

A test case of how a process of dedicated cherry picking can produce a false appearance of program effectiveness was provided by Gorman and Huber (2009), in a demonstration exercise involving reanalysis of data from a large evaluation of the DARE (Drug Abuse Resistance Education) program that had been conducted by University of Kentucky researchers. The original evaluation concluded that DARE was ineffective in reducing adolescents' substance use (e.g., Clayton et al., 1996). However, Gorman and Huber, by dividing and slicing the data set in various ways, were able to show that numerous statistically significant treatment versus control differences could be produced at the seventh grade follow-up. One of their strategies was to conduct multiple subgroup analyses—e.g., by both gender and initial drug use status—for multiple drugs. Their point was to demonstrate that evaluation data can be manipulated to produce apparent evidence of effectiveness, which may in turn be sufficient to land programs on lists of approved, "evidence-based" drug prevention interventions (see Chapter 5).

The simplest remedy for these manipulations would be for evaluators to highlight their core analysis early on, as part of their evaluation plan, as discussed in Chapters 7 and 8. This early declaration provides a basis for understanding which analyses are considered to be top priority and which analyses are considered secondary, even though they might certainly be informative. This commitment discourages the possibility of cherry picking one's findings after the results are in.

Internal Validity

Considerations of internal validity when drawing study conclusions refer to those conclusions that address the cause of the results, most notably whether the delivery of the intervention caused any observed change in the outcome scores. How confident can we be in our conclusion about causality? That is, is there only one viable explanation for the results, or were there any plausible rival hypotheses that the study wasn't able to rule out?

Error 7 addresses the need to account for a broken-down design. A design may be quite strong before it is implemented, but once the study is underway it can become weakened in various ways (Reichardt, 2019). One area of breakdown that often occurs is study attrition, when participants leave the study before it is completed. This is an especially concerning problem when the level of attrition differs across the study conditions, being more pervasive in one or another of the sample groups. One can hypothesize reasons why participants may be especially likely to drop out of either the *program* condition (e.g., program participation is burdensome on daily schedules) or the *control* condition (e.g., participants feel they are spending a lot of time answering evaluators' questions and not getting anything in return). A certain amount of attrition should always be expected to occur if a study takes any length of time, but when it becomes extensive it can be a serious threat to the study. Evaluators might not know how to incorporate the effect of attrition into their conclusions, and therefore might just ignore it.

Another breakdown in design can come from a compromised randomization procedure. Some members of the control group may have found ways to switch over into the treatment group, or vice-versa. This could happen, for example, in a classroom-based evaluation study in which some parents feel strongly about their children being in either the new curriculum class or the traditional class, as a result of which the school administrators accommodate those families in order to maintain harmony.

Error 8 is rigidity or overcautiousness in the process of drawing conclusions from the data analyses. Different types of analysis contribute different insights, and it can be beneficial to plan for flexibility in one's analytic approach. An example is how to handle attrition from the intervention when it occurs over the course of the study. Relying solely on an Intention-to-Treat analysis framework (see Chapter 8), in which all originally assigned program participants are included in the analysis, even if they dropped out of the program midway and even if they never participated at all, is clearly conservative. Secondary analyses that focus on those individuals who had at least some minimal threshold of experience with the intervention (which can be defined in multiple ways), and which also take into account levels of program dosage, will allow for a more complete picture and deeper understanding of the program.

Construct Validity

With construct validity, our concern is whether the constructs implied in our conclusions match up appropriately with the realizations of those constructs as actually embodied in the evaluation study. For example, do the intervention(s), participants, and outcomes described in those conclusions follow from those that were part of the evaluation?

Error 9 involves potential discrepancies involving the intervention, e.g., the intervention as understood by stakeholders and the intervention that was actually delivered in the evaluation study. Interventions can, and often do, break down in any number of ways between the stages of planning and implementation. In Chapter 7, we saw an extreme case of this, the delivery of a 2-year-long preschool program that was interrupted by a major earthquake (Moreno et al., 2011). Under more ordinary circumstances, interventions can change form and go off-course due to vicissitudes in timing, physical space, available resources, presenter readiness, participant demand, or philosophical differences between principal players. They can also *improve* midcourse due to program staff members' alert adaptations to program elements that are not working well.

As a result, when the evaluator draws conclusions about intervention effectiveness, there needs to be clarity about how the intervention was delivered in this particular instance. Devoting attention in the evaluation to program implementation and fidelity will help to ensure that this occurs.

Similarly, Error 10 involves the correct interpretation and portrayal of the measured outcomes. Chapter 5 discussed how conceptions about constructs follow a sequence of ever-increasing specificity, such that initial conversations with stakeholders focus on general constructs and, through a series of steps, become operationalized into the measures that are used in the evaluation study. The process of drawing conclusions from the evaluation can often follow the opposite path. Colloquial, nontechnical statements about the study conclusions are likely to return to the general constructs that are found in everyday speech. Thus, for example, stakeholders may state: "This evaluation found that the new curriculum was superior to the standard curriculum in boosting students' reading skills." The fact that the reading test may have been either the Iowa Test of Basic Skills, the Woodcock Reading Mastery Test, a different standardized test, or a locally developed test becomes lost in the shuffle. Program stakeholders, guided by the evaluators, need to bear in mind that the accuracy of this conclusion is based on the use of a very specific outcome measure.

Specificity in describing the outcome measure can also help to ensure that the rigor of the measurement strategy is properly communicated. For example, if an evaluation of an academic skills program measures school grades through the use of students' self-report, the strong susceptibility of that measurement strategy to inflated estimates would make it advisable to refer to the outcome in the evaluation conclusions as "self-reported grades." Whether or not the program increased actual grades is open to conjecture, since actual grades were not observed.

External Validity

External validity bears close correspondence to construct validity in that we are talking about generalizing from the particulars of the study to the relative abstraction of the underlying concepts. But whereas construct validity focuses on the constructs that are represented by the study's samples, treatments, observations, and settings, external validity focuses on the generality of the casual relationship. Shadish et al. (2002) described it as follows: "For external validity generalizations, the inference concerns whether the size or direction of a causal relationship changes over persons, treatments, settings, or outcomes" (p. 94).

Error 12 addresses the potential pitfalls of overgeneralizing, that is, drawing broad conclusions from one study. An example of accuracy concerns regarding this form of validity was provided in Case Study 3.1. Recall that researchers in Washington State conducted a rigorous study to evaluate a school-based smoking prevention program. The results were disappointing, and led the authors to conclude that school-based programs, even those based on accepted "best practices," do not work. Thus the researchers were generalizing from their specific case of a school-based program to all instances of school-based smoking prevention efforts. I argued that the sweeping generalization contained in their conclusion might well be over-stated and was open for debate. Although their report indicated that the curriculum adhered to the conception of best practices that was in effect at the time the program was developed, nevertheless their study necessarily incorporated very specific instances of curriculum, measures, geographical location, and other contextual features. Generalization usually comes down to a process of argument, insight, and persuasion.

The Validity of Conclusions From House's Validity Perspective

In assessing validity, the Campbellian perspective focuses on truth and accuracy, in various forms. As we saw in Chapter 3, House's perspective differs in several ways. First, he spoke of validity as a feature of the evaluation itself, rather than solely of inferences, judgments, and knowledge claims. Second, he expanded the validity concept to include three distinct criteria: truth, coherence, and justice. Let's consider each of those criteria in turn, to see how they might help us understand the formulation of strong evaluation conclusions.

Truth

For an evaluation to be *true*, its conclusions must flow soundly from the design and analysis stages of the study, and must address the evaluation study's guiding questions. These aspects of accuracy have been treated in detail above through the discussion of the Campbellian four-part validity model. But House adds a new dimension to these considerations through his conceptualization of evaluation as a process of argument.

By framing evaluation as argument, House characterizes its primary goals as persuasion and practical utility, rather than a search for certainty and universal truth. This view has attained wide acceptance in recent years, largely due to House's writings, but it was unusual at the time of his 1980 book. In this respect evaluation differs from scientific inquiry, which is more concerned with describing, understanding, and predicting phenomena without regard for particular audiences who receive the information (although the extent to which objectivity in science is possible is a fundamental issue of debate within the philosophy of science). House wrote that he treats "science as an argument aimed at a universal audience and hence concerned with establishing long-term generalizations, and evaluation as an argument aimed at particular audiences dealing with context-bound issues" (House, 1980, pp. 84–85). In the case of evaluation, there is little question that the specific audiences for the evaluative information play a crucial role in determining the form of that information.

In the time that has elapsed since 1980, House also wrote more explicitly about the need for evaluation to be free of deliberate bias, considering this to be a feature of the "truth" dimension of evaluation validity. He used pharmaceutical drug studies as a prototypical example that sharply illustrates the problem of bias in evaluation:

> Companies have found ways to meet technical standards while biasing findings, such as suppressing negative results, publishing data selectively, censoring what they provide to data banks, and paying large consulting fees to those serving on FDA approval committees. In these circumstances the arguments for validity via technical adequacy fall short....That the study be true is still relevant, and we still necessarily depend on arguments to establish validity, but the particular arguments to ensure validity have shifted. (House, 2014, pp. 12–13)

What guidance for the development of evaluation conclusions can House's perspective on evaluation-as-argument provide? Primarily, it highlights the central importance of the audiences for a given evaluation. Conclusions need to be written so as to be accessible to the identified primary audiences. Usually, they can be developed using language that is comprehensible to all audiences, although in some cases it may be advantageous to express them in a more technical form for the evaluation's more sophisticated audiences. Thus, if a conclusion is written and presented in a way that is not clear and understandable to one or more of the primary audiences, its validity will be compromised, according to House.

House also maintained that the evaluation audience must play an active role in the assessment of an evaluation's conclusions. "Whoever the audience, in argumentation, the audience must share responsibility....It must actively choose how much it wishes to believe....This rational decision belongs to the audience, not to the evaluator" (House, 1980, p. 76).

Bottom line: As an evaluator, you must express your conclusions in a way that will be clear and persuasive for the evaluation's audiences, while also being accurate.

Coherence

For House, the *coherence* of an evaluation refers to how it is shaped and presented. If evaluation is seen as a process of argument, then the way that argument is framed and articulated will affect its persuasiveness. The relationship of coherence to truth is analogous to the relationship of form to content.

A coherently presented evaluation will be more convincing, more compelling, and more effective as a motivator for action in response to the findings. It creates a set of connections—a narrative—that links together the evaluation's components, *viz.*, the introduction of the social problem, the proposed intervention as a strategy for mitigating the problem, the collection and presentation of evidence (whether quantitative, qualitative, or both), and ultimately a judgment about the intervention's effectiveness and success in addressing the problem.

Not all evaluations are successful in achieving this goal. For example, Davidson (2014) describes an evaluation project on which she served as an advisor. She was involved in the development of the evaluation questions but did not participate in the data collection or analysis. She writes:

> When the first draft of the report came through, I was dismayed to see that the researchers had completely missed a critically important aspect of what we were doing that seemed blindingly obvious to me. The whole point of framing the evaluation around high-level questions in the first place was that we would actually answer them.
>
> As one might expect from highly competent applied researchers, the data collection instruments and the evidence collected were fine....The real issue lay in the coherence of how it was woven together—particularly the evaluative reasoning. Instead of considering the evidence as a set and weaving it together to create a compelling answer to that question, the evidence was laid out in separate sections (surveys and then interviews) and never synthesized, let along interpreted evaluatively to say how good the results were. (p. 35)

In other words, the problem with the evaluation lay in the deficiencies of its conclusions. The various findings from the study were presented without being integrated into a coherent whole message, and the form of the conclusions left the evaluation questions unanswered. Davidson contends that the ability to achieve this integration—that is, to bring evidence to bear in the practical sphere of interpreting social problems and making decisions about potential solutions—is one component of the evaluator's skill set that places evaluation apart from basic or applied research.

Justice

Given evaluation's focus on determining worth, the dimension of justice comes into play with consideration of the essential question: worthwhile for whom? Different stakeholder groups have diverse sets of interests that are not always consistent, or even compatible, with each other. Some stakeholder groups may get left out of the evaluation planning process and may not be considered over the course of the evaluation study. In this way, House (1980, 1993) contended, the determination of an intervention's worth becomes an inherently political issue. House also noted that the stakeholder groups that tend most often to be left out of the evaluation process are those from the less advantaged and less powerful strata of society. A commitment to social justice in evaluation will require that these voices be acknowledged, included, and given weight. The unequal power dynamics that underlie many evaluation contexts are also a central concern of Kirkhart's view of multicultural validity (Kirkhart, 2005, 2010; see Chapter 3).

As an example of the social justice implications that may be inherent in any evaluation, House reflected on his evaluation of an academic program for gifted students, which used the practice of ability-based grouping:

> In retrospect, the major weakness was that we did not investigate possible deleterious effects from grouping talented children together. We did investigate the effects on the gifted children themselves, but we did not investigate the effects on nongifted students nor consider the broader social impact on the class system. Admittedly, these are not easy questions to resolve, partly because they have not been asked often enough. But they should have been addressed more than they were. (House, 1980, p. 131)

How can the evaluator accommodate an array of diverse stakeholder interests in developing conclusions about an intervention's value? House (1995) provided a detailed analysis of this question, which builds on the components of evaluation logic for making judgments of value. To recap Scriven's four-step model described earlier in this chapter, these judgments require that the evaluator determine the criteria of interest, determine which of those criteria are more and less important, assess the performance in each of the criteria, and finally arrive at an integrated synthesis. Very often, stakeholders will disagree about what the criteria should be or how heavily each criterion should count. Nevertheless, House (1995) contended that it is often—certainly not always—possible for the evaluator to arrive at a single unified synthesis that incorporates these differences:

> Do we send our evaluation reports to our clients and let them decide how they wish to balance test scores against interviews, or correlations with discriminant analyses? Not likely. There is a sense in which evaluators have knowledge and information with which to balance these sometimes conflicting considerations. I believe the same is true regarding stakeholder views and interests if we understand what we are and are not doing. (pp. 41–42)

To be clear, much of the attention to ensuring social justice in an evaluation must occur early in the process, well before the development of conclusions, particularly in the planning stage in which the intervention's stakeholders are identified and included. But as illustrated here, conclusions play a significant role in an evaluation's achieving justice as well because they reflect the synthesis of what has been learned.

Chapter Summary

- Validity, as usually defined, refers to the accuracy or truth of an inference. Viewed in this light, validity concerns are closely linked to the conclusions and recommendations that form the final phase of an evaluation study.

- A general logic of evaluation, proposed by Michael Scriven, consists of four steps: (1) determining criteria of merit; (2) determining standards of merit; (3) measuring performance; and (4) synthesizing the results to produce an overall judgment. The skill of synthesis comes into play when the evaluator, working together with stakeholders, must consider all the information and new knowledge that has been generated by the study and incorporate it into a set of conclusions and recommendations. Scriven has written that synthesis is "the key cognitive skill in evaluation."

- The recommendations from an evaluation are usually of great interest to stakeholders. Well-designed recommendations should lead logically out of the study's conclusions, but they may also involve additional complexities if they require consideration of factors that are external to the specifics of the evaluation study that has just been completed.

- Program and policy recommendations lay out potential options for action. But the identification of available options will depend on how the problem and its possible solutions have been framed. Ernest House has noted that people routinely frame complex social problems in terms of simplifying metaphors, which can be limiting with regard to the range of possible solutions that one will consider. Evaluators and stakeholders need to be aware of these limiting tendencies and strive for openness and creativity in their thinking about social issues and problems.

- The Campbellian validity model presents a framework through which the accuracy of evaluative conclusions, in terms of their links to the findings and analyses of the evaluation study, can be assessed.

- House's validity model can also be useful in assessing the strength and quality of evaluation conclusions. To fulfill the *truth* criterion, conclusions must be accurate, convincing, and free from bias. To fulfill the *coherence* criterion, they must be persuasive and compelling. Finally, to fulfill the *justice* criterion, they must reflect the interests of all stakeholder groups rather than just those stakeholders wielding the most power and influence.

Questions for Reflection—Chapter 9

1. What are some of the particular challenges involved with synthesizing an evaluation's results to arrive at valid conclusions and recommendations?

2. As this chapter describes, people tend to use metaphors to understand a social problem, and these metaphors can shape what get proposed as suggested solutions to the problem. Describe an example from your experience in which a social problem can be framed using different metaphors.

   • What are recommendations for dealing with the problem that might logically flow from each of those metaphors? To what degree do those metaphors diverge?

3. How does the concept of *justice* relate to the development of an evaluation study's conclusions and recommendations?

   • In this phase of the evaluation process, how are different stakeholder groups impacted by placing priority on a justice perspective?

   • What are some of the approaches to developing recommendations that can help to ensure an emphasis on justice?

• References •

AERA, APA, and NCME. (1954). *The standards for educational and psychological testing.* American Psychological Association.

AERA, APA, and NCME. (2014). *The standards for educational and psychological testing.* American Psychological Association. https://www.testingstandards.net/open-access-files.html

American College Health Association. (2012). Position statement on tobacco on college and university campuses. *Journal of American College Health, 60,* 266–267. doi: 10.1080/07448481.2012.660440

American Evaluation Association. (2011). *Public statement on cultural competence in evaluation.* Author. www.eval.org

American Nonsmokers' Rights Foundation. (2022). *Smokefree and tobacco-free U.S. and tribal colleges and universities.* https://no-smoke.org/wp-content/uploads/pdf/smoke-freecollegesuniversities.pdf

Anastasi, A. (1986). Evolving concepts of test validation. *Annual Review of Psychology, 37,* 1–15.

Angoff, W. H. (1988). Validity: An evolving concept. In H. Wainer and H. I. Braun (Eds.), *Test validity* (pp. 19–32). Lawrence Erlbaum Associates.

Archibald, T. (2020). What's the problem represented to be? Problem definition critique as a tool for evaluative thinking. *American Journal of Evaluation, 41*(1), 6–19. doi: 10.1177/1098214018824043

Babor, T. F., Caulkins, J., Fischer, B., Foxcroft, D., Medina-Mora, M. E., Obot, I., Rehm, J., Reuter, P., Room, R., Rossow, I., & Strang, J. (2019). Drug policy and the public good: A summary of the second edition. *Addiction, 114,* 1941–1950. doi: 10.1111/add.14734

Bandalos, D. L. (2018). *Measurement theory and applications for the social sciences.* Guilford.

Banta, T. W. (Ed.). (2004). *Hallmarks of effective outcomes assessment.* Jossey-Bass.

Barrett, C. B. (2010). Measuring food insecurity. *Science, 327*(5967), 825–828. doi: 10.1126/science.ll82768

Baumrind, D. (1991). Parenting styles and adolescent development. In R. M. Lerner, A. C. Petersen, & J. Brooks-Gunn (Eds.), *The encyclopedia of adolescence* (Vol. 2, pp. 746–758). Garland.

Baumrind, D. (2013). Authoritative parenting revisited: History and current status. In R. E. Larzalere, A. S. Morris, & A. W. Harrist (Eds.), *Authoritative parenting: Synthesizing nurturance and discipline for optimal child development* (pp. 11–34). American Psychological Association.

Bennett, B. L., Deiner, M., & Pokhrel, P. (2017). College anti-smoking policies and student smoking behavior: A review of the literature. *Tobacco Induced Diseases, 15,* 11. doi: 10.1186/s12971-017-0117-z

Bhatti, B., Derezotes, D., Kim, S.–O., & Specht, H. (1989). In A. M. Mecca, N. J. Smelser, & J. Vasconcellos (Eds.), *The social importance of self-esteem* (pp. 24–71). University of California Press.

Billingsley, K. L. (2010, July 29). *Retrospective: A state of esteem?* Cal Watchdog. https://calwatchdog.com/2010/07/29/retrospective-a-state-of-esteem/

Bittner, A., & Goodyear-Grant, E. (2017). Sex isn't gender: Reforming concepts and measurements in the study of public opinion. *Political Behavior, 39*(4), 1019–1041. doi: 10.1007/s11109-017-9391-y

Blalock, H. M., Jr. (1982). *Conceptualization and measurement in the social sciences.* SAGE.

Boring, E. G. (1923). Intelligence as the tests test it. *New Republic, 36,* 35–37.

Borsboom, D., Cramer, A. O. J., Kievit, R. A., Scholten, A. Z., & Franić, S. (2009). The end of construct validity. In R. Lissitz (Ed.), *The concept of validity* (pp. 135–170). Information Age Publishing.

Boruch, R. F. (1997). *Randomized experiments for planning and evaluation: A practical guide.* SAGE.

Braverman, M. T. (2013). Negotiating measurement: Methodological and interpersonal considerations in the choice and interpretation of instruments. *American Journal of Evaluation, 34*(1), 99–114. doi: 10.1177/1098214012460565

Braverman, M. T. (2019). Measurement and credible evidence in Extension evaluations. *Journal of Human Sciences and Extension, 7*(2), 88–107. https://jhsonline.com/

Braverman, M. T., Brenner, J., Fretz, P., & Desmond, D. (1993). Three approaches to evaluation: A ropes course illustration. In M. A. Gass (Ed.), *Adventure therapy: Therapeutic applications of adventure programming* (pp. 357–370). Kendall/Hunt.

Braverman, M. T., Ceraso, M., Sporrer, F., & Rockler, B. E. (2021). Five-year changes in support for tobacco control policy options among students, faculty and staff at a public university. *Preventive Medicine, 142,* Article 106359. doi: 10.1016/j.ypmed.2020.106359

Braverman, M. T., Chin Young, J., King, N. J., Paterson, C. A., & Weisskirch, R. S. (2002). Career awareness and part-time work examined in lives of high school seniors. *California Agriculture, 56*(2), 55–60. doi: 10.3733/ca.v056n02p55

Braverman, M. T., Geldhof, G. J., Hoogesteger, L. A., Johnson, J. A. (2018). Predicting students' noncompliance with a smoke-free university campus policy. *Preventive Medicine, 114,* 209–216. doi: 10.1016/j.ypmed.2018.07.002

Braverman, M. T., Hoogesteger, L. A., & Johnson, J. A. (2015). Predictors of support among students, faculty and staff for a smoke-free university campus. *Preventive Medicine, 71,* 114–120. doi: 10.1016/j.ypmed.2014.12.018

Bruine de Bruin, W. (2011). Framing effects in surveys: How respondents make sense of the questions we ask. In G. Keren (Ed.), *Perspectives on framing* (pp. 303–324). Psychology Press.

Buckley, J., Archibald, T., Hargraves, M., & Trochim, W. M. (2015). Defining and teaching evaluative thinking: Insights from research on critical thinking. *American Journal of Evaluation, 36*, 375–388. doi: 10.1177/1098214015581706

California State Department of Education. (1990). *Toward a state of esteem. The final report of the California task force to promote self-esteem and personal and social responsibility.* ISBN: 0-8011-0846-2 Eric Document #ED 321-170.

Cameron, R., Best, J. A., & Brown, K. S. (2001). Re: Hutchinson smoking prevention project: Long-term randomized trial in school- based tobacco use prevention—Results on smoking. *Journal of the National Cancer Institute, 93*(16), 1267–1268. doi: 10.1093/jnci/93.16.1267-a

Campbell, D. T. (1957). Factors relevant to validity of experiments in social settings. *Psychological Bulletin, 54*, 297–312. doi: 10.1037/h0040950

Campbell, D. T. (1986). Science's social system of validity-enhancing collective belief change and the problems of the social sciences. In D. W. Fiske & R. A. Shweder (Eds.), *Metatheory in social science: Pluralisms and subjectivities* (pp. 108–135). University of Chicago Press.

Campbell, D. T., & Fiske, D. W. (1959). Convergent and discriminant validation by the multitrait-multimethod matrix. *Psychological Bulletin, 56*, 81–105. doi: 10.1037/h0046016

Campbell, D. T., & Stanley, J. C. (1966). *Experimental and quasi-experimental designs for research.* Rand McNally.

Chaloupka, F. J., Powell, L. M., & Warner, K. E. (2019). The use of excise taxes to reduce tobacco, alcohol, and sugary beverage consumption. *Annual Review of Public Health, 40*, 187–201. doi: 10.1146/annurev-publhealth-040218-043816

Chaplowe, S., & Cousins, J. B. (2016). *Monitoring and evaluation training: A systematic approach.* SAGE.

Chen, H. T. (2015). *Practical program evaluation: Theory-driven evaluation and the integrated evaluation perspective* (2nd ed.). SAGE.

Chen, H. T., Donaldson, S. I., & Mark, M. M. (Eds.). (2011). *Advancing validity in outcome evaluation: Theory and practice* (Vol. 130). New Directions for Evaluation.

Chong, D., & Druckman, J. N. (2007). Framing theory. *Annual Review of Political Science, 10*, 103–126. doi: 10.1146/annurev.polisci.10.072805.103054

Clark, H. H., & Schober, M. F. (1992). Asking questions and influencing answers. In J. M. Tanur (Ed.), *Questions about questions: Inquiries into the cognitive bases of surveys* (pp. 15–48). Russell Sage Foundation.

Clayton, R. R., Cattarello, A. M., & Johnstone, B. M. (1996). The effectiveness of Drug Abuse Resistance Education (Project DARE): 5-year follow-up results. *Preventive Medicine, 25*, 307–318. doi: 10.1006/pmed.1996.0061

Clayton, R. R., Scutchfield, F. D., & Wyatt, S. W. (2000). Hutchinson smoking prevention project: A new gold standard in prevention science requires new transdisciplinary thinking. *Journal of the National Cancer Institute, 92*(24), 1964–1965. doi: 10.1093/jnci/92.24.1964

Cohen, J. (1990). Things I have learned (so far). *American Psychologist, 45*(12), 1304–1312. doi: 10.1037/0003-066X.45.12.1304

Cohen, J. (1994). The earth is round (p<.05). *American Psychologist, 49*(12), 997–1003. doi: 10.1037/0003-066X.49.12.997

Converse, J. M., & Presser, S. (1986). *Survey questions: Handcrafting the standardized questionnaire.* SAGE.

Cook, T. D., & Campbell, D. T. (1979). *Quasi-experimentation: Design and analysis for field settings.* Rand McNally.

Coyle, K., Anderson, P., Laris, B. A., Barrett, M., Unti, T., & Baumler, E. (2021). A group randomized trial evaluating High School FLASH, a comprehensive sexual health curriculum. *Journal of Adolescent Health, 68*, 686–605. doi: 10.1016/j.jado health.2020.12.005

Crockenberg, S. B., & Soby, B. A. (1989). Self-esteem and teenage pregnancy. In A. M. Mecca, N. J. Smelser, & J. Vasconcellos (Eds.), *The social importance of self-esteem* (pp. 125–164). University of California Press.

Crockett, L. J., & Hayes, R. (2011). Parenting practices and styles. In B. B. Brown & M. J. Prinstein (Eds.), *Encyclopedia of adolescence* (Vol. 2, pp. 241–248). Academic Press.

Cronbach, L. J. (1982). *Designing evaluations of educational and social programs.* Jossey-Bass.

Cronbach, L. J. (1988). Five perspectives on validity argument. In H. Wainer & H. I. Braun (Eds.), *Test validity* (pp. 3–17). Lawrence Erlbaum Associates.

Cronbach, L. J. (1990). *Essentials of psychological testing* (5th ed.). HarperCollins.

Cronbach, L. J., Ambron, S. R., Dornbusch, S. M., Hess, R. D., Hornik, R. C., Phillips, D. C., Walker, D. F., & Weiner, S. S. (1980). *Toward reform of program evaluation.* Jossey-Bass.

Cronbach, L. J., & Meehl P. E. (1955). Construct validity in psychological tests. *Psychological Bulletin, 52*, 281–302. doi: 10.1037/h0040957

Davidson, E. J. (2014). How "beauty" can bring truth and justice to life. In J. C. Griffith & B. Montrosse-Moorhead (Eds.), *Revisiting truth, beauty, and justice: Evaluating with validity in the 21st century* (Vol. 142, pp. 31–43). New Directions for Evaluation. doi: 10.1002/ev.20083

Davis, K., Christodoulou, J., Seider, S., & Gardner, H. (2011). The theory of multiple intelligences. In R. J. Sternberg & S. B. Kaufman (Eds.), *The Cambridge handbook of intelligence* (pp. 485–503). Cambridge University Press.

Detry, M. A., & Lewis, R. J. (2014). The intention-to-treat principle: How to assess the true effect of choosing a medical treatment. *JAMA, 312*(1), 85–86. doi: 10.1001/jama.2014.7523

DeVellis, R. F. (2017). *Scale development: Theory and applications* (4th ed.). SAGE.

Dillman, D. A., Smyth, J. D., & Christian, L. M. (2014). *Internet, phone, mail, and mixed-mode surveys: The tailored design method* (4th ed.). Wiley.

Doepke, M., & Zilibotti, F. (2019). *Love, money and parenting: How economics explains the way we raise our kids.* Princeton University Press.

D'Onofrio, C. N., Moskowitz, J. M., & Braverman, M. T. (2002). Curtailing tobacco use among youth: Evaluation of project 4-Health. *Health Education and Behavior, 29*(6), 656–682. doi: 10.1177/109019802237937

Druckerman, P. (2019, February 7). The bad news about helicopter parenting: It works. *New York Times.* https://www.nytimes.com/2019/02/07/opinion/helicopter-parents-economy.html

Dumanovsky, T., Huang, C. Y., Bassett, M. T., & Silver, L. D. (2010). Consumer awareness of fast-food calorie information in New York City after implementation of a menu labeling regulation. *American Journal of Public Health, 100*(12), 2520–2525. doi: 10.2105/AJPH.2010.191908

Edwards, J. R., & Bagozzi, R. P. (2000). On the nature and direction of relationships between constructs and measures. *Psychological Methods, 5*(2), 155–174. doi: 10.1037//1082-989X.5.2.155

Embretson, S. (1983). Construct validity: Construct representation versus nomothetic span. *Psychological Bulletin, 93*, 179–197. doi: 10.1037/0033-2909.93.1.179

Esbensen, F.–A., Matsuda, K. N., Taylor, T. J., & Peterson, D. (2011). Multimethod strategy for assessing program fidelity: The national evaluation of the revised G.R.E.A.T. program. *Evaluation Review, 35*(1), 14–39. doi: 10.1177/0193841X 10388126

Fallin, A., Roditis, M., & Glantz, S. A. (2015). Association of campus tobacco policies with secondhand smoke exposure, intention to smoke on campus, and attitudes about outdoor smoking restrictions. *American Journal of Public Health, 105*, 1098–1100. doi: 10.2105/AJPH.2014.302251

Ferber, R. (1956). The effect of respondent ignorance on survey results. *Journal of the American Statistical Association, 51*(276), 576–586. doi: 10.1080/01621459.1956. 10501347

Fischer, B., Daldegan-Bueno, D., & Reuter, P. (2021). Toward a "post-legalization" criminology for cannabis: A brief review and suggested agenda for research priorities. *Contemporary Drug Problems, 48*(1), 58–74. doi: 10.1177/0091450920977976

Funnell, S. C., & Rogers, P. J. (2011). *Purposeful program theory: Effective use of theories of change and logic models.* Jossey-Bass.

GenIUSS Group [Gender Identity in U.S. Surveillance]. (2013). *Gender-related measures overview.* The Williams Institute, UCLA School of Law. https://williamsinstitute. law.ucla.edu/wp-content/uploads/Gender-Related-Measures-Overview-Feb-2013.pdf

Glantz, S. A., & Bareham, D. W. (2018). E-cigarettes: Use, effects on smoking, risks, and policy implications. *Annual Review of Public Health, 39*, 215–235. doi: 10.1146/ annurev-publhealth-040617-013757

Glick, J. L., Theall, K., Andrinopoulos, K., & Kendall, C. (2018). For data's sake: Dilemmas in the measurement of gender minorities. *Culture, Health & Sexuality, 20*(12), 1362–1377. doi: 10.1080/13691058.2018.1437220

Gorber, S. C., Schofield-Hurwitz, S., Hardt, J., Levasseur, G., & Tremblay, M. (2009). The accuracy of self-reported smoking: A systematic review of the relationship between self-reported and cotinine-assessed smoking status. *Nicotine & Tobacco Research, 11*(1), 12–24. doi: 10.1093/ntr/ntn010

Gorman, D. M., & Huber, J. C., Jr. (2009). The social construction of "evidence-based" drug prevention programs: A reanalysis of data from the Drug Abuse Resistance Education (DARE) program. *Evaluation Review, 33*(4), 396–414. doi: 10.1177/0193 841X09334711

Griffith, J. C., & Montrosse-Moorhead, B. (Eds.). (2014). *Revisiting truth, beauty, and justice: Evaluating with validity in the 21st century* (Vol. 142). New Directions for Evaluation.

Groves, R. M. (1989). *Survey errors and survey costs*. Wiley.

Haertel, E. H. (2006). Reliability. In R. L. Brennan (Ed.), *Educational measurement* (4th ed., pp. 65–110). Praeger.

Hannon, P. A., Hammerback, K., Kohn, M. J., Kava, C. M., Chan, K. C. G., Parrish, A. T., Allen, C., Helfrich, C. D., Mayotte, C., Beresford, S. A., & Harris, J. R. (2019). Disseminating evidence-based interventions in small, low-wage worksites: A randomized controlled trial in king county, Washington (2014–2017). *American Journal of Public Health, 109*(12), 1739–1746. doi: 10.2105/AJPH.2019.305313

Hayat, M. J., Staggs, V. S., Schwartz, T. A., Higgins, M., Azuero, A., Budhathoki, C., Chandrasekhar, R., Cook, P., Cramer, E., Dietrich, M. S., Garnier-Villarreal, M., Hanlon, A., He, J., Hu, J., Kim, M., Mueller, M., Nolan, J. R., Perkhounkova, Y., Rothers, J., ... & Ye, S. (2019). Moving nursing beyond p<.05. *International Journal of Nursing Studies, 95*, A1–A2. doi: 10.1016/j.ijnurstu.2019.05.012

Hayes, A. F. (2013). *Introduction to mediation, moderation, and conditional process analysis: A regression-based approach.* Guilford.

Holleman, B. C. (2006). The meanings of 'yes' and 'no'. An explanation for the forbid/ allow asymmetry. *Quality and Quantity, 40*, 1–38. doi: 10.1007/s11135-005-4479-6

Holl, K., Niederdeppe, J., & Schuldt, J. P. (2018). Does question wording predict support for the Affordable Care Act? An analysis of polling during the implementation period, 2010-2016. *Health Communication, 33*(7), 816–823. doi: 10.1080/1041 0236.2017.1315676

Hood, S., Hopson, R. K., & Kirkhart, K. E. (2015). Culturally responsive evaluation: Theory, practice, and future implications. In K. E.Newcomer, H. P. Hatry, & J. S. Wholey (Eds.), *Handbook of practical program evaluation* (4th ed., pp. 281–317). Wiley.

House, E. R. (1977). *The logic of evaluative argument.* Center for the Study of Evaluation, UCLA Graduate School of Education.

House, E. R. (1980). *Evaluating with validity.* SAGE.

House, E. R. (1983). How we think about evaluation. In E. R.House (Ed.), *Philosophy of evaluation* (Vol. 19, pp. 5–25). New Directions for Evaluation. doi: 10.1002/ev.1342

House, E. R. (1993). *Professional evaluation: Social impact and political consequences.* SAGE.

House, E. R. (1995). Putting things together coherently: Logic and justice. In D. M. Fournier (Ed.), *Reasoning in evaluation: Inferential links and leaps* (Vol. 68, pp. 33–48). New Directions for Evaluation. doi: 10.1002/ev.1018

House, E. R. (2008). Blowback: Consequences of evaluation for evaluation. *American Journal of Evaluation, 29*(4), 416–426. doi: 10.1177/1098214008322640

House, E. R. (2011). Conflict of interest and Campbellian validity. In H. T. Chen, S. I. Donaldson, & M. M. Mark (Eds.), *Advancing validity in outcome evaluation: Theory and practice* (Vol. 130, pp. 69–80). New Directions for Evaluation. doi: 10.1002/ev.366

House, E. R. (2014). Origins of the ideas in evaluating with validity. In J. C. Griffith & B. Montrosse-Moorhead (Eds.), *Revisiting truth, beauty, and justice: Evaluating with validity in the 21st century* (Vol. 142, pp. 9–15). New Directions for Evaluation. doi: 10.1002/ev.20081

Hox, J. J., Moerbeek, M., & van de Schoot, R. (2017). *Multilevel analysis: Techniques and applications* (3rd ed.). Routledge.

Huang, F. L., & Cornell, D. G. (2015). The impact of definition and question order on the prevalence of bullying victimization using student self-reports. *Psychological Assessment, 27*(4), 1484–1493. doi: 10.1037/pas0000149

Hurlbert, S. H., Levine, R. A., & Utts, J. (2019). Coup de grâce for a tough old bull: "Statistically significant" expires. *The American Statistician, 73*, 352–357. doi: 10.1080/00031305.2018.1543616

Hyland, P., Boduszek, D., Dhingra, K., Shevlin, M., & Egan, A. (2014). A bifactor approach to modelling the Rosenberg self-esteem scale. *Personality and Individual Differences, 66*, 188–192. doi: 10.1016/j.paid.2014.03.034

Johnson, M. B., Lange, J. E., Voas, R. B., Clapp, J. D., Lauer, E., & Snowden, C. B. (2006). The sidewalk survey: A field methodology to measure late-night college drinking. *Evaluation Review, 30*(1), 27–43. doi: 10.1177/0193841X04273255

Johnson, R. L., & Morgan, G. B. (2016). *Survey scales: A guide to development, analysis, and reporting*. Guilford.

Jones, L. K., & Lohmann, R. C. (1998). The career decision profile: Using a measure of career decision status in counseling. *Journal of Career Assessment, 6*(2), 209–230. doi: 10.1177/106907279800600207

Kaiser Family Foundation. (2019). *Public opinion on single-payer, national health plans, and expanding access to Medicare coverage.* https://www.kff.org/slideshow/public-opinion-on-single-payer-national-health-plans-and-expanding-access-to-medicare-coverage/. Accessed on October 19, 2019.

Kaminsky, A. (2000). Beyond the literal: Metaphors and why they matter. In R. K. Hopson (Ed.), *How and why language matters in evaluation* (Vol. 86, pp. 69–80). New Directions for Evaluation. doi: 10.1002/ev.1173

Kane, M. T. (2013). Validating the interpretations and uses of test scores. *Journal of Educational Measurement, 50*, 1–73. doi: 10.1111/jedm.12000

Kirkhart, K. E. (2005). Through a cultural lens: Reflections on validity and theory in evaluation. In S. Hood, R. Hopson, & H. Frierson (Eds.), *The role of culture and cultural context: A mandate for inclusion, the discovery of truth and understanding in evaluative theory and practice* (pp. 21–39). Information Age Publishing.

Kirkhart, K. E. (2010). Eyes on the prize: Multicultural validity and evaluation theory. *American Journal of Evaluation, 31*(3), 400–413. doi: 10.1177/1098214010373645

Knowlton, L. W., & Phillips, C. C. (2013). *The logic model guidebook: Better strategies for great results* (2nd ed.). SAGE.

LaFrance, J., Kirkhart, K. E., & Nichols, R. (2015). Cultural views of validity: A conversation. In S. Hood, R. Hopson, & H. Frierson (Eds.), *Continuing the journey to reposition culture and cultural context in evaluation theory and practice* (pp. 49–72). Information Age Publishing.

Leviton, L. C. (2017). Generalizing about public health interventions: A mixed-methods approach to external validity. *Annual Review of Public Health, 38,* 371–391. doi: 10.1146/annurev-publhealth-031816-044509

Leviton, L. C., & Trujillo, M. D. (2017). Interaction of theory and practice to assess external validity. *Evaluation Review, 41*(5), 436–471. doi: 10.1177/0193841X15 625289

Lipsey, M. W. (1990). *Design sensitivity: Statistical power for experimental research.* SAGE.

Lipsey, M. W. (1993). Theory as method: Small theories of treatments. In L. B. Sechrest & A. G. Scott (Eds.), *Understanding causes and generalizing about them* (Vol. 57, pp. 5–38). New Directions for Program Evaluation. doi: 10.1002/ev.1637

Lipsey, M. W., & Hurley, S. M. (2009). Design sensitivity: Statistical power for applied experimental research. In L. Bickman & D. J. Rog (Eds.), *The Sage handbook of applied social research methods* (2nd ed., pp. 44–76). SAGE.

Mark, M. M. (2000). Realism, validity, and the experimenting society. In L. Bickman (Ed.), *Validity and social experimentation: Donald Campbell's legacy* (Vol. 1, pp. 141–166). SAGE.

Martin, M. J., Bascoe, S. M., & Davies, P. T. (2011). Family relationships. In B. B. Brown & M. J. Prinstein (Eds.), *Encyclopedia of adolescence* (Vol. 2, pp. 84–94). Academic Press.

Masten, A. S. (2014). *Ordinary magic: Resilience in development.* Guilford.

Masten, A. S., & Monn, A. R. (2015). Child and family resilience: A call for integrated science, practice, and professional training. *Family Relations, 64,* 5–21. doi: 10.1111/fare.12103

Mathison, S. (2018). Does evaluation contribute to the public good? *Evaluation, 24*(1), 113–119. doi: 10.1177/1356389017749278

Maxwell, S. E., Delaney, H. D., & Kelly, K. (2018). *Designing experiments and analyzing data: A model comparison perspective* (3rd ed.).Routledge.

McKillip, J. (1989). Evaluation of health promotion media campaigns. In M. T. Braverman (Ed.), *Evaluating health promotion programs* (Vol. 43, pp. 89–100). New Directions for Evaluation.

McKnight, P. E., McKnight, K. M., Sidani, S., & Figueredo, A. J. (2007). *Missing data: A gentle introduction.* Guilford.

McWilliams, C. (2018). *What does being gifted really mean?* Michigan State University Gifted and Talented Education. https://gifted.msu.edu/about/226/what-does-being-gifted-really-mean

Mead, L. M. (2016). On the "how" of social experiments: Using implementation research to get inside the black box. In L. R. Peck (Ed.), *Social experiments in practice: The what, why, when, where, and how of experimental design and analysis* (Vol. 152, pp. 73–84). New Directions for Evaluation. doi: 10.1002/ev.20206

Mecca, A. M. (1989). Foreword. In A. M. Mecca, N. J. Smelser, & J. Vasconcellos (Eds.), *The social importance of self-esteem* (pp. vii–ix). University of California Press.

Mecca, A. M., Smelser, N. J., & Vasconcellos, J. (Eds.). (1989). *The social importance of self-esteem.* University of California Press.

Messick, S. (1981). Constructs and their vicissitudes in educational and psychological measurement. *Psychological Bulletin, 89*(3), 575–588. doi: 10.1037/0033-2909.89.3.575

Messick, S. (1989). Validity. In R. L. Linn (Ed.), *Educational measurement* (4th ed., pp. 13–103). American Council on Education and Macmillian Publishing Company.

Messick, S. (1995). Validity of psychological assessment: Validation of inferences from persons' responses and performances as scientific inquiry into score meaning. *American Psychologist, 50*(9), 741–749. doi: 10.1037/0003-066X.50.9.741

Meyer, J. P. (2010). *Reliability.* Oxford University Press.

Moreno, L., Treviño, E., Yoshikawa, H., Mendive, S., Reyes, J., Godoy, F., Del Rio, F., Snow, C., Leyva, D., Barata, C., Arbour, M. C., & Rolla, A. (2011). Aftershocks of Chile's earthquake for an ongoing, large-scale experimental evaluation. *Evaluation Review, 35*(5), 103–117. doi: 10.1177/0193841X11400685

Munafò, M. (2019). Are e-cigarettes tobacco products? *Nicotine & Tobacco Research, 21*(3), 267. doi: 10.1093/ntr/nty130

Murphy, K. R., Myors, B., & Wolach, A. (2014). *Statistical power analysis: A simple and general model for traditional and modern hypothesis tests* (4th ed.). Routledge.

National Conference of State Legislatures. (2017, May 3). *Alternative nicotine products, electronic cigarettes.* http://www.ncsl.org/research/health/alternative-nicotine-products-e-cigarettes.aspx. Accessed on August 17, 2019.

National Institute on Drug Abuse. (2018, January 5). *Tobacco, nicotine, and e-cigarettes.* https://www.drugabuse.gov/publications/research-reports/tobacco-nicotine-e-cigarettes

Nature This Week. (2018). Anatomy does not define gender. *Nature, 563*(7729), 5. doi: 10.1038/d41586-018-07238-8

Overholt, J. R., & Ewert, A. (2015). Gender matters: Exploring the process of developing resilience through outdoor adventure. *Journal of Experiential Education, 38*(1), 41–55. doi: 10.1177/1053825913513720

Pardo, B., & Reuter, P. (2018). Narcotics and drug abuse: Foreshadowing of 50 years of change. *Criminology & Public Policy, 17*(2), 419–436. doi: 10.1111/1745-9133.12363

Patton, M. Q. (2008). *Utilization-focused evaluation* (4th ed.). SAGE.

Pawson, R., Wong, G., & Owen, L. (2011). Known knowns, known unknowns, unknown unknowns: The predicament of evidence-based policy. *American Journal of Evaluation, 32*(4), 518–546. doi: 10.1177/1098214011403831

Peck, L. R. (2020). *Experimental evaluation design for program improvement.* SAGE.

Peters, S. J. (2022). The challenges of achieving equity within public school gifted and talented programs. *Gifted Child Quarterly, 66*(2), 82–94. doi: 10.1177/0016986221100253511002535

Peterson, A. V., Jr., Kealey, K. A., Mann, S. L., Marek, P. M., Sarason, I. G. (2000). Hutchinson Smoking Prevention Project: Long-term randomized trial in school-based tobacco use prevention—Results on smoking. *Journal of the National Cancer Institute, 92*(24), 1979–1991. doi: 10.1093/jnci/92.24.1979

Pierce, J. P., Choi, W. S., Gilpin, E. A., Farkas, A. J., Merritt, RK. (1996). Validation of susceptibility as a predictor of which adolescents take up smoking in the United States. *Health Psychology, 15*, 355–361. doi: 10.1037/0278-6133.15.5.355

Poropat, A. E. (2009). A meta-analysis of the five-factor model of personality and academic performance. *Psychological Bulletin, 135*(2), 322–338. doi: 10.1037/a001 4996

Porter, J. M., Rathbun, S. L., Bryan, S. J., Arseniadis, K., Caldwell, L. P., Corso, P.S., Lee, J. M., & Davis, M. (2018). Law accommodating nonmotorized road users and pedestrian fatalities in Florida, 1975 to 2013. *American Journal of Public Health, 108*(4), 525–531. doi: 10.2105/AJPH.2017.304259

Presser, S. Couper, M. P., Lessler, J. T., Martin, E., Martin, J., Rothgeb, J. M., & Singer, E. (2004a). Methods for testing and evaluating survey questions. *Public Opinion Quarterly, 68*(1), 109–130. doi: 10.1093/poq/nfh008

Presser, S. Rothgeb, J. M., Couper, M. P., Lessler, J. T., Martin, E., Martin, J., & Singer, E. (2004b). *Methods for testing and evaluating survey questionnaires.* Wiley.

Price, L. R. (2017). *Psychometric methods: Theory into practice.* Guilford.

Rafferty, J. (2018). *Gender identity development in children.* HealthyChildren.org (website of the American Academy of Pediatrics). https://www.healthychildren.org/English /ages-stages/gradeschool/Pages/Gender-Identity-and-Gender-Confusion-In-Children.aspx

Reichardt, C. S. (2019). *Quasi-experimentation: A guide to design and analysis.* Guilford.

Renzulli, J. S. (1986). The three-ring conception of giftedness: A developmental model for creative productivity. In R. J. Sternberg & J. E. Davidson (Eds.), *Conceptions of giftedness* (pp. 53–92). Cambridge University Press.

Reuter, P. (2013). "Why has U.S. drug policy changed so little over 30 years?" In M. H. Tonry (Ed.), *Crime and justice in America: 1975–2025* (pp. 75–140). University of Chicago Press.

Roda, A. (2015). *Inequality in gifted and talented programs: Parental choices about status, school opportunity, and second-generation segregation.* Palgrave Macmillan.

Rodriguez, S., & Acree, J. (2021). Discourses of belonging: Intersections of truth, power, and ethics in evaluation with migrant youth. *American Journal of Evaluation, 42*(2), 276–292. doi: 10.1177/1098214020963837

Rosenfeld, B., Imai, K., & Shapiro, J. N. (2016). An empirical validation study of popular survey methodologies for sensitive questions. *American Journal of Political Science, 60*(3), 783–802. doi: 10.1111/ajps.12205

Rossi, P. H., Lipsey, M. W., & Henry, G. T. (2019). *Evaluation: A systematic approach* (8th ed.). SAGE.

Rousseau, D. M., & Gunia, B. C. (2016). Evidence-based practice: The psychology of EBP implementation. *Annual Review of Psychology, 67*, 667–692. doi: 10.1146/ annurev-psych-122414-033336

Rutter, M. (2012). Resilience as a dynamic concept. *Development and Psychopathology, 24,* 335–344. doi: 10.1017/S0954579412000028

Schneiderman, L., Furman, W. M., & Weber, J. (1989). Self-esteem and chronic welfare dependency. In A. M. Mecca, N. J. Smelser, & J. Vasconcellos (Eds.), *The social importance of self-esteem* (pp. 200–247). University of California Press.

Schwandt, T. A. (2015). *Evaluation foundations revisited: Cultivating a life of the mind for practice.* Stanford University Press.

Schwarz, N. (1999). Self-reports: How the questions shape the answers. *American Psychologist, 54*(2), 93–105. doi: 10.1037/0003-066X.54.2.93

Schwarz, N., & Oyserman, D. (2001). Asking questions about behavior: Cognition, communication, and questionnaire construction. *American Journal of Evaluation, 22*(2), 127–160. doi: 10.1177/109821400102200202

Scriven, M. (1991). *Evaluation thesaurus* (4th ed.). SAGE.

Scriven, M. (1994). The final synthesis. *Evaluation Practice, 15*(3), 367–382. doi: 10.1177/109821409401500317

Scriven, M. (2012). The logic of valuing. In G. Julnes (Ed.), *Promoting valuation in the public interest: Informing policies for judging value in evaluation* (Vol. 133, pp. 17–28). New Directions for Evaluation. doi: 10.1002/ev.20003

Sedgwick, P. (2014). Explanatory trials versus pragmatic trials. *BMJ, 349,* g6694. doi: 10.1136/bmj.g6694

Shadish, W. R., Cook, T. D., & Campbell, D. T. (2002). *Experimental and quasi-experimental designs for generalized causal inference.* Houghton-Mifflin.

Singal, A. G., Higgins, P. D. R., & Waljee, A. K. (2014). A primer on effectiveness and efficacy trials. *Clinical and Translational Gastroenterology, 5,* e45, doi:10.1038/ctg.2013.13

Singleton, R. A., Jr., & Straits, B. C. (2018). *Approaches to social research* (6th ed.). Oxford University Press.

Sireci, S. G. (2009). Packing and unpacking sources of validity evidence: History repeats itself again. In R. W. Lissitz (Ed.), *The concept of validity: Revisions, new directions, and applications* (pp. 19–38). Information Age Publishing.

Skager, R., & Kerst, E. (1989). Alcohol and drug use and self-esteem: A psychological perspective. In A. M. Mecca, N. J. Smelser, & J. Vasconcellos (Eds.), *The social importance of self-esteem* (pp. 248–293). University of California Press.

Smelser, N. J. (1989). Self-esteem and social problems: An introduction. In A. M. Mecca, N. J. Smelser, & J. Vasconcellos (Eds.), *The social importance of self-esteem* (pp. 1–23). University of California Press.

Soares, J. A. (Ed.). (2020). *The scandal of standardized tests: Why we need to drop the SAT and ACT.* Teachers College Press.

Sternberg, R. J. (2011). The theory of successful intelligence. In R. J. Sternberg & S. B. Kaufman (Eds.), *The Cambridge handbook of intelligence* (pp. 504–527). Cambridge University Press.

Strong, D. R., Hartman, S. J., Nodora, J., Messer, K., James, L., White, M., Portnoy, D. B., Choiniere, C. J., Vullo, G. C., & Pierce, J. (2015). Predictive validity of the expanded susceptibility to smoke index. *Nicotine & Tobacco Research, 17*(7), 862–869. doi: 10.1093/ntr/ntu254

Sussman, S. & Stacy, A. W. (1994). Five methods of assessing school-level daily use of cigarettes and alcohol by adolescents at continuation high schools. *Evaluation Review, 18*(6), 741–755. doi: 10.1177/0193841X9401800606

Sussman, S., Hansen, W. B., Flay, B. R., & Botvin, G. J. (2001). Re: Hutchinson smoking prevention project: Long-term randomized trial in school- based tobacco use prevention—Results on smoking. *Journal of the National Cancer Institute, 93*(16), 1267. doi: 10.1093/jnci/93.16.1267

Taylor-Powell, E. (2002). *Water quality program: Logic model, evaluation questions, indicators.* University of Wisconsin Extension. https://fyi.extension.wisc.edu/pro-gramdevelopment/files/2016/03/WaterQualityProgram.pdf

Thompson, B. (1996). AERA editorial policies regarding statistical significance testing: Three suggested reforms. *Educational Researcher, 25*(2), 26–30. doi: 10.3102/00131 89X025002026

Tolstoy, L. (1961). *Anna Karenina* (Translated by D. Magarshack; originally published 1878). New American Library.

Tourangeau, R., Conrad, F. G., Couper, M. P., & Ye, C. (2014). The effects of providing examples in survey questions. *Public Opinion Quarterly, 78*(1), 100–125. doi:10.1093/poq/nft083

Tourangeau, R., Rips, L. J., & Rasinski, K. (2000). *The psychology of survey response.* Cambridge University Press.

Tourangeau, R., & Yan, T. (2007). Sensitive questions in surveys. *Psychological Bulletin, 133*(5), 859–883. doi: 10.1037/0033-2909.133.5.859

Urbina, S. (2004). *Essentials of psychological testing.* Wiley.

U.S. Department of Health and Human Services [USDHHS]. (2012). *Preventing tobacco use among youth and young adults: A report of the surgeon general.* U.S. Department of Health and Human Services, Centers for Disease Control and Prevention, Office on Smoking and Health. https://www.cdc.gov/tobacco/sgr/2012/

U.S. Department of Health and Human Services [USDHHS]. (2014). *The health consequences of smoking—50 Years of progress: A report of the surgeon general.* U.S. Department of Health and Human Services, Centers for Disease Control and Prevention, Office on Smoking and Health. https://www.cdc.gov/tobacco/sgr/50th-anniversary/

U.S. Department of Health and Human Services [USDHHS]. (2016). *E-cigarette use among youth and young adults: A report of the surgeon general.* U.S. Department of Health and Human Services, Centers for Disease Control and Prevention, Office on Smoking and Health. https://www.cdc.gov/tobacco/sgr/e-cigarettes/

U.S. Department of Health and Human Services [USDHHS]. (2019). *Quick facts on the risks of E-cigarettes for kids, teens, and young adults.* Centers for Disease Control and Prevention, Office on Smoking and Health. https://www.cdc.gov/tobacco/basic_information/e-cigarettes/Quick-Facts-on-the-Risks-of-E-cigarettes-for-Kids-Teens-and-Young-Adults.html

Vasconcellos, J. (1989). Preface. In A. M. Mecca, N. J. Smelser, & J. Vasconcellos (Eds.), *The social importance of self-esteem* (pp. xi–xxi). University of California Press.

Wang, T. W., Gentzke, A., Sharapova, S., Cullen, K. A., Ambrose, B. K., & Jamal, A. (2018). Tobacco product use among middle and high school students—United States, 2011–2017. *MMWR Morbidity & Mortality Weekly Report, 67*, 629–633. doi: 10.15585/mmwr.mm6722a3

Wasserstein, R. L., Schirm, A. L., & Lazar, N. A. (2019). Moving to a world beyond "p<.05." *The American Statistician, 73*(Suppl. 1), 1–19. doi: 10.1080/00031305.2019.1583913

Weiss, C. H. (2000). Which links in which theories shall we evaluate? In P. J. Rogers, T. A. Hacsi, A. Petrosino, & T. A. Huebner (Eds.), *Program theory in evaluation: Challenges and opportunities* (Vol. 87, pp. 35–45). New Directions for Evaluation. doi: 10.1002/ev.1180

Weiss, C. H., Murphy-Graham, E., Petrosino, A., & Gandhi, A. G. (2008). The fairy godmother—And her warts: Making the dream of evidence-based policy come true. *American Journal of Evaluation, 29*(1), 29–47. doi: 10.1177/1098214007313742

Whittington, A., & Aspelmeier, J. E. (2018). Resilience, peer relationships, and confidence: Do girls' programs promote positive change? *Journal of Outdoor Recreation, Education, and Leadership, 10*(2), 124–138. doi: 10.18666/JOREL-2018-V10-I2-7876

Willson, S., & Miller, K. (2014). Data collection. In K. Miller, V. Chepp, S. Willson, & J. L. Padilla (Eds.), *Cognitive interviewing methodology* (pp. 15–33). Wiley.

Windle, G., Bennett, K. M., Noyes, J. (2011). A methodological review of resilience measurement scales. *Health and Quality of Life Outcomes, 9*, 8. http://www.hqlo.com/content/9/1/8. doi: 10.1186/1477-7525-9-8

Worrell, F. C., & Erwin, J. O. (2011). Best practices in identifying students for gifted and talented education programs. *Journal of Applied School Psychology, 27*(4), 319–340. doi: 10.1080/15377903.2011.615817

Worrell, F. C., Subotnik, R. F., Olszewski-Kubilius, P., & Dixson, D. D. (2019). Gifted students. *Annual Review of Psychology, 70*, 551–576. doi: 10.1146/annurev-psych-010418-102846

Yarbrough, D. B., Shulha, L. M., Hopson, R. K., & Caruthers, F. A. (2011). *The program evaluation standards: A guide for evaluators and evaluation users* (3rd ed.). SAGE.

Ziliak, S., & McCloskey, D. (2008), *The cult of statistical significance: How the standard error costs us jobs, justice, and lives.* University of Michigan Press.

Zuckerman, M. (2007). *Sensation seeking and risky behavior.* American Psychological Association.

Zumbo, B. D. (2009). Validity as contextualized and pragmatic explanation, and its implications for validation practice. In R. W. Lissitz (Ed.), *The concept of validity: Revisions, new directions, and applications* (pp. 65–82). Information Age Publishing.

• Index •

Accuracy, 3, 10, 15, 164
  in evaluation, 3–5, 4 (table)–5 (table)
  statistical conclusion validity, 43, 51
  truth and, 17, 18, 32
Acree, J., 48
Ad hoc variables, 204–207
Adolescents, career awareness in, 8–9
Affordable Care Act (ACA), 143
Afterschool homework assistance,
  38–39
Alcohol use, 122–123
Alternative nicotine products, 103
American Academy of Pediatrics, 105
American Educational Research
  Association, 18
American Evaluation Association (AEA), 47
American Psychological Association, 18,
  19
Americans for Nonsmokers' Rights
  (ANR), 59
Anastasi, A., 21
Angoff, W. H., 25
Anna Karenina, 7
ANOVA framework, 204, 209
Argument
  evaluation as, 9–10
  validity measurement, 31–32
Assimilation effects, 149
Auxiliary measurement theories,
  116–117

Bandalos, D. L., 119
Baumrind, D., 85–86
Bias in measurement and evaluation, 4,
  29, 30, 45, 88, 92, 119, 121–122,
  132–152, 172, 178, 185, 202, 232,
  235
  apply to all respondents, 133
  cultural and economic bias, 29, 30,
    49, 223
  dealing with, 133
  measurement assumptions, 132
  mono-operation, 43
  sampling bias, 7, 159, 177, 182, 203
  socioeconomic and cultural, 30

Biochemical measurement, 121–122
Biological sex, 124
Black box approach, 70
Blalock, H. M., 87, 116–117, 119, 151
Boring, E., 22
Boruch, R. F., 162, 211
Braverman, M. T., 9, 77, 93 (table), 94,
  125–127, 137–138, 156 (figure),
  204–207
Bullying, 148

California Assembly Bill 3659, 105
California Task Force to Promote Self-
  Esteem and Personal and Social
  Responsibility, 105–109
Campbell, D. T., 11, 30, 35–44, 50, 60,
  154, 155, 164, 192
Campbellian validity model
  construct validity, 38–39, 229–230
  data interpretation errors, 224, 224
    (table)–226 (table)
  external validity, 35–38, 230–231
  internal validity, 35–38, 228–229
  statistical conclusion validity, 43–44,
    227–228
Career awareness, 8–9
Cause-probing designs, 36
Ceiling effect, 136–139
Cherry picking, 224 (table)
Children, Youth and Families at Risk
  (CYFAR), 76–78
Chong, D., 146
Cigarette smoking, measurement of,
  121–123
Civic engagement, 116
Clark, H. H., 146
Cognitive interviewing, 130–131
Cognitive processes, 24
Cohen, J., 196–199
Coherence (House validity model), 44,
  221, 232–233
Cohort comparison group design, 155
College graduation, 89
Conceptualizing variables, 87
Concurrent validity, 22, 23

Construct confounding, 43
Construct-irrelevant variance, 27
Construct underrepresentation, 27, 28
Construct validity, 11, 24–25, 38–39,
 51, 117, 170–171, 184, 229–230
  behavioral observations, 12
  conceptualization, 12
  definition of, 12
  errors, 225 (table)–226 (table)
  evaluation plans, 13
  misapprehension of, 84–86
  program theory, 13
  proxy variables, 96–97
  social observations, 12
  tests and, 19–22, 20 (table)
Constructs
  definition (table), 20
  and tests, 19–22
  and variables, 93 (table), 94 (table),
   96–105
  intervention as construct, 55–59
Content validity, 23–24
Contrast effects, 149
Converse, J. M., 141
Cook, T., 11, 38–44, 50
Copyright infringement, 129
Core analysis, 162, 178
  cause and effect, 192
  mediation and moderation, 193–194
Correlates, 95–96
Correlational approach, 19
Counterfactual condition, 154, 156–157
Criterion-related validity, 22–23
Cronbach, L. J., 11, 20–22, 24–26, 31,
 37, 38, 59, 169, 213, 217
Cronbach's alpha, 118
Culturally responsive evaluation (CRE),
 47
Culture, definition of, 47
Cyberbullying, 148

Daily exercise, 89
Data analysis
  ad hoc variables, 204–207
  ANOVA framework, 204
  benefits, 187
  coherence, 208
  core analysis, 192–194
  data collection, 188
  dichotomous dependent variable,
   208
  evaluation measures and scores,
   208–209
  evaluation participants, 209–211
  evaluation questions, 212–213

and evaluation validity, 188–192
  fishing expeditions, 207–208
  group membership, breakdowns, 211
  intention-to-treat (ITT) framework,
   210–211
  missing data, 203
  multilevel analysis, multiple-site
   evaluations, 202
  null hypothesis significance testing
   (NHST), 194–202
  ordinal logistic regression, 209
  pre-post control group study, 204
  program fidelity, analysis of, 211–212
  program dosage, 209–210
  program-outcome relationship, 204
  p-values, 198–200
  rigor, 208
  threshold strategy, 211
  transparency, 207–208
  treatment-on-the-treated (TOT), 210
  two-way analysis of variance, 209
Davidson, E. J., 233
Demographic variables, 84, 95, 124
Descriptive questions, 153–154
Design alignment, evaluation
   questions, 172–173
DeVellis, R. F., 119
Dillman, D. A., 129, 130, 135, 139, 141,
 149
Doonesbury, 106
Druckman, J. N., 146

E-cigarettes, 58
  introduction and proliferation of, 103
Effectiveness trials, 57
Efficacy trials, 57
Electronic nicotine delivery systems
   (ENDS), 103
Endorsement experiment, 136
Error, 117
  random, 132
  systematic, 132, 149
Erwin, J. O., 99
Esbensen, F.-A., 67–68, 219
Evaluation. *See also* Evaluation design
  accuracy in, 3–5, 4 (table)–5 (table)
  as argument, 9–10
  constructs, 87–89
  cultural influences in, 47–50
  definition of, 3, 15
  intervention, 70–72, 71 (table)
  operationalizing in, 14
  plan, 5, 6, 13
  questions, 5–7
  validity of, 44–47

Evaluation design
    construct validity, 170–171
    control/comparison, 160
    core analysis, 162
    data collection, 158
    design alignment, evaluation
        questions, 172–173
    elements, 157–163
    experimental design, 161
    external validity, 169–170
    function of, 153–157
    HealthLinks intervention, 157
    internal validity, 163–164, 164
        (table)–168 (table), 168–169
    interrupted time-series (ITS), 161
    intervention delivery, 158
    limitations and weaknesses, 179
    menu labeling regulation, 179–183
    multiple posttests, 162
    multiple pretests, 161–162
    power analysis, 177–178
    program condition, 159–160
    quasi-experimental design, 161
    randomized assignment, 161
    regression model, 163
    resources, 179, 185
    sample attrition, 158
    sample size, 158
    single-group pre-post design, 160
    standard business as usual, 160
    statistical analysis, 176–177
    statistical conclusion validity, 171–172
    statistical random error, 176
    study conditions, choice of, 159–161
    study participants, 157–159
    transparency and protections, 178, 185
    treatment group, 160
"Evidenced-based" (as variable), 100–101
Evidence-based intervention (EBI), 76, 78
Experimental validity, 37
Explanatory questions, 154
Explanatory trials, 57–58
External validity, 11, 35–38, 50, 55, 76,
    169–170, 184, 230–231
    disagreement, 56
    errors, 226 (table)

Factor analysis, 19
Federal drug control policy, 223
Fidelity of intervention delivery
    conceptualizing, 66
    definition of, 66
    measuring, 68
    multicomponent conception of, 66–68
    standards of, 69–70

Fishing expeditions, data analysis, 207–208
Fiske, D., 30
Floor effect, 136–139
Food and Nutrition Technical
    Assistance (FANTA), 128
Food insecurity, 119
Foster group homes, evaluation of, 73–74
Framing effects, 141–148
    controlling, 147–148
Funnell, S. C., 62, 64

Gender, 12–13, 47, 104–105, 124, 135, 228
    gender identity, 13, 105, 124, 135
    social conceptions of, 13
Generalization, external validity, 169
Giftedness, 98–99
Groves, R., 140–141

HealthLinks intervention, 157
Healthy eating, 14, 92
House, E. R., 11, 31, 44–47, 51, 90, 173,
    178, 187, 188, 199, 217, 221, 222
    validity perspective, 231–234
4-H Youth Development Program, 65,
    211–212
Hypothesized causal variables, 95

Iatrogenic program effects, 84
Illegal drug use, 90
Implementation evaluation, 70–71
Information feedback systems, 66
Intelligence, measurement of, 22, 99
Intention-to-treat (ITT) framework,
    210–211
Internal consistency, 118
Internal replicability analyses, 201
Internal validity, 11, 35–38, 50, 184,
    191–192, 228–229
    characteristics, 163–164
    control/comparison group, 168–169
    errors, 225 (table)
    plausible rival hypotheses, 164
    threats minimization, 173–174, 175
        (figure), 185
    threats to, 164, 164–168 (table)
Interrater reliability, 118
Interrupted time-series (ITS), 161
Intervention, 55
    as construct, 55–59
    evaluating independently
        functioning sites, 72–74
    evaluation activities, 70–72, 71 (table)
    fidelity, 66–70
    interaction of, 59–60
    labels, 76–78

local adaptations, 74–76
logic model, 62–64, 63 (figure)
logistics of implementation, 62–64
as planned, 64–65
planned and as delivered, 57–58
program monitoring, 65–66
program theory, 61–62, 62 (figure)
ITS. *See* Interrupted time-series (ITS)
ITT framework. *See* Intention-to-treat
(ITT) framework

Johnson, R. L., 129
Joint Committee on Standards for
Educational Evaluation, 3
Justice (House validity model), 44,
233–234

Kane, M., 31
Kirkhart, K., 11, 48, 49 (table), 51, 223, 234

Learning in Communities (LinC), 156
Leviton, L. C., 60, 75
Lipsey, M. W., 154, 201
List experiment, 136
Local adaptations, 74–76
Logic model, 62–64, 63 (figure)
Logic of evaluation (Scriven's), 218–219,
235

Management information system (MIS), 65
Mark, M. M., 36
Masten, A. S., 101
Mathison, S., 48
McKnight, P. E., 203
Measurement strategies, 113
acceptability, 121
auxiliary measurement theories,
116–117
bias and error, 132–149
Campbell's validity typology, 114,
114–115 (table)
credibility, 120
data collection, 120
electronic and mechanical, 131
extant measures, 127–129
government or institutional records,
131–132
multiple measures, 121–123
own measures, 129–131
pilot testing and refining, 130–131
potential bias, 119
reliability of, 117–119
replication study, 125–127
single item/scale, 123–125
validation studies, 120

Medicare-for-all, 143–144
Meehl, P. E., 11, 20, 21, 24
Mental Measurements Yearbook
(MMY), 128
Messick, S., 20, 25, 26, 30, 32
Meyer, J. P., 119
Monitoring and Evaluation, 65
Monitoring program implementation,
65–66
Monn, A. R., 101
Mono-operation bias, 43
Morgan, G. B., 129
Multicultural validity, 11, 48–50, 49
(table)
Multilevel analysis, multiple-site
evaluations, 202
Multitrait-multimethod matrix, 30, 37
Multiple posttests, 162
Multiple pretests, 161–162
Murphy, K. R., 201

National Cancer Institute Expert
Advisory Panel, 56
National Council on Measurement in
Education, 18
National Institute of Food and
Agriculture (NIFA), 76
Nicotine metabolites, 121
Nonattendance, 121
Normative questions, 154
Null hypothesis, 45
Null hypothesis significance testing
(NHST)
decision process, 198
dependence reduction, 199–201
reverse probability, 196
statistical reasoning, 202
validation study, 197
visual literacy, 194

Operationism, 22
Operationalization, 14, 15, 87, 90, 95,
113, 115, 151, 170, 172, 184, 214,
218

Parenting skills, 89, 92
Parenting styles, 84–86
Patton, M. Q., 42, 61, 65, 72–74, 76, 97,
213, 220–221, 227
Pearson, K., 19
Peck, L. R., 155
Peterson, A. V., 56
Physical activity, 92
Pipeline logic model, 64
Plagiarism, 129

Plausible rival hypotheses, 36, 50, 164, 174
Pragmatic trials, 58
Predictive validity, 22, 23
Pre-post control group study, 204
Presser, S., 141
Pretest-posttest nonequivalent
    comparison group study, 155
Pretest-posttest randomized
    experimental study, 155
Prevention programs, 222
Price, L. R., 119
Process evaluation, 70–71
Program Evaluation Standards, The,
    3–5, 4–5 (table), 15
Program logic models, 64
Program–pretest interaction, 60
Program theory, 13, 76, 89
    independent variables, 95
    of interventions, 61–62, 62 (figure)
Project 4-Health, 72, 211–212
Proxy variables, 96–97
PSAs. See Public service announcements
Psychological Bulletin, 35
Psychological test, 20, 21
Psychological theory, 12
Psychological traits, 12, 21
Psychometrics, 12, 17, 25, 35
Public service announcements (PSAs), 193

Quality teaching, 90
Question order, 148–149, 150 (table)
Question wording effects, 141–148

Random error, 132
Randomization process, 184
Randomized controlled trials (RCTs), 45
    smoking prevention, 39–42
Randomized response technique, 136
Regular smoking, 90
Reichardt, C. S., 154, 155
Reliability, 67, 91–92, 115 (table), 117–119,
    124, 139, 145, 151, 178, 191
    alternate forms, 118
    definitions of, 117
    internal consistency, 118
    interrater, 118
    test–retest, 118–119
Renzulli, J. S., 99
Resilience, 101–102
Respondents' tendencies, 140–141
Response alternatives, 145–146
Reuter, P., 223
Robert Wood Johnson Foundation
    (RWJF), 75

Rodriguez, S., 48
Rogers, P. J., 62, 64
Rosenberg Self-Esteem Scale, 23
Rossi, P. H., 72

SAT test, 29
Schober, M. F., 146
School-based cigarette and alcohol use,
    measuring, 122–123
School-based tobacco prevention, 56,
    57
Schwandt, T. A., 10, 153, 202, 218, 219
Schwarz, N., 145
Scriven, M., 218–219
Selection-maturation interaction effect,
    174, 175 (figure)
Selection variables, 95
Self-assessments of learning, 97–98
Self-esteem, 23, 105–109, 128
Self-report, 121
Sensitive subject matter, 134–136
Sex as one gender-relevant variable, 105
    biological, 124
Sexual health, 61, 62 (figure)
Shadish, W. R., 11, 12, 38–44, 50, 114,
    155, 163, 169, 189, 191, 217
Shorter-term variables, 97
Single-group pre-post design, 160, 182–183
Single-item measures, 123, 124
Single-pretest design, 174
Sireci, S. G., 19
Small theories (of interventions), 61
Smoking cessation programs, 14
Smoking prevention RCT, 39–42
Social justice, 11
Socioeconomic bias, 30
Spearman, C., 19
Split-sample experiments, 131
Stakeholders, 46, 87, 88, 110
    construct, 90
Standard notation of research design
    impact designs, 155
    Learning in Communities (LinC)
        academic success program, 156
Standards for educational and psychological
    testing, 18–22, 24, 26, 27, 32
Stanley, J. C., 35, 37, 60, 154, 155, 164
Statistical conclusion validity, 11,
    43–44, 51, 171–172, 184, 227–228
    data interpretation errors, 224
        (table)–225 (table)
    type I and type II errors, 189–191, 190
        (table)
Statistical random error, 176

Statistical significance testing. *See* Null hypothesis significance testing (NHST)
Sternberg, R. J., 99
Systematic error, 132, 149

Testing, 60
Test–retest reliability, 118–119
Test scores, 32
Test validation, 26
  consequences of, 30–31
  internal structure, 28
  relations to other variables, 29–30
  response processes, 28
  test content, 27–28
Theoretical constructs, 25
Theory of change, 61
Thompson, B., 201
Tobacco-free campuses, 59
Tobacco prevention strategy, 56
Tobacco products, 104
Tobacco taxation policy, 78
Tobacco use (as variable), 102–104
Tolstoy, L., 7
Tourangeau, R., 134, 135, 139, 146, 147
Triangulation, 121
Trudeau, G., 106
Trujillo, M. D., 60
Truth (House validity model), 44, 231–232
Type I and Type II errors, 43, 100, 177, 189–191, 195, 197, 201, 213

Unitary concept, 26
US Department of Agriculture, 128
US Food and Drug Administration (FDA), 103
US National Health Policy survey, Kaiser Family Foundation, 143–144
Utility, 3
Utilization-focused evaluation, 97

Vaccination program, 95
Validity, 3, 10, 15
  and research designs, 35–44
  argument perspective, 31–32
  conceptualization of, 17–19
  construct, 11–13, 24–25
  content, 23–24

  criterion-related, 22–23
  cultural influences in, 47–50
  definition of, 18, 37, 217
  of evaluations (House model), 44–47
  external, 11, 35–38
  internal, 11, 35–38
  measurement and, 114–119
  multicultural, 48–51, 49 (table)
  psychometric, 17
  Standards, 19
  statistical conclusion, 11
  tripartite view, 22–26
  truth function of, 18
  unitary view, 26–30
Vaping, 103
Variables, 83
  conceptualizing, 87
  constructs relationships to, 87–89
  convenience of selection, 97–98
  correlates, 95–96
  definition of, 89
  demographic, 84
  evidence-based, 100–101
  gender, 104–105
  giftedness, 98–99
  hypothesized causal variable, 95
  identification of, 84, 86, 89–90
  instruments, 91–92, 94 (figure)
  levels of specificity, 92
  measurement strategies, 90–91, 93 (table)
  outcomes, 94–95
  proxy, 96–97
  resilience, 101–102
  selecting, 109–110
  selection variables, 95
  tobacco use, 102–104
Vasconcellos, A. J., 105–106, 108

Water quality education program for farmers, 63 (figure)
Weiss, C., 64, 100
Wording choices, 142–144
Worrell, F. C., 99

Yan, T., 135

Zumbo, B., 12, 25